SOCIAL COMMUNICATION

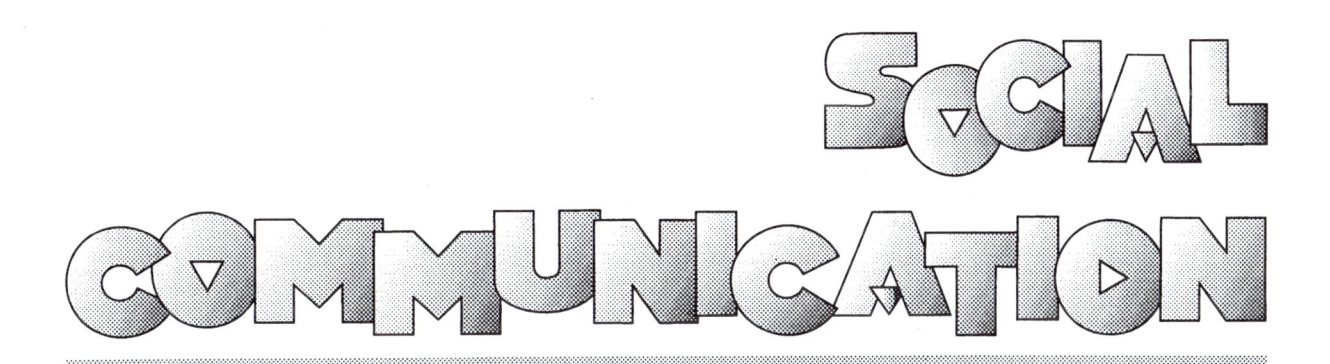

Activities for Improving Peer Interactions and Self-Esteem

M. Ann Marquis, M.S., CCC-SLP
Department of Communicative Disorders
University of New Mexico
Albuquerque, New Mexico

Elaine Addy-Trout, M.S., CCC-SLP
Speech-Language Pathologist
Aztec, New Mexico

Thinking Publications
Eau Claire, Wisconsin

© **1992 Thinking Publications®**
A Division of McKinley Companies, Inc.

Thinking Publications grants limited rights to individual professionals to reproduce and distribute pages that indicate duplication is permissible. Pages can be used for student instruction only and must include Thinking Publications' copyright notice. All rights are reserved for pages without the permission-to-reprint notice. No part of these pages may be reproduced in any form, electronic or mechanical, including photocopy, recording, or any information storage and retrieval system without permission in writing from the publisher.

08   07   06   05   04   03   11   10   9   8   7   6   5

Library of Congress Cataloging-in-Publication Data

Marquis, M. Ann.
  Social communication : activities for improving peer interactions and self-esteem / M. Ann Marquis, Elaine Addy-Trout.
    p.   cm.
  Rev. ed. of: CASE Study. 1992.
  Includes bibliographical references (p.   ).
  ISBN 0–930599–75–6
  1. Learning disabled youth—Language. 2. Communication—Study and teaching (Secondary). 3. Self-esteem in adolescence. 4. Interpersonal relations. I. Addy-Trout, Elaine. Marquis, M. Ann. CASE study. III. Title.
  LC4704.5.M38 1995   95–18855
  371.91'4—dc20   CIP

Printed in the United States of America

THINKING PUBLICATIONS®
A Division of McKinley Companies, Inc.

424 Galloway Street
Eau Claire, WI 54702-0163
(715) 832-2488
Fax (715) 832-9082

DEDICATION

This book is dedicated to self-knowledge,
respect for life, and world responsibility.

Table of Contents

Preface vii

Introduction 1
    A Model of Self-Esteem 1
    Rationale for Combining Communication and Self-Esteem 4
    Language Intervention 13
    How to Use This Book 16

Section 1: Developing a Group Concept 29

Section 2: Communicating with Others 61

Section 3: Understanding Oneself 97

Section 4: Exploring Self-Concept 137

Section 5: Defining Self-Esteem 169

Section 6: Decision Making and Problem Solving 201

Section 7: Analyzing Family Issues 233

Section 8: Social Values and Myths 261

Section 9: Differences and Similarities Among People 289

Section 10: Examining Our Role in the World 325

Appendix A: Communication Summation Forms 359

Appendix B: *Social Communication* Goals and Objectives 361

Appendix C: Low Self-Esteem Symptom Checklist 364

Appendix D: Closure Activity—Suggestions for Ending the Group ... 368

References 369

PREFACE

This project evolved from working with communicatively impaired, secondary-school students over the past five years. Its foundation is in pragmatic communication development. The focus was influenced by students who continually talked with us about their lack of self-confidence, their view of themselves as failures, and their fears about their futures. During those five years, there were few bright and shining faces eager to explore what was around the next corner. In fact, many couldn't imagine that there could be adventures for them at all.

To teach effective social communication skills without addressing the area of self-esteem seemed not to take the whole communicative context into account. With that idea in mind, we did extensive readings in the areas of psychology, counseling, and sociology. From our investigation, we chose concepts that seemed particularly relevant to communicating, getting along with others, and exploring how people develop knowledge of the world. This project is based on that search and our notion that appropriate communication is dependent upon a healthy self-esteem.

During our background reading for this book, we discovered ideas captured by others that inspired us. We found Bourgault's (1991) description of adolescents who wander around in a social and academic twilight zone to be particularly poignant:

> Throughout their academic career, these students experience social and academic exclusion from their class and peers. They often have poor feelings of self-worth, have had little social and academic success, and express anger in various ways. Generally, they are educationally unmotivated and have a classic case of "BA" (bad attitude). By the time these adolescents reach junior high and high school, they have given up on themselves and on the educational process. (pp. 358–359)

We liked Pickering's (1991) definition of communication as an ever-changing process involving the total personality: "It involves tacit knowledge as well as explicit knowledge, emotion as well as reason, thought as well as action, body as well as mind. The gestalt of an individual is what is involved in communication" (p. 270).

The idea of the integration of communication functions is of utmost importance to us. To blend the elements of interpersonal interaction into a whole, we have chosen to focus on the topic of self-esteem within a communicative framework. We agree with Butler (1985), who discusses the interdisciplinary nature of our profession: "Will it always be necessary to borrow, reaching out to other disciplines? Most assuredly. The scope of research in language is too broad to be encompassed by a single discipline" (p. iv).

Our own professional discipline is communication disorders. Blending our discipline's knowledge with that of others for the benefit of the people we serve was foremost in our minds when we developed *Social Communication: Activities for Improving Peer Interactions and Self-Esteem*. We hope that participants in your program find this resource as helpful as our students have.

We wish to thank the open-minded students and professionals who ventured into unknown territory with us and contributed significantly to the evolution of this endeavor. We also wish to thank our friends and family for their encouragement.

INTRODUCTION

Social Communication: Activities for Improving Peer Interactions and Self-Esteem was developed to help professionals facilitate social communication and peer interaction among adolescents with learning disabilities and communication impairments. This resource is based on pragmatic language theory and the development of self-esteem. The activities in this book can be used to supplement other communication goals or can be used as the primary focus of a communication development program.

Self-esteem can be described as pride in oneself while self-concept is considered to be a collection of traits by which individuals describe themselves; it is their thoughts and feelings about themselves. In this collection of traits, "there may be areas in which the individual feels good and other areas in which the individual does not feel so good" (Sweeney and Zionts, 1989). A study of adolescent self-concept reveals multiple traits which can function independently or as a whole (Ellis and Davis, 1982). Accordingly, the various dimensions of the adolescent's self-concept include: self-acceptance, self-security, social confidence, self-assertion, family affiliation, peer affiliation, teacher affiliation, and school affiliation.

A Model of Self-Esteem

In developing *Social Communication: Activities for Improving Peer Interactions and Self-Esteem,* we have drawn on several models and theories of self-esteem that interrelate with the task of communication development (Borba, 1989; Branden, 1987; California Task Force to Promote Self-Esteem and Personal and Social Responsibility, 1990; Dembrowsky, 1988; Reasoner, 1982). In addition to describing self-esteem as having pride in oneself, we found the California Task Force to Promote Self-Esteem and Personal and Social Responsibility (1990) definition to be particularly captivating and succinct:

> Self-esteem is appreciating my own worth and importance and having the character to be accountable for myself and to act responsibly towards others. (p. 22)

Our model of self-esteem is based primarily on the models of Dembrowsky (1988) and the California Task Force to Promote Self-Esteem and Personal and Social Responsibility (1990). Specifically, we view self-esteem as reflecting the following five areas:

1. *Appreciating My Self-Worth* means realizing my value to myself, to others, and to the world. This sense of myself is based on my unique abilities and is not measured against those of others. What I do in the world makes a difference.

Social Communication

2. *Appreciating the Worth of Others* involves respecting, accepting, and supporting others. This idea also means that I express my feelings to others, take risks, and forgive others. It means that I value cultural and ethnic differences in society.

3. *Relating Effectively to Others* requires that I communicate as clearly and as honestly as I can. I strive to create mutual understanding and a sense of cooperation. I express myself assertively and ask for help when I need it.

4. *Being Accountable for Myself* involves taking responsibility for my own decisions, actions, statements, choices, attitudes, and well-being. Acting responsibly means not blaming others or circumstances for my mistakes. Being accountable means being a person of integrity. It also means thinking about the future and my place in it.

5. *Solving Problems and Pursuing Goals* requires that I make commitments to live successfully through demanding and challenging times. I face problems directly and set specific goals that reflect my accountability. I pursue my goals until I have reached them because I feel empowered.

Who Can Benefit from this Book?

Social Communication is appropriate for adolescents who are entering middle adolescence (12–16 years) or who are older. The language level of the material is at approximately the 10- to 12-year-old level based on Wallach and Miller (1988). Keep in mind that those individuals who present communication disorders or language-learning disabilities are usually delayed in language development. The material is meant for individuals who are beginning the transition into the formal operational period of cognitive development. Most of the material is also applicable to individuals in the concrete operational stage; however, students will need help considering hypothetical situations.

The activities are designed primarily for adolescents who have communication disorders or who are labeled *language-learning disabled*. Groups of three to eight participants result in the best implementation of the program. *Social Communication* is also possible to use with larger groups, as well as during one-to-one interactions.

Some activities in *Social Communication* need special consideration to determine whether they are appropriate for certain groups of adolescents. Professionals should scrutinize each lesson ahead of time and decide whether the group that will be involved in the lesson is either too young developmentally for the activity or too impaired emotionally, thus necessitating a counselor to be present or nearby. These activities are marked with code letters that refer to one of the two caveats in *Social Communication*:

1. (HS) is used to code lessons that may be developmentally more appropriate for high school students (i.e., 15 years and older) and less appropriate for students in the middle grades and junior high school. Typically, lessons marked with an (HS) use content that is beyond the realm of interest of most youths below 15 years of age (i.e., the topic of the activity may be an inappropriate vehicle for teaching communication skills to young adolescents). Sample topics include marriage, career planning beyond high school, and intimacy in relationships.

2. (C) is used to designate activities that may require the presence of a counselor because of the potential for evoking strong emotional reactions, especially from youth with severe emotional impairments. These activities are probably best used when adult facilitators have ready access to counselors. Team teaching can be an especially effective technique for these lessons. Whenever activities in *Social Communication* result in responses that are outside the realm of the facilitator to accommodate, a counselor should be consulted immediately. Activities marked with a (C) use content vehicles such as these to teach communication skills: personality analysis, family problems, and hypothetical life-threatening situations (e.g., who should survive out of a small group with limited supplies).

These caveats are intended to assist professionals in using *Social Communication* effectively and ethically. Each activity must be examined before use with adolescents to make certain the lesson's objectives are appropriate to the communication goals established for each individual.

Who Can Implement the Program?

Social Communication is designed to be used by speech-language pathologists and educators, both special and regular. This resource may also be used as a tool for counselors, social workers, or psychologists to develop effective interpersonal communication skills in individuals with language disorders. *Social Communication* is an ideal vehicle for teaming, consulting, and communicating between professionals.

What Is Included in This Program?

Social Communication has three parts: an *Introduction*, 100 activities, and an *Appendix*. The *Introduction* provides the information needed to implement the activities appropriately. It includes a discussion of self-esteem, communication development, and professional roles, as well as ideas to facilitate group interaction. *Appendix A* includes two Communication Summation Forms, *Appendix B* includes a list of goals and objectives, *Appendix C* is a Low Self-Esteem Symptom Checklist, and *Appendix D* has suggestions for a closure activity.

Social Communication

The 100 activities are organized into 10 sections. The first two sections, *Developing a Group Concept* and *Communicating with Others*, focus on building group cohesiveness. These two sections lay the groundwork for and encourage the relationship stage of group process. The exploration stage is emphasized in the next two sections, *Understanding Oneself* and *Exploring Self-Concept*. Activities in these two sections focus on investigating the details of how self-concept develops. The next three sections, *Defining Self-Esteem, Decision Making and Problem Solving,* and *Analyzing Family Issues,* correspond to the revealing stage of group interaction. Activities in these areas offer participants the opportunity to examine issues on a more personal level and share them with the group if they choose to do so. Participants experience an ongoing reorganization of their communication skills, behaviors, beliefs, and thoughts as they proceed through the remaining three sections, *Social Values and Myths, Differences and Similarities Among People,* and *Examining Our Role in the World.*

A discussion section precedes each area, explaining how self-esteem issues can be integrated into each activity. Each activity includes detailed suggestions for communication development. The areas and activities are hierarchically arranged to facilitate comfortable and noncompetitive group interaction. After the first two sections establish basic group interaction guidelines and communication strategies, the program moves the individual from a personal perspective to a familial-social perspective to a world perspective.

A closure activity is included in *Appendix D*. It can be adapted to correlate with particular group needs. All groups have their own time line, dynamics, and orientation. An important guideline is to allow groups to progress at their own pace.

Rationale for Combining Communication and Self-Esteem

The Evolving Definition of Communicative Competence

Over the last decade, professionals who serve individuals with speech, language, and communication disorders have evolved from teaching isolated language skills to promoting effective interpersonal communication (Craig, 1983; Larson and McKinley, 1985; Prutting, 1982; Spekman and Roth, 1984). Achieving communicative competence requires focusing on the broad spectrum of linguistic and cognitive goals, as well as conversational effectiveness (Blank and Marquis, 1987; Hoskins, 1990; Prutting, 1982).

This shift in pragmatic communication perspective presents a more holistic intervention orientation. Prizant, Audet, Burke, Hummel, Maher, and Theadore (1990) state that:

This change in expertise reflects a growing sensitivity to the complex interrelationships among speech, language, and communicative competence, and emotional well-being. Furthermore, considerations of contexts of treatment and the mutual influence between communicatively impaired persons and their social environment have expanded greatly. (p. 191)

How we see ourselves is central to emotional well-being and successful relationships. The value we place on ourselves is the measure of our self-esteem. The measure of our self-esteem is directly correlated to communicative competence. We become comfortable with interpersonal communication not only because we have acquired the mechanics of conversation, but because we have the self-confidence to present ourselves in a straightforward manner that reflects a degree of comfort in our communication style. The professional who provides communication remediation, intervention, or enhancement without addressing self-esteem issues on some level is once again teaching aspects of communication in isolation.

Communicative Competence as a Way to Reduce Frustration

In their discussion of successful intervention practices with students who are language disordered, Wiig and Semel (1984) explain that including an exploration of self-concept improves motivation and relieves anxieties:

Often these children express frustrations reflecting conflicts in self-perception and in the development of the self, the ideal self, and the public self. Descriptions by the child that reflect how he believes himself to be (self-concept), how he wishes to be (ideal self), and how he wants others to perceive him (public self) may suggest discrepancies and conflicts which may need to be resolved. Self-acceptance seems essential to the outcome of intervention. (p. 584)

As children with communication problems become adolescents, they are increasingly aware of themselves as being unsuccessful and "different." Klecan-Aker (1985) states that "any therapy program must take into account the emotional and psychological problems that accompany a language or learning disorder in the young adolescent" (p. 53). Klecan-Aker goes on to explain that language specialists must take such factors into account, rather than focusing only on linguistic and syntactic goals.

Communicative Competence and Literacy

Miller (1990) indicates that our feelings of competency are vital to how we see our place in the world. Her discussion on literacy stresses the importance of engaging in activities that provide personal meaning that is self-reinforcing rather than externally motivated. Her definition of literacy negates the restricted idea of literacy as being able to read and write. Instead, she views literacy as cultural participation, as arising out of shared events and experiences, and as emerging from communicative interactions about those experiences. She explains that becoming literate means being able to think in certain ways that allow for participation in cultural activities not available to those who have not acquired necessary experiences. "These ways of thinking gradually come to constitute one's intelligence, or what and how one knows" (Miller, 1990, p. 3).

Types of Competences

Two significant intelligence "competences" discussed by Miller (1990) are *intrapersonal competence* and *interpersonal competence*. Intrapersonal competence is the degree to which people know themselves. One's intrapersonal intelligence develops from family experiences and contributes to the formation of self-concept and self-esteem. Intrapersonal competence involves knowledge of oneself in varying situations and includes knowing how one responds under specific conditions across other competences (linguistic, spatial, bodily-kinesthetic, logical-mathematical, and musical). According to Miller, "because self-concept is an integrative phenomenon, it includes knowledge of self across learning domains, with self-esteem reflecting the value people place on their competence across domains" (p. 12).

Interpersonal competence involves knowing that other people are unique personalities with their own experiences, motivations, emotions, and beliefs. Interpersonal communication is based on being able to read others' behaviors and take their perspective. Miller (1990) states that "much of interpersonal competence relies on the ability to engage in communicative interactions with others, much of which involves significant linguistic ability" (p. 12). Intrapersonal and interpersonal competence can be seen as the self. The self monitors and integrates all learning domains. It provides access to one's feelings and acts in an information-processing capacity. If the self is weak or lacking in esteem, monitoring and processing information from other domains is likely to be impaired. Self-esteem then can be seen as central to the development of communicative competence and success in all areas of life.

By taking Miller's view that intelligence is a set of competences monitored by the self, clinicians and educators can begin to see communication intervention in new ways. Miller suggests that we build programs and curricula that help individuals discover what their competences are and how they can be improved or expanded. She goes on to say that:

> These same educators and professionals can help children and adolescents develop a self-concept that is centered on a set of intelligences defined in terms of the sort of things they do and that enables them to participate in meaningful ways with others in their lives. (p. 22)

The development of a strong, healthy self-concept is at the heart of *Social Communication: Activities for Improving Peer Interactions and Self-Esteem*.

Significant Others and Self-Esteem

As the child grows toward adolescence, those significant people in the immediate environment with whom he or she has relationships change from parents to others in the expanding community (Winne, Woodlands, and Wong, 1982). *Significant other* is a term used to describe someone in the environment who is a source of influence, whose opinion is valued or strongly desired, and who is considered by the adolescent as credible (Beane and Lipka, 1986; Galbo, 1984; Juhasz, 1985; Street, 1988). "Family, school, peers—all 'significant others'—share a responsibility in forming the social personality [of the youth]" (Wilkerson, Protinsky, Maxwell, and Lentner, 1982, p. 137).

For the adolescent, there are multitudes of significant others to enhance or lower the student's self-esteem, self-identity, and learning motivation (Peck, 1981). In attempting to discern who would be chosen as significant others, Peck (1981) found that an individual perceived to have high ability to perform a particular task was predicted to be accepted as a significant other by adolescents with learning problems. Teachers, speech-language pathologists, counselors, and other professionals are frequently included in this category.

Battle and Blowers (1982) found that "definitions of self-worth are made in terms of comparisons of oneself with others and that in the absence of objective standards of comparison, individuals will employ significant others in their environment as the basis for forming estimates of self-worth" (p. 101). *Social Communication* activities encourage participants to analyze how people influence each other.

Self-Esteem and Communication Skills

Social Communication does not suggest that speech-language pathologists or teachers take over the roles of psychologists or counselors. Developing self-esteem is not a substitute for psychological intervention. The suggestion is made, however, that professionals look at communication success as dependent upon self-knowledge and self-esteem. These areas, as well as the general area of interpersonal communication, originated from studies done in psychology. Nonverbal communication, for example, was once an area of research and intervention not associated with the field of communication disorders. This is no longer the case. A mingling of disciplines is taking place. People are good communicators because they have self-confidence and effective communication skills.

As clinicians and educators seek to further their understanding of communication, they find themselves becoming increasingly interdisciplinary in their study. Knowledge of intrapersonal and interpersonal constructs can help a clinician or teacher better understand the gestalt of an individual's assets and deficits, the social meaning of those assets and deficits, and the adaptive strategies in use by the individual (Pickering, 1991).

An ongoing argument ensues over which comes first—a communication disorder or lowered self-concept. By late childhood or adolescence, this debate is moot. By focusing on the emotional impact that a communication disorder has on personality development, speech-language pathologists and teachers can help individuals with communication disabilities better understand their strengths and weaknesses, their feelings regarding their problems, and the impact that a communication disorder can have on one's life ambitions (Hartzell, 1984; Klein, Moses, and Altman, 1988). In the past decade, counseling clients about their disorders has become an aspect of holistic speech-language intervention programs (Larson and McKinley, 1985; Simon, 1985; Wiig and Semel, 1984).

Social Communication leads individuals to explore all aspects of themselves both intra- and interpersonally. In this way, counseling about problem communication areas is woven into activities throughout the book. By pairing an emphasis on communication and self-esteem, individuals become more communicative because self-esteem is elevated. Conversely, improving communication skills can lead to higher self-esteem.

Self-Esteem and Academic Performance

Self-esteem and academic achievement have been shown to be interrelated, but in some cases it is not known if poor achievement affects self-esteem or vice versa (Patten, 1983). Teaching communication and social skills across settings is an effective approach to improving self-confidence and academic performance. Students with social perception or self-concept deficits should be identified and the deficits dealt with as quickly as possible to prevent future difficulties.

Self-concept has been significantly related to educational development, including interpersonal behavior patterns, self-attributions about success or failure, and academic achievement (Coleman, 1983; Mboya, 1989; Winne et al., 1982). A study reported by Kershner (1990) revealed that students with "relatively high IQs who also feel good about themselves and are confident in their ability to cope with peer/family relationships, family dynamics, and school demands are more likely to be successful learners" (p. 368). Kershner found that self-concept, and not IQ alone, was a significant predictor of increased learning within the remedial context.

Self-Esteem and Students with Learning Disabilities

Students "who despite adequate intellectual potential, repeatedly experience academic failures at school are at high risk for developing poor self-concepts, low self-confidence, and the behaviour patterns which typically accompany such occurrences" (Wilchesky and Reynolds, 1986, p. 411). The description of average potential accompanied by underachievement can precipitate a vicious cycle of failure, intellectual self-doubt, and lowered self-expectation. Special-needs adolescents often display feelings of frustration, poor self-concept, social withdrawal, depression, despair, and anxiety (Canino, 1981; Coleman, 1983; Knoff, 1983; Peck, 1981; Zarb, 1984). Continued failure can result in a lack of motivation, lowered expectations, feelings of shame and sadness, lowered intensity of performance, and less persistence when faced with future academic tasks (Palmer, Drummond, Tollison, and Zinkgraff, 1982).

Adolescents with learning disabilities have not only displayed lower self-concepts than their "normally achieving" peers, but also lower levels of academic achievement and social competencies (Gresham, Evans, and Elliott, 1988; Kershner, 1990; Sweeney and Zionts, 1989). Adolescents with learning disabilities will compare themselves to peers to gauge not only academic ability, but also social acceptance (Winne et al., 1982).

Self-Efficacy and Students with Learning Disabilities

Self-efficacy is the feeling or belief that one can control one's life. Self-efficacy focuses on the individual's perception of the degree to which events and outcomes can be produced and regulated (Gresham et al., 1988). Motivationally, this can be described as an internal locus of control.

In an attempt to reintegrate the student with learning disabilities into the regular education classroom, special education personnel may unwittingly cause the student to develop a poor sense of self-efficacy. These students, due to past academic and/or social failures in the regular education setting, may feel that they cannot achieve and therefore will fail (Cooley and Ayres, 1988; Gresham et al., 1988; Haynes, 1990). Many of these students attribute failure to factors outside their control. Their locus of control is external. They attribute success to luck or task ease (Canino, 1981; Stevens and Pihl, 1987; Zarb, 1984)

Learned helplessness is a term used to describe the behavior of individuals who act helplessly because they think they cannot affect positive outcomes of events. Many teachers perceive pupils with learning disabilities as displaying more learned helplessness than other students. According to Galbo (1984), learning disabled students exhibit less persistence and response initiative on academic and nonacademic tasks than do normally achieving pupils. These students have also been distinguished from their peers due to increased requesting behaviors, indicating a possible lack of basic information or a lack of self-assurance (Markoski, 1983). Conversely, some students with learning disabilities do not request additional assistance with tasks to prevent calling attention to their lack of knowledge, and therefore fail to complete or incorrectly complete academic tasks, thus perpetuating the cycle of failure. These students can be perceived as lower functioning, lacking motivation, or simply stubborn.

Students affected by a poor sense of self-efficacy experience feelings of not being able to maintain effective control over their lives and destinies (Wilkerson et al., 1982). This lack of control, and the subsequent belief that they cannot achieve like other students, often results in lowered ability or a self-fulfilling prophecy of failure. This attitude of failure "undermines motivation, limits interest patterns, heightens negative affect (i.e., loss of self-esteem), and retards intellectual growth" (Canino, 1981, p. 481). According to Waksman (1984), "positive self-descriptions are important for school achievement, social effectiveness, reduced anxiety, and acceptance by others" (p. 277–278).

Social Communication

Gresham, Evans, and Elliott (1988) found that students with learning disabilities "typically failed on academic tasks; were poorly accepted, rejected, or neglected by their nonhandicapped peers; experienced difficulties in interactions with nonhandicapped peers" (p. 232). Haynes (1990) recommends that school-based interventions motivate these students and give them a sense of empowerment and control. Self-efficacy is enhanced by using the ideas presented in Communication Strategies for Group Participants (see page 16).

Professionals should remain aware that self-efficacy and the concept of an internal locus of control are based in Western thought and are widely embraced by the American school system. This cultural orientation may not be shared by persons from minority or Third World cultures. *Social Communication* should be used judiciously with these persons.

Social Acceptance and Perceptions

Adolescents, as a group, are prone to self-doubt, self-consciousness, and defensiveness. When combined with lowered self-confidence, this can be a social disaster. Self-esteem and social perception deficits of students with learning disabilities have been studied extensively. "Social perception deficits are viewed as the most serious of all types of learning disabilities" (Minskoff, 1980, p. 118). Social perception involves that ability to "read" social messages consisting of both verbal content and nonverbal cues. Wilchesky and Reynolds (1986) found that many adolescents with learning disabilities experience significant difficulty in processing information from the social environment, and integrating and adapting to that information. Because of deficits in social perception, these students many times do not perceive their poor social status and they overestimate their social acceptance (Minskoff, 1980).

The social stigma of academic failure or underachievement can have a detrimental effect not only on underachievers, but on the perceptions of those around them. Studies have found that students with learning disabilities were less accepted by their peers than students who progress and achieve normally (Coleman, 1983; Madden and Slavin, 1983; Prillaman, 1981; Sabornie, Kauffman, Ellis, Marshall, and Elksnin, 1987-1988; Toro, Weissburg, Guare, and Liebenstein, 1990; Wanat, 1983; Zarb, 1984). Deficient interpersonal skills have been targeted as a possible reason for the student with learning disabilities' poor peer relations. According to Baum, Duffelmeyer, and Geelan (1988), 41.57 percent of senior high school students with learning disabilities were perceived by their teachers as manifesting deficits in social interactions.

Oral communication abilities of students who are learning disabled also influence their social competence. Students displaying difficulty following communication rules, such as interrupting their conversational partners, failing to give or respond to feedback, or producing ambiguous remarks, are not likely to be popular conversational or social partners (Mathinos, 1988). "Social competence is now generally acknowledged to be as necessary as academic achievement for children to be prepared to deal with life's challenges" (Wojnilower and Gross, 1988, p. 109). Students with learning disabilities have been found to generate fewer alternatives for solving social problem situations. Also, they display lower frustration tolerance and adaptive assertiveness than their normally achieving peers (Toro et al., 1990). Social perception and communicative difficulties not only influence relations with peers, but also relations with teachers and others in the learning disabled adolescent's environment.

Teacher Acceptance and Perceptions

Numerous studies have documented the student with learning disabilities' relationship with both regular and special education teachers and the teachers' perceptions of the difficulties these students present in the academic setting. According to a study cited by Markoski (1983), "both classmates and teachers are more likely to ignore the learning disabled student than his counterpart" (p. 606). West, Jones, and McConahay (1981) found that according to learning disabled student participants, 41 percent of teacher behaviors toward the student with learning disabilities were positive, indicating that over half of teacher behaviors were not positive. This figure was derived from the perceptions of students with learning disabilities. Peck (1981) states that a person's early experiences in an unrewarding environment "make him or her hypersensitive to censure and inclined to see censure where none is intended" (p. 449).

Just as the student's perception of a teacher can influence academic achievement, a teacher's perception of a student is an important variable in influencing the way the teacher responds to the student. Bryan (1974) found that students with learning disabilities were twice as likely to receive criticism from a teacher in comparison to "normal" students. It has been established that teachers perceive differences not only in academic ability of learning disabled and "normal" students but also in social behavior, and they show bias in favor of the "normal" student. These perceptions can affect student/teacher interactions, referrals, and programming decisions (Center and Wascom, 1986). Teacher-student relationships can have a direct effect on academic performance and self-esteem.

Improving Self-Esteem

Research has demonstrated that teachers can improve their students' self-concepts by making positive comments to them and creating an atmosphere of security in the classroom (Mboya, 1989; Street, 1988). According to Wilkerson et al. (1982), teachers need to be sensitive to issues such as trust and confidence in self and others, self-esteem, and a sense of adequacy and accomplishment. The teacher should not only be familiar with a student's achievement and cognitive ability but also understand and appreciate the student as a social being. Most special education teachers and speech-language pathologists, while being aware of the multiple deficits displayed by their students, have been encouraged to emphasize academics or linguistic skills. Current research, however, emphasizes the need to alter curriculum to include such areas as self-esteem, social and classroom interaction, and self-disclosure.

Teachers need to encourage students to express feelings, work through conflicts, and improve self-concept (Margalit, 1985). A majority of high school programs emphasize academic/remedial/tutorial goals or preparation for postschool work and independent living skills. Special education programs designed specifically for students who are learning disabled do not appear to have a significant impact on social acceptance and self-esteem (Gresham and Elliott, 1987; Knoff, 1983; Prillaman, 1981; Sabornie et al., 1987-1988; Wanat, 1983). A case can be made for addressing the "here and now" needs of exceptional students in high school that extend beyond their academic difficulties (Calhoun and Beattie, 1987). "The purpose of education has to be the development of individual potentials, not just academic potential" (Wanat, 1983, p. 37).

Battle and Blowers (1982) show that teachers who attend to the affective needs of their students significantly improve their pupils' perceptions of self-worth. Direct teaching of peer interaction skills in a small-group situation can also help improve self-esteem. Teachers, as group leaders or facilitators, can help students examine a wide range of self-esteem and social problem-solving situations. Small-group interaction can help adolescents learn and practice alternatives to their usual responses to interpersonal problems (Juhasz, 1985; Toro et al., 1990; Waksman, 1984). Materials that effectively teach social skills are *SSS: Social Skill Strategies (Books A and B)* (Gajewski and Mayo, 1989), *Scripting: Social Communication for Adolescents* (Mayo and Waldo, 1986), and *Skillstreaming the Adolescent: A Structured Learning Approach to Teaching Prosocial Skills* (Goldstein, Sprafkin, Gershaw, and Klein, 1980).

Self-concept enhancement in the educational curriculum may help individuals to become more realistic and self-accepting (Sweeney and Zionts, 1989). Madden and Slavin (1983) proposed a cooperative learning situation involving small groups to decrease social differences and promote understanding between student group members. Through small-group cooperation, greater academic achievement and enhanced self-concept resulted. Teachers, speech-language pathologists, and other significant adults can facilitate this process by guiding group members through the activities found in *Social Communication*.

World Knowledge and Communication

By helping individuals assess their self-concept and their roles in varying relationships, we are helping them to be communicative members of a group, a community, our society, and the world. We are helping them to find their niche. We are helping them to find out how the world works.

We all bring different experiences to the intervention setting or the classroom. Our experiences can be considered our world knowledge. World knowledge is based on how we interact with others, who we have interacted with, and what events we have experienced. Throughout lifelong development, our experiences are continually revising our expectations, and those expectations reflect how we will communicate (Milosky, 1990). It is through our ability to communicate that we align our notions of the real world with the daily requirements of living (Butler, 1990). This world view has implications for professionals. Communication goals cannot be considered only as language or vocabulary, but must be seen as "pockets of information about the world" (Milosky, 1990). The focus of intervention then becomes teaching individuals how to use language to investigate the myriad of possibilities and options that exist for them.

Activities in *Social Communication* such as "Gender Identification," "Defining Prejudice," and "Examining Social Myths" allow students to compare their experiences of the world across a wide spectrum. In interaction with others, individuals have the opportunity to take peers' and professionals' perspectives, acquire new information, share experiences, and participate in discussions about the implications of the topic at hand.

Language Intervention

Interpersonal Communication and Pragmatics

When considering how to facilitate communication, it is widely agreed that pragmatic language development is a crucial aspect of an intervention program (Donahue and Bryan, 1984; Fey and Leonard, 1983; McKinley and Lord Larson, 1985; Prutting and Kirchner, 1983; Wilkenson and Milosky, 1987). Pragmatic language development is embedded in interpersonal communication development. Pickering (1991) underscores the fact that communication is a complex phenomenon, encompassing more than oral language. Suggested constructs about communication were presented by Pickering as follows:

1. We cannot *not* communicate.
2. We express feelings, perceptions, and experiences in a variety of ways in addition to talking.
3. In communication between people, there is simultaneous involvement of both individuals.

Communication can also be described in terms of three components: linguistic rules, cognitive and social knowledge, and pragmatic rules (Prutting, 1982). Pragmatic language skills allow us to be sensitive to others, to understand the importance of nonverbal communication, and to establish rapport and relationships with others. Pragmatics emphasizes the appropriateness of language to specific situations and to cultural norms in general.

For some individuals for whom academic success is limited, it may be appropriate to place pragmatics in the center stage of their educational process. A pragmatic focus is particularly important for individuals who will pursue work rather than higher education after high school.

Regardless of their career focus, many individuals with communication disorders experience difficulties with the social use of language. In examining pragmatic problems in youth who are language-learning disabled, Spekman and Roth (1984) list the following problems:

1. difficulty in comprehending and producing communicative meanings;
2. inability to take a listener's perspective;
3. insufficient knowledge about communication responsibility and communicator assertiveness; and
4. inability to monitor the adequacy of previous messages.

These areas of concern have been interwoven into the general focus of *Social Communication*. Skills in these areas are the communicative framework from which group interaction operates. They should be kept foremost in the minds of individuals during all aspects of the program, including developing vocabulary, improving syntax, listening, conversing, and writing.

A Focus on Discourse

The purpose of *Social Communication: Activities for Improving Peer Interactions and Self-Esteem* is to facilitate effective discourse. According to Larson and McKinley (1987), discourse can be separated into two categories: conversations and narrations. Conversations are a process by which two or more people share verbal and nonverbal messages in relatively spontaneous and unstructured situations. Conversation involves interaction in which ideas, feelings, and experiences are shared. It is a foundation for most relationships, allowing people to talk directly to one another about matters of mutual focus.

Narrations are extended monologues that are primarily concerned with metaphor and credibility and have their own structure and intent (Sutton-Smith, 1986; Van Dongen and Westby, 1986; Wallach and Miller, 1988). Typically, narrations are a recollection or an account of past experiences. They can also be a current synopsis of an idea or opinion (Heath, 1986). Hopefully, narrations take a serial and chronological form and utilize a consistent point of view (Wallach and Miller, 1988). Roth and Spekman (1986) explain the difference between narrations and conversations as follows:

1. Narrations are more extensive than conversations and usually more detailed and complicated.
2. Narrations include opening and closing statements and proceed in an orderly manner to a logical resolution.
3. Narrations carry the expectation that the speaker maintains a monologue and the listener passively listens.

In terms of social interaction, narrations are embedded within conversations. It is up to the speaker to include an appropriate narration in a verbal exchange in an organized, coherent, and interesting manner.

Discourse Guidelines

Effective discourse requires that participants know and use discourse guidelines. Cooperation is required. Grice (1975) elaborated on cooperation during discourse and proposed four categories that reflect speaker cohesiveness:

1. Quantity—Do not say more or less than the listener can comfortably process.
2. Quality—Do not say anything that is false or for which you lack adequate evidence.
3. Relation—Speak about things that are relevant to the situation.
4. Manner—Speak clearly and lucidly. Avoid ambiguity.

Damico (1991), using Grice's framework, developed a way of analyzing and assessing discourse to classify problem language behaviors. Damico's *Clinical Discourse Analysis* emphasizes the underlying conditions of discourse rather than its surface structure. Damico suggests that discourse be examined as follows:

1. Quantity
    a. Insufficient information for the listener
    b. Nonspecific vocabulary
    c. Redundancy
    d. Inappropriate need for repetition
2. Quality
    a. Inaccurate messages
3. Relation
    a. Poor topic maintenance
    b. Inappropriate response
    c. Irrelevant questions
    d. Situational inappropriateness
    e. Inappropriate speech style
4. Manner
    a. Linguistic nonfluency; repetitions, unusual pauses, hesitations
    b. Revisions
    c. Delays before responding
    d. Failure to structure discourse
    e. Turn-taking problems
    f. Gaze inefficiency
    g. Inappropriate intonation

Under normal circumstances, pragmatic skills and linguistic skills are generally learned through discourse. Additionally, peer interaction skills such as turn-taking, interpreting nonverbal communication, and giving attention to another person are modeled during discourse. Effective discourse, therefore, may well be the end goal of language intervention (Brinton and Fujiki, 1989; Damico, 1991; Hoskins, 1990; Snow, Midkoff-Borunda, Small, and Proctor, 1984; Wells, 1981).

How to Use This Book

The activities in *Social Communication* are designed to be motivating and relevant to adolescents, to explore the idea of self-esteem across topics, and to facilitate meaningful conversation and open discussion. All topics were chosen not only to encourage discourse, but to sustain it for a significant period of time (usually 45 to 60 minutes) across conversational turns. The sustained development and analysis of a topic is central to *Social Communication*. Since all topics are based on the concept of self-esteem, verbal interaction evolves naturally because of associated underlying themes. Activities will be more pertinent and more effectively generalized if group discourse is incorporated whenever possible.

Social Communication is not intended, however, to teach basic conversational skills such as, taking turns, requesting clarification, or introducing, maintaining, or changing a topic. Individuals participating in *Social Communication* activities should have some degree of skill in these areas. Presumably, individuals with communication impairments may need further work in specific conversational skill areas; however, the goal of conversation in this program is the exchange of ideas, not the mechanics of how to do so. For materials that focus on direct remediation of conversational mechanics, see Brinton and Fujiki (1989), Hoskins (1987), and Schwartz and McKinley (1984).

Hoskins (1990) suggests that in the conversational approach to communication remediation, foundation skills are not taught as prerequisites to conversation, but are learned as needed in developing conversational abilities. For example, a new term may be learned while listening to another, or a new way of asking for clarification or adding new information may be observed during conversation.

If necessary, basic conversational rules may be posted for easy observation as a reminder of how successful conversation works. Figure 1 on page 17 from Schwartz and McKinley (1984) can be a helpful guide.

Communication Strategies for Group Participants

Listed next are other rules and communication strategies that should be used by group participants throughout all activities. They are meant to serve as

RULES OF CONVERSATION

SPEAKER
1. Be polite
2. Be orderly
3. Be relevant
4. Be brief

Take turns
Stay on topics
Signal transitions

LISTENER
1. Pay attention
2. Engage in eye contact
3. Indicate level of understanding
4. Avoid interruptions

BOTH SPEAKER AND LISTENER CAN BE THE STARS IN A CONVERSATION!

Figure 1. Basic conversational rules. From *Daily Communication* (p. 123) by L. Schwartz and N. McKinley, 1984, Eau Claire, WI: Thinking Publications. Reprinted with permission.

guidelines for effective intrapersonal and interpersonal competence in a school/clinic setting and in relationships of all kinds. They are emphasized in the first two sections of *Social Communication*:

1. Say only as much as you are comfortable saying, but be truthful.
2. Use *I* messages. Instead of saying, "People are glad that you came," say, "I'm glad that you came."
3. Use constructive feedback. Instead of saying, "That was a dumb thing to say," say, "Would you explain what you meant?" Avoid put-downs.
4. Be an active listener. Pay attention when people talk. Think about what they are saying. Ask questions about what others are saying.
5. Be sensitive to others' feelings. People's feelings can be hurt very easily.
6. Keep what is said in the group confidential.
7. Develop your sense of humor. Not everything is serious.

When a group is first brought together, these strategies should be briefly discussed. Participants should know why they are important. Strategies 2, 3, and 4 have been expanded into activities included in the second section. It would be helpful to post this list so that group participants have access to it at all times.

Program Structure

Social Communication is an integrated series of sequenced activities. Each activity is based on the idea that participants have experienced the ones that precede it. The scope of this program is to move participants from an understanding of the group, to an understanding of themselves, and then to an understanding of their place in the world. Although activities can be used out of sequence, participants' acquisition of discourse skills and self-esteem concepts will be more effectively facilitated if the activities are done in sequence.

Social Communication

The flow of activities is arranged to establish some form of group communication, to help participants focus on personal issues, and then to move participants into thinking about social and global concerns. If, however, your group has already covered material in particular sections, or if you want to adapt the material to be more relevant for your group, do so. Some activities may be redundant for particular groups. Some groups may benefit from redundancy. It is important that participants understand the concept of self-esteem discussed in Section 5, Activity 1—"Analyzing the Concept of Self-Esteem," page 170, and Activity 9—"Developing Self-Esteem," page 194, before doing any activities in Sections 6–10. Conversely, Sections 1–4 do not include specific discussion of self-esteem.

If you want to eliminate activities within sections or rearrange the order of activities within sections, do so. Adapt the order and number of activities to fit your group. If you skip activities and participants appear to be having difficulty with particular concepts, refer back to information in activities that you did not cover. The concepts in the first two sections are crucial to successful group interaction.

Social Communication is organized into 10 areas with 10 discourse-based activities in each area. The 100 activities are divided into the following sections:

1. *Developing a Group Concept*
2. *Communicating with Others*
3. *Understanding Oneself*
4. *Exploring Self-Concept*
5. *Defining Self-Esteem*
6. *Decision Making and Problem Solving*
7. *Analyzing Family Issues*
8. *Social Values and Myths*
9. *Differences and Similarities Among People*
10. *Examining Our Role in the World*

We think such a path will foster adolescents' sense of confidence and responsibility so necessary for success in the adult world. Activities and sections are arranged to reflect Hartzell's (1984) reminder that:

> In human life there is no period as characterized by change as adolescence. Some of the changes are physical.... The emotions also experience change—the desire for liberation, the fear of failure, the fear of being different, the thrill of physical love, the awareness of a mature body. Finally, changes affect intellect, bringing concern about world problems, sensitivity to human suffering, curiosity about the laws of nature, and passion for the pursuit of truth. (p. 8)

Group Interaction

Language intervention with adolescents is most beneficial when conducted in groups (Hoskins, 1990; Larson and McKinley, 1987; Nelson, 1989; Schwartz and McKinley, 1984). Group interaction is the ideal setting for promoting interpersonal communication skills. Groups provide natural communication contexts and the opportunity to give support to others and to observe that others also have communication difficulties. In addition, because group members participate in rendering judgments on their own and their peers' performances, the evaluation of ongoing communicative behaviors is not the sole province of the professional, making interactions more relevant and realistic (Larson and McKinley, 1985).

As a group becomes more cohesive, individuals have the opportunity to see themselves as helping others to be more communicative (Berg and Wages, 1982). Individuals with communication disorders may never have had the opportunity to see themselves as helpers. This interactional giving and receiving of support can help develop a self-image that has previously been hidden. The dual role process also facilitates trust among group members. When working with groups, several variables need to be considered: structure, language level, relationships, size, and space.

Structure

Common communication goals, age, and developmental levels of adolescents make a structured group experience most effective. Structuring also provides security for group members. The primary structure of *Social Communication* is dictated by the topics and the format of activities. Open and comfortable discussion, however, is built into each activity. Structure is also attained by working within a defined time frame (intervention session, class period, etc.). Group members know when a group begins and ends. This kind of orientation gives definition to member and facilitator expectations and carries with it the expectation of personal responsibility within a fixed time period (Berg and Wages, 1982).

Language Level

Group members should have basic social communication skills (such as turn-taking and topic maintenance) that allow for effective group interaction. Individuals should be at similar language levels to promote group compatibility (Larson and McKinley, 1987). An individual language assessment should be done for each participant before beginning any language remediation program. Individuals whose language levels are greatly disparate should probably not participate in the same group.

Relationships

Groups go through a natural process or progression as people get to know each other. The facilitator should be aware of the group level of relationship.

How a group functions will depend on its participants. General stages may be observed as follows:

1. *The relationship stage*—Individuals establish an identity within the group.
2. *The exploration stage*—Individuals share information about themselves and begin seeking information about others.
3. *The revealing stage*—Individuals engage in more self-disclosure and greater feelings of intimacy and trust.
4. *The reorganization stage*—Individuals may reorganize their ways of responding, behaving, and thinking.
5. *Closure*—Individuals reflect on what they have experienced and discuss how it feels to terminate a group.

If groups become cohesive, each stage allows group members to become more open about themselves, which in turn makes discussions more meaningful.

Larson and McKinley (1987) stress that "group members should perceive one another as equal in status if they are going to work cooperatively with one another, rather than competitively" (p. 161). Although it is not always possible to have group members of equal status, professionals can help to equalize relationships by being aware of the differences in the amount of participation among group members. Aspects of group dynamics that should be noted are:

1. Who talks? For how long? How often? Who doesn't talk?
2. Do you see any shift in the communicative pattern (e.g., talkative people become quiet, quiet people suddenly become talkative)? Is there a reason for this within the group interaction?
3. How are silent people treated? Is their silence part of their communication impairment? Are they actively listening?
4. Who do people look at when they talk?
5. Who talks after whom, or who interrupts?
6. What style of communication is used (e.g., assertions, aggressions, questions, tone of voice, gestures, etc.)?
7. Is there a natural group leader other than you? How does that person affect the group?

Size

The size of a communication remediation group is quite frequently determined by the number of students in a classroom or by students' schedules. Ideally, group participation should be limited to eight members. Many times, however, there is no choice as to how large a group may be, particularly in the school setting. Realistically, however, no more than 10 to 12 individuals per group should be considered if everyone is going to have the opportunity to communicate. If your situation dictates that you have a large group, be sure to engage everyone at least once in the activity discussion. Smaller groups of two to three are also effective. Activities in *Social Communication* can also be used for one-to-one intervention.

Various group compositions are recommended for particular activities. There are reasons for this. Some activities are better suited for small groups, some for large. Listed below are group compositions and some reasons for using them:

1. *Pairs*—Dyads offer the maximum in peer communication. Pairing is much less threatening than speaking in a larger group and is an ideal way for participants to establish rapport or discuss sensitive topics. To facilitate interaction with numerous people, vary partners frequently.

2. *Small groups*—Many activities include discussions for four to six participants. Some groups allow each person to participate and get feedback from others. To facilitate a variety of experiences within the group, vary subgroup composition frequently (i.e., don't let the same people always group together during discussions or games). If your group does not have four people, proceed with the discussion with two or three.

3. *Large groups*—Groups containing eight or more participants give people a chance to hear many opinions and respond to them. To include everyone in large group discussions, directly encourage those participants who may be reticent about talking publicly. If your group is not this large, the attention given to each participant can be easily adapted.

Space

Although space considerations may be dictated by facility assignments, group interaction will be enhanced if the size of the room is comfortable for the size of the group. Also, it would be helpful if participants feel that privacy is facilitated by a lack of outside interruptions.

Directions

To expand discussion and facilitate writing skills, most activities have accompanying activity pages, personal assessments, or "quizzes." To maintain interest and facilitate discourse skills, various activities such as role plays and games have been included. All written materials are designed to be easily read by participants who find reading difficult. The readability level of the written material is at approximately the fourth grade level, based on the Flesch-Kincaid Index (Readability Plus, 1988). If reading is a problem, read the material to the participants.

Activity Format

Activities are arranged in a specific format designed to facilitate discourse. Most activities take 45 to 60 minutes to complete. The time it takes to complete some activities will vary depending on group levels and interest. Some

Social Communication

facilitators may choose to do more than one topic per session, whereas others may find it desirable to extend a particular activity to an additional session. As with any communication development program, facilitators need to plan for variations.

Each activity contains a language purpose, a self-esteem focus, important vocabulary to be defined and discussed, and necessary materials. Each activity also contains a framework to follow. Although activity discussions proceed in a predetermined manner, the suggestions of what to say are meant to be used flexibly and to be adapted to your personal teaching style. The suggestions are not meant to be read verbatim to students. Discourse ideas presented in the Process section of each activity are designed to be scaffolds on which to hang your own experiences, knowledge, and focus. Embellish these ideas with your own communication style. During all discussions, however, the following guidelines should be modeled:

1. Listen attentively.
2. Ask questions.
3. Contribute to the conversation when you have something relevant to say.
4. Talk about personal experiences only when you are comfortable doing so.
5. Be sensitive to the feelings of others.

Activities are introduced by talking to participants about what they will be doing and why. The objective of this conversation is to give participants the opportunity to understand the relevancy of the topic both communicatively and interpersonally.

Each activity is concluded with a summary discussion that synthesizes and integrates participants' ideas. It is particularly in this last segment that sustained discourse can be encouraged.

Communication Summation Forms are available for participants to evaluate their role and interaction during activity discussions. These forms can be used whenever you want to emphasize self-assessment strategies or to assess group functioning as a whole. Information from these forms can also be used to facilitate discussion about how the group is functioning. The forms are located in *Appendix A*.

Process Steps

To keep the focus on discourse, proceed in the following manner for each activity:

1. Introduce the topic by writing the name of the activity on a chalkboard or where everyone can see it.
2. Define the words included in the Vocabulary section. These words are critical to understanding the focus of the activity. If appropriate, ask students to look up the words in the dictionary, or give them the definitions yourself. Only words that can be found in the dictionary are

included in the Vocabulary section. Engage participants in a brief discussion about where they have heard the word used before or about a situation that reflects an appropriate use of the word. Sometimes words have been included in the Vocabulary section more than once throughout the program. Use your own judgment about which words participants need to define before beginning the discussion process. The discussion process begins with the assumption that participants have a basic understanding of the vocabulary words listed. Phrases or concepts that need to be defined (e.g., body image) but cannot be found in the dictionary are defined in the activity itself. Sometimes a definition is provided and other times participants are guided to "discover" the definition through the questions that are posed.

3. Begin the actual "Process" discussion by talking about why the topic is relevant and important to learn. By helping participants to identify how and why a particular topic affects their lives, you are promoting a more effective learning situation. You are incorporating participants into the learning process by showing them that you have no hidden agendas.

4. Expand on the topic by following the "Process" steps and incorporating your own ideas whenever possible. Most activities use a brainstorming technique to generate ideas for discussion. When brainstorming, encourage participants to think of as many ideas as possible. Guidelines for brainstorming can be found in Section 1, Activity 1—"Group Interaction," p. 30.

5. Use the written materials to help expand conversation. Weave ideas from the activity pages and quizzes to sustain the topic. Adapt written materials to fit your needs. For example, if time is short, discuss ideas on activity pages rather than having participants complete them. Sections of activity pages can be collapsed or expanded into more extensive writing assignments.

6. Conclude the topic discussion by synthesizing ideas and comments.

7. Use the Communication Summation Forms found in *Appendix A* to assess (and to help participants assess) the success of individual and group interaction, if appropriate to the situation. This is a helpful way to tie up loose ends.

Written Materials

Since many activities build on each other, a notebook of activity pages, assessments, and quizzes can be compiled. The notebook will be helpful to review ideas as participants move through the program. There are exceptions to the suggestion, however. Very personal information, such as that included on the Stress Test on page 122, should be kept at each participant's discretion. A general rule of thumb is to have participants keep only those written assignments with which they are comfortable. Written material that participants consider personal or private should be disposed of at their discretion.

Supplemental Materials

A chalkboard and chalk, flip chart and markers, or some other easily visible writing surface should be available for all activities. Participants should always have pencils or pens.

Facilitator Preparation

Since almost all materials are included in *Social Communication*, preparation is not a lengthy process. However, you should be familiar with the activity content and structure before beginning any group interaction. You will need to set aside time to think about the grouping of participants during activities and to duplicate written material.

Role of the Facilitator

Facilitating communication groups necessitates that professionals have a strong orientation in communication development as well as personal knowledge of their own communication style (Pickering, 1991). The end goal of this intervention program is improved interpersonal communication. This means that the adult in the communication process must be comfortable as the group facilitator as well as being cognizant of personal communication attributes and weaknesses. Being comfortable and at ease as a facilitator are skills that develop over time. By following group process suggestions, adults can develop their own sense of self-confidence as effective facilitators.

The quality of interpersonal communication influences our relationships, and there is strong evidence that the relationship between teachers and students affects the educational process (Center and Wascom, 1986; Galbo, 1984; Peck, 1981). Students' improved abilities in the area of interpersonal communication are directly related to the teachers' awareness of their own effective communication style. Specifically, the facilitator's ability to communicate warmth, empathy, respect, concreteness, self-disclosure, genuineness, immediacy, and confrontation significantly improves students' interpersonal communication skills as well as general cognitive growth (Robinson and Brosh, 1980).

In addition to focusing on what happens between people, it is also necessary for the facilitator to provide an environment that maximizes learning. Larson and McKinley (1987) explain that:

> During mediation, the adult transmits the meaning underlying an object, event, or experience (i.e., interprets *why* something exists, happens, or may occur), and guides the adolescent to comprehend this meaning. (p. 186)

In such an environment, the adult explains why an idea or activity is important and links communication and self-esteem goals and objectives. The end goal of mediation is to help adolescents become more capable of monitoring and changing their own progress.

Listed below are ways in which interpersonal communication can be mediated and/or enhanced. The following ideas, some of them adapted from Cormier and Hackney (1987), should be used throughout the duration of the group:

1. *Use specific language in a context that is appropriate to the activity.* If you feel that important vocabulary terms or concepts are difficult, explain them and tell the group why they are important and how they relate to life. In this way, semantics are precise, and language stays at a comfortable comprehension level.

2. *Keep group participants on the activity topic.* If they wander off, explain how an off-topic remark makes it difficult to follow a conversation.

3. *Look for opportunities to help group members become aware that their concerns are shared.* Ask, "Who else has this concern? Has anyone else felt this way?" Seeing similarities between themselves and others reduces participants' anxiety and promotes group cohesion. Your goal is to eliminate apprehension about self-expression in a group and to help participants to universalize their experiences.

4. *Redirect comments and questions to you back to the group.* For example, say, "Steve, you've had that experience. What happened to you?" Redirecting promotes involvement and helps prevent you from being the center of attention.

5. *Establish links between group participants by pointing out similarities in what people say, have experienced, or feel.* Linking promotes interaction and discussion.

6. *Promote creativity and participation by teaching the group to brainstorm.* Brainstorming delays evaluation until all suggestions are offered. Since no suggestions initially are discarded, any potential feelings of rejection are softened. Brainstorming can be especially valuable when the group offers ideas to one of its members.

7. *Stop discouraging or destructive remarks.* Point out why disparaging remarks may be hurtful or may hamper group dynamics. One helpful strategy is to teach participants to use *I* messages. Using *I* messages is a strategy described in Communication Strategies for Group Participants (see page 16), and is also included in Section 2, Activity 8—"Being Assertive" (see page 85). "Constructive Criticism" is another communication strategy and is also an activity in *Section 2: Communicating with Others* (see page 66).

8. *Summarize, clarify, and paraphrase.* These skills focus discussion, help participants assimilate what they have learned, and let you know how well a topic has been understood. Asking for clarification models the necessity of doing so, while requiring the speaker to use his or her own words to convey the message learned.

9. *Teach participants to listen actively.* Active listening is a strategy included in Communication Strategies for Group Participants (see page 16) and is also the basis for Section 2, Activity 6—"Active Listening" (see page 76).

10. *Be aware of the emotional, cognitive, and social limitations of the group.* Don't push the group or individual participants into uncomfortable areas. If a particular discussion seems difficult for someone, require that only the written portion of an activity be done, or if someone becomes overly agitated, ask him or her just to listen to the remainder of the discussion. Accept as much participation as a person can comfortably give.

11. *Be aware of feelings that may arise during activities.* Dealing with the topic of self-esteem is bound to generate feelings on some level. Realistic interpersonal communication and feelings are inseparable, and to express those feelings increases communication possibilities. Sometimes being aware of feelings is enough. It should be a participant's choice to express those feelings or not to express them. Holistic communication includes feelings and emotion.

12. *Be aware of the difference between developing communication skills and counseling.* To foster understanding of communication difficulties, professionals may need to counsel individuals about their communication problems (Schwartz and McKinley, 1984; Simon, 1985; Wiig and Semel, 1984). Because lowered self-esteem is frequently associated with a communication problem, it is also beneficial to talk about feelings in the classroom or therapy setting. Such discussions are particularly important in settings where counselors are not routinely available. Larson and McKinley (1987) suggest that "providing release and support for feelings associated with the communication disorder might involve discussing frustration, anger, and rejection that adolescents have felt" (p. 164).

Activities in *Social Communication* were designed to tap into and generate emotions about how one feels about oneself, how one views interpersonal communication, and how one fits into a cultural and world community. Topics do not include extremely sensitive areas such as suicide, domestic violence, incest, or rape. These kinds of issues need to be referred to trained counselors or psychologists. According to Larson and McKinley (1987), "It is unethical and impossible to try to handle all of the problems associated with adolescence within the confines of the speech-language program" (p. 192). Dealing with self-esteem issues, however, presents a perfect opportunity for educators, speech-language pathologists, counselors, and other related professionals to share their overlapping areas of expertise. Developing self-esteem is also an ideal situation for collaboration among professionals.

It is possible that some activities may inadvertently trigger comments or emotions that are outside of the scope of the group, especially among individuals with emotional disturbance or behavioral disorders.

Activities that have the potential to generate intense feelings have been coded with a (C), indicating the need for caution and/or a suggestion that they may be more comfortably discussed with the aid of a counselor.

13. *Keep the conversational focus on group members, not on yourself.* The group facilitator should establish a balance between offering personal ideas and anecdotes and sharing the conversational spotlight with participants.

14. *Promote self-efficacy.* See pages 9–10 for a discussion of this topic.

The role of the facilitator is crucial to successful group communication. The facilitator's comfort level and ease of interaction provides the model for participants to follow. In addition to facilitating the group, being an active participant in group discussions is a powerful way to enhance and encourage group dynamics.

New Role for the Speech-Language Pathologist

An understanding of the relationship between self-esteem and communication impairments is being emphasized by researchers in speech-language pathology who deal with individuals who have emotional/behavioral disorders. Most speech-language clinicians have certainly been challenged by the behavioral and emotional demands of some of their clients. Additionally, speech-language pathologists are increasingly acting as consultants and facilitators in behaviorally disordered classrooms, in psychiatric hospitals and treatment centers, and even in courtroom settings (Hoskins, 1990; Prizant et al., 1990).

As new data are gathered that indicate the prevalence of co-occurrence of communication disorders and emotional/behavioral disorders (Baker and Cantwell, 1985; Baltaxe and Simmons, 1988, 1990; Burke, 1990; Camarata, Hughes, and Ruhl, 1988), it is crucial that speech-language pathologists understand that "disorders of the development of language are likely to be central to the development of human personality" (Gualtieri, Koriath, Van Bourgondien, and Saleeby, 1983; Prizant and Wetherby, 1990). Additionally, because of the close relationship between communication disorders and emotional/behavioral disorders, goals for individuals should not be handled in an isolated and fragmented manner by speech-language pathologists and teachers (Audet and Hummel, 1990; Prizant et al., 1990).

Prizant et al. (1990) also speculate that because of the correlation between communication disorders and emotional/behavioral disorders, speech-language pathologists will be called upon to play a larger and more complex role in serving these individuals, as well as interacting with mental health professionals. Prizant et al. (1990) also suggest that speech-language pathologists become more familiar with the literature and issues of psychotherapy.

Maintaining an Emotionally Safe Environment

All communication development groups must be psychologically safe for participants. Participants need to feel that if they risk saying something personal, absurd, cynical, or inaccurate, there will be a safe environment that is free of criticism. As with all realistic interpersonal communication, we cannot be protected from honest feedback. A facilitator can, however, maintain a communicative atmosphere that reduces fear and defensiveness.

Certain safeguards can be taken to attain comfortable group dynamics:

1. Screen out individuals who may not be appropriate for group communication. Interpersonal communication will be hampered if one person always monopolizes the group focus. Communication groups may not be appropriate for individuals who are extremely hostile or extremely emotionally labile, or who have unusual problems with impulse control.

2. Work with extremely hostile or emotional people individually. Since these individuals are frequently the ones who need the most help with self-esteem, it would be appropriate and very beneficial to intervene on a one-to-one basis. After self-esteem has been improved, that individual may be reintroduced back into the group. A counselor should be involved on a consultation basis to assist in developing strategies for extremely difficult individuals. In some cases, referring difficult cases to a counselor would be more appropriate than addressing self-esteem issues in the classroom setting.

3. Be sure to leave enough time at the end of a discussion to address how people are feeling. Get closure before the group separates.

4. Be aware of cultural differences between all group participants. Not all cultures value the same interactional behaviors. For example, direct, assertive eye contact may be considered to be rude in some cultures. Cultural sensitivity and receptivity are crucial when considering any communication intervention.

Section 1: Developing a Group Concept

This section lays the foundation for group interaction. Activities emphasize development of connections, cooperation, and trust. Participants learn about group involvement and cohesiveness in a way that is not intimidating. They also learn that others have communication difficulties. As the group becomes unified, individuals have the opportunity to see themselves as helping others to be more communicative.

Comfortable peer interaction is established in this first section. *It is important to set a tone based on comfort, confidentiality, and confidence.* To help create an effective, communicative group, review the suggestions for group interaction on pages 19–21. The first activity introduces discussion guidelines for group interaction and is the first step for group participants to get to know each other. (See pages 17 and 22 for more information on guidelines.)

As in all activities in *Social Communication: Activities for Improving Peer Interactions and Self-Esteem*, the communication focus is on discourse. The activities are designed to provide the content for discussion.

Activities in this section include:

		Page
1.	Group Interaction	30
2.	Group Interviews: Getting to Know Each Other	32
3.	Sharing Who I Was, Am, and Will Be	35
4.	Cooperation	38
5.	Sharing Mementos	42
6.	Predicting Another's Answers (C)	44
7.	Group Problem Solving	47
8.	Recognizing Communication Differences Among Group Members	51
9.	Establishing Group Trust (IIS)	55
10.	Trusting Others	58

Social Communication

Activity 1—Developing a Group Concept
Group Interaction

Language Purpose:

1. To identify guidelines for communication during group interaction
2. To define the concept of *brainstorming*
3. To use a *brainstorming* strategy to help find information

Self-Esteem Focus:

To establish group expectations and communication techniques

Materials:

none

Vocabulary:

brainstorm, expectation, generate, guideline, interaction

Process:

(Note: This activity was designed to introduce participants to group interaction. The guidelines for this activity are purposefully general to give maximum flexibility to group compositions.)

1. Explain that for a group to function comfortably and efficiently, it is helpful to establish guidelines and discuss expectations. Ask participants what might happen if people did not have guidelines for group communication. Also ask them to give examples of situations where they have to follow guidelines. Are guidelines and expectations the same?

2. Express your expectations for group interaction and initiate a discussion about possible guidelines or rules. For example:

   a. Only one person talks at a time.
   b. Respect others' rights to talk or to remain silent.
   c. Keep what is said in the group within the group.
   d. Try to talk about yourself, not about others.

   Go into some detail about why each guideline is important and what the consequences will be if some participants have difficulty following the guidelines. These should be group decisions. After guidelines have been determined, post them for use in subsequent activities.

3. Explain that you are now going to introduce a group technique called "brainstorming" that will be used frequently in group interaction. It is

designed to facilitate group involvement. Ask participants to guess what *brainstorming* might mean.

4. Present the concept of *brainstorming*. Explain that the term means thinking of as many ideas as possible that go with a particular concept. The purpose of brainstorming is to generate ideas. The quantity, not quality, of ideas is important. Each idea generated is written for all participants to see. Initially, all ideas are included without judgment or comment. After all ideas have been listed, the group then decides which of the suggested responses will be used for discussion.

5. With the group, decide how brainstorming ideas are to be shared (e.g., one person talks at a time, each person takes a turn, a person with an idea just says it, etc.).

6. Do a very general brainstorming activity. For example, participants may list interesting discussion topics for the group. Brainstorm for three minutes. As a group, choose the two most interesting topics. If necessary, do an additional general brainstorming activity.

7. Conclude the activity with a discussion about individual participation in the activity. Was working as a group to do this activity comfortable? Why or why not? Did everyone participate? If some group members didn't participate, what held them back? How might a group change over time? Are there changes students would like to see in the group?

Social Communication

Activity 2—Developing a Group Concept
Group Interviews: Getting to Know Each Other

Language Purpose:

1. To concentrate attention on a speaker
2. To question another person for information
3. To report information to a group

Self-Esteem Focus:

To establish basic connections between group members

Materials:

Group Interview activity page

Vocabulary:

interview, interviewee

Process:

1. Explain that group interaction is more successful if participants really know each other. Ask participants what they have experienced when getting to know other people. How do people get to know each other?
2. Explain that one of the best ways to get to know another person is to find out what that person thinks and what that person has done. Ask, "What's the best way to find out what people think?" (Answer: Ask them.)
3. Explain that participants will be asking each other questions that will then be shared with the large group. Select either Format A or B in process step 4.
4. *Format A:* Choose a partner for each participant. Distribute the *Group Interview* activity page to each person. Instruct partners to ask each other all the questions on the activity page and any other questions that might be interesting to the group. Allow about 10 minutes per person (i.e., 20 minutes for the partnership). When all questioning is completed, ask participants to report their findings about their partners. Encourage other participants to ask additional questions.

    Format B: Put the questions from the *Group Interview* activity page on cards. Put them face down on a table. Ask participants to take two cards each and to choose one to answer. Each participant answers his or her

Developing a Group Concept: Group Interviews

own chosen question for the group, and then chooses another group member to answer the remaining question.

5. Conclude the activity with a discussion of the interview process. Did participants prefer to be the interviewer or interviewee? Why? Did they learn anything interesting about anyone? Did they learn anything that surprised them? Do they have anything in common with other people in the group? Did learning information about other participants help them to feel more comfortable? How?

Social Communication

GROUP INTERVIEW

Directions: Ask your partner each question and record a brief answer. If the interviewee doesn't want to answer your question, move on to the next question. If the interviewee says, "I don't know," say something like "Take a guess" or "Give it a try."

1. Where were you born?

2. How would your parents have described you as a small child?

3. What is your definition of a good parent?

4. What kind of music do you like?

5. What is your favorite movie? Why?

6. What is your most valued possession?

7. Who would you most like to be like?

8. What is your definition of a friend?

9. What kind of job would you most like to have in the future?

10. What is the most important thing that people should know about you?

Activity 3—Developing a Group Concept
Sharing Who I Was, Am, and Will Be

Language Purpose:

1. To describe past, present, and future interests
2. To report information about another person

Self-Esteem Focus:

To develop an understanding of individuals within the group

Materials:

Who I Was, Am, and Will Be activity page

Vocabulary:

fantasy, imagine, paraphrase

Process:

1. Ask why it is important to learn about individuals within the group. What group strengths can be gained from understanding others in the group?

2. Distribute the *Who I Was, Am, and Will Be* activity page. Explain that this activity page necessitates that participants try as best they can to remember the past. If participants say they can't remember, tell them to try to imagine how they felt when they were 10 years old. Also, encourage them to fantasize about what they will be doing in five years. Participants may write their responses on the activity page or mentally prepare oral answers. When all participants have completed the activity page, break them into small groups, preferably consisting of four people who don't know each other well.

3. Explain that participants are to share their answers, beginning with the first category on the activity page. When all four group members have shared answers, then go on to the second category, and so on.

4. Tell small-group members that they are each to report on (i.e., summarize) another member's responses. This should be a paraphrasing of what that group member said, not a reading from the activity page. Every participant should make a report. Make report assignments ahead of time, or wait until all responses have been shared and then randomly make report assignments.

5. Conclude the activity with a discussion. Ask if participants learned anything new about their small-group members. Why is it important for

group members to know about each other's past, present, and future? Do group members feel they need to know another person well in order to interact with that person in a group situation? Why or why not?

Developing a Group Concept: Sharing Who I Was, Am, and Will Be

Who I Was, Am, and Will Be

Directions: Fill in the blanks after thinking about your past and present. Then think about five years from now and answer those questions.

When I was 10 years old . . .

Wish: _____

Main interest: _____

Biggest problem: _____

Major accomplishment: _____

My hero: _____

Description of myself: _____

Right now in my life . . .

Wish: _____

Main interest: _____

Biggest problem: _____

Major accomplishment: _____

My hero/mentor: _____

Description of myself: _____

Five years from today . . .

Wish: _____

Main interest: _____

Biggest problem: _____

Major accomplishment: _____

My role model: _____

Description of myself: _____

© 1992 Thinking Publications
Duplication permitted for educational use only.

Social Communication

Activity 4—Developing a Group Concept
Cooperation

Language Purpose:

1. To define *cooperation*
2. To define problems nonverbally and determine solutions

Self-Esteem Focus:

To increase awareness of the importance of the individual in group problem solving

Materials:

cooperation puzzles, envelopes

Vocabulary:

cooperation, enhance

Process:

1. Prepare ahead of time one set of cooperation puzzles for each small group you intend to form during this activity. (Read the instructions on pages 40–41 now.)
2. Ask participants to give examples of when other people have cooperated with them. Ask them why it is important to cooperate in group activities.
3. Brainstorm a meaning for *cooperation*. What is required to create a cooperative environment?

    Examples: Agreeing on the problem.

    Being willing to help.

    Working as a group.

    Thinking of others, not only of oneself.

4. Divide into small groups (four people per group is ideal).
5. Distribute the envelopes containing the cooperation puzzles. Each small group receives four envelopes.
6. Instruct participants within each small group that there are enough pieces in their envelopes to form four squares of the same size. There is to be no verbal communication while constructing the squares. No one may ask or indicate that they need a specific piece. Participants may, however, give puzzle pieces to others within their small groups.

7. Allow enough time for all small groups to complete their puzzles.
8. Conclude the activity with a discussion concerning problems encountered in the exercise. How did it feel to work in a group? What was the strategy of the small groups? How did the members feel when one person finished a square and did not look to see if it benefited the rest of the group? How did participants feel when one person did not see what was needed to attain completion for the larger group? How did that one person feel? Did you learn anything about yourself or others?

Ideas for this activity were adapted from Coleman (1980).

Social Communication

Cooperation Puzzle Instructions

Materials:

poster board, scissors, pencil, ruler, envelopes

Directions:

1. Cut a set of four 4-by-4-inch squares out of poster board for each small group that will participate in this activity.
2. Cut the 4-by-4-inch squares into three pieces each, as pictured below. By using 2-inch and 4-inch pieces, pieces may be interchanged, but there will be only one solution which will make four 4-by-4-inch squares.
3. Mix up the cut pieces for one set of puzzles and randomly place three pieces in each of four envelopes.
4. Label the envelopes by groups of four to ensure that each small group will have pieces for four 4-by-4-inch square puzzles within those envelopes (i.e., A-1, A-2, A-3, A-4; B-1, B-2, B-3, B-4; etc.).

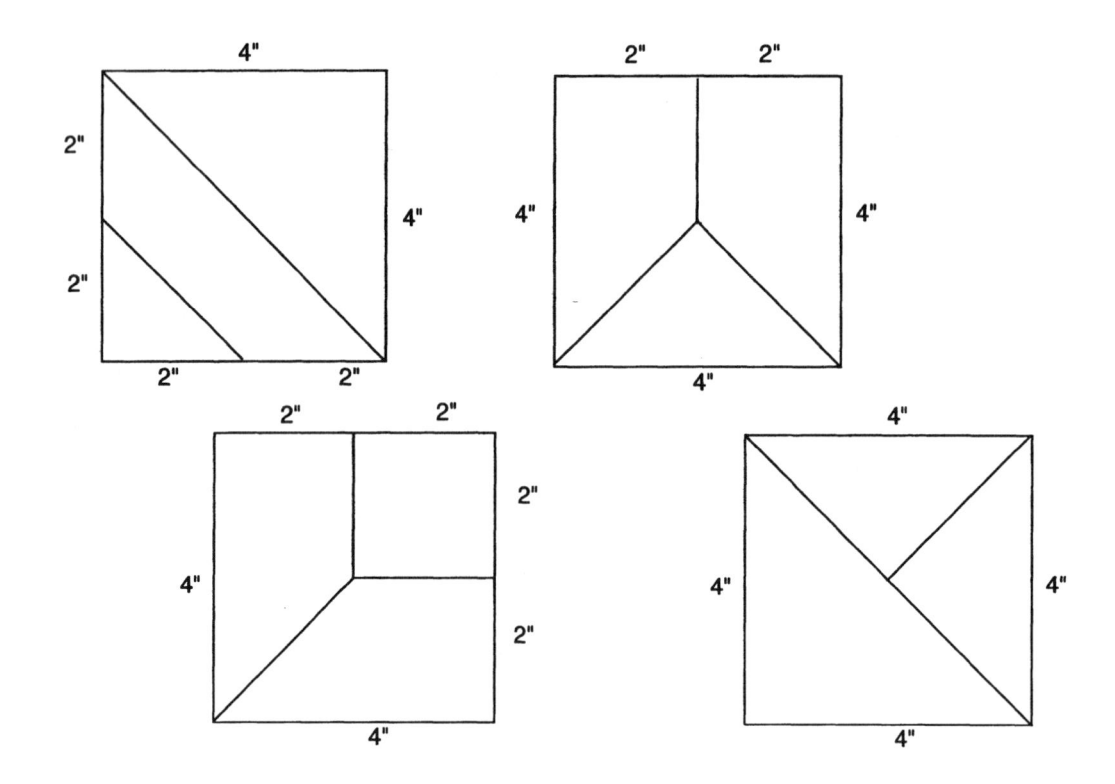

Developing a Group Concept: Cooperation

(Note: To simplify the activity, glue a magazine photograph to the poster board before cutting it. To complicate the activity, use only one envelope for each small group with pieces for all puzzles in that one envelope. To make a large group cooperation activity, do the following:

1. Divide the large group into four smaller groups.
2. Using one set of puzzles, place three puzzle pieces in each envelope. [Assemble one envelope for each small group.] Of the three puzzle pieces, one piece should belong to another group's puzzle. This will require small groups to cooperate with one another to complete the puzzles. Make sure your room is large enough to allow groups to work comfortably.)

Social Communication

Activity 5—Developing a Group Concept
Sharing Mementos

Language Purpose:

1. To organize appropriate mementos and describe them
2. To explain why particular mementos are important

Self-Esteem Focus:

To increase self-awareness and share important aspects of one's life with group members

Materials:

lunch-size paper bags, poster board

Vocabulary:

cohesive, insight, interest, memento, priority

Process:

(Note: This is a two-day activity. Homework is required.)

1. Ask participants why it is important to continue to share individual interests and priorities with others in the group.
2. Distribute paper bags to group members.
3. Tell participants that they are to take the bags home and put in three to five items that would help others know them better. The items could be actual objects, photos, or anything else that would give others insight into their lives.
4. Remind participants that they should not include anything that would make them feel uneasy or uncomfortable.
5. Explain to participants that you have already collected a few items from your home. Share the contents of your bag and the meaning behind each item.
6. Instruct participants to bring their bags back the next day.

The following session:

7. Ask for volunteers to share the contents of their bags and suggest that participants ask questions of each other about the mementos. (This may take more than the allotted time and may need to be continued.) When everyone has had a chance to share their mementos, ask the following questions:

Developing a Group Concept: Sharing Mementos

    a. Have the participants learned anything new about themselves or others?

    b. Has it helped them become more cohesive as a group? Why or why not?

8. Conclude the activity with a discussion. If there was one bag for the entire group, what would the members include in it? Write or have group members gather or illustrate the group bag items. These might include words that describe the group, significant group activities, shared group interests, a group picture, etc. Also, group members could collectively decide which item to include from each participant's bag to create a group memento.

(Note: If you think that many participants will forget to bring in mementos, modify the activity by letting them cut meaningful pictures from magazines that represent things that are important to them. Another option is to name and describe their mementos on note cards.)

Social Communication

Activity 6—Developing a Group Concept
Predicting Another's Answers (C)

Language Purpose:

1. To predict another's responses to predetermined questions
2. To compare and contrast partner responses

Self-Esteem Focus:

To increase knowledge about group members and improve observation skills

Materials:

Predicting Another's Answers activity pages

Vocabulary:

observation, predict

Process:

1. Explain to participants that the purpose of this activity is to help them get to know other group members better and improve their observation skills.
2. Ask participants why it may be important to be able to predict another's answers. If participants are able to predict another's answers, what does that mean? How does that help communication within the group?
3. Instruct group members to pair up with someone they don't know well. When in pairs, tell group members to sit back to back or put a barrier between them so they can't see each other.
4. Distribute the *Predicting Another's Answers* activity pages.
5. Tell participants to answer the questions, first predicting what their partners will say or do and then answering the questions for themselves.
6. Ask participants to compare and contrast their predictions with the actual answers of their partners.
7. Conclude the activity with a discussion. Were any predictions accurate? Why or why not? Did discussing the answers help participants get to know another group member better? Did participants learn anything new about themselves? Was making predictions about another person helpful? Why or why not? Had participants ever tried to make predictions about other people? What kind? Were they right?

Developing a Group Concept: Predicting Another's Answers

PREDICTING ANOTHER'S ANSWERS

Directions: Under the "Partner" column, write the answers you think your partner will give about himself or herself. Under the "Self" column, answer the questions for yourself. Answer honestly.

           Partner   **Self**

1. You find a $20 bill. What do you do with it? _____

2. You failed to study for a test. What do you do? _____

3. You arrive at class 45 minutes late. What do you say? _____

4. You want to buy a friend a special gift, but you don't know what he/she likes. What do you do? _____

5. A stray animal follows you home. What do you do? _____

6. You really want to ask someone out, but you are afraid to. What do you do? _____

7. You just flunked an important test. What do you do? _____

© 1992 Thinking Publications
Duplication permitted for educational use only.

Social Communication

                                                      Partner   **Self**

8. What do you like to do in your spare time? _____ _____

9. You don't have enough money to buy something you want. What do you do? _____ _____

10. You just got a speeding ticket while driving the family car. What do you do? _____ _____

11. Your parents don't like the person you're dating. What do you do? _____ _____

12. A grandparent buys you something you don't like. What do you do? _____ _____

13. You break a lamp at home. What do you do? _____ _____

14. You see a car run over an animal. What do you do? _____ _____

15. Your teacher asked you to bring a sample of your favorite music to school. What kind do you bring? _____ _____

Activity 7—Developing a Group Concept
Group Problem Solving

Language Purpose:

1. To examine problems jointly and determine what needs to be done
2. To consider alternative solutions to problems
3. To analyze roles within a group

Self-Esteem Focus:

To establish group rapport

Materials:

Problem Situation I: The Blizzard or *Problem Situation II: The Fire* activity page (Choose the situation most appropriate for your group.)

Vocabulary:

analyze, eliminate, feedback, rapport, realistic, recorder, role, solution

Process:

(Note: The primary focus of this activity is on group interaction, not problem-solving strategies. Problem solving is addressed more fully in *Section 6: Decision Making and Problem Solving*.)

1. Explain that this activity involves analyzing a problem and then discussing possible solutions to the problem. Tell participants that they will be working in small groups. Ask if anyone has had experience solving problems as a group (possible experiences may have been within their families, at work, with a group of friends). Ask when or why solving problems as a group could be helpful.

2. Divide participants into small groups (three to four people is an ideal number). Give each group a copy of one problem situation included in this activity (or create your own). Read the problem aloud to all participants.

3. Tell each group to choose a recorder who will list important information and then report it to the large group. Give the groups a minute to decide who the recorder will be.

4. Explain that the task for each group is to talk about the problem situation and to complete the following steps to solve the problem:

   a. determine the main problem
   b. list possible solutions to the problem (brainstorm)
   c. eliminate solutions that aren't realistic

47

Social Communication

     d. choose the best solution

     e. decide on a plan of action for the solution

    Give participants as much help with these concepts as is necessary for their level of understanding. Allow 10 to 15 minutes to discuss the situation and formulate a plan of action.

5. Ask the groups to come back together. Have each group recorder report all information discussed. Groups can give each other feedback about their decisions.

6. Conclude with a discussion about such ideas as:

    a. the problems that arose in making group decisions

    b. the roles within the group (How was the recorder chosen? Did everyone contribute to the problem-solving process? Was one person the leader?)

    c. **the comfort level and rapport between people**

Developing a Group Concept: Group Problem Solving

✤ ❈ ✤ ❈ ✤ Problem Situation I: ✤ ❈ ✤ ❈ ✤

The Blizzard

You and your small sister are traveling across the country by car to visit your parents. As you approach the Rocky Mountains, you find yourself in the middle of a major blizzard. There is so much snow on the road that you can no longer drive. You have seen no other cars. You think that there is a small town about a mile down the road. You are not sure if your sister could walk the mile in the snow, but if you leave her in the car or if you stay in the car, you are afraid you both may freeze to death. What are you going to do?

Social Communication

Problem Situation II: THE FIRE

You wake up in the middle of the night to the smell of smoke. You turn on the lamp beside your bed and walk toward the door to see what the problem is. If there is a fire, you need to warn the other people in the house. As you go to open the door, you touch it and realize that it is hot. You don't know what to do. If you open the door, there may be fire in the hall. If you take the time to climb down from your second-story window, the others may burn. What are you going to do?

Activity 8—Developing a Group Concept
Recognizing Communication Differences Among Group Members

Language Purpose:

1. To assess interactive communication styles
2. To compare and contrast extrovert/introvert communication styles

Self-Esteem Focus:

To increase understanding of individual communication styles

Materials:

Communication Style activity pages, magazines, bulletin board or large paper

Vocabulary:

communication, extrovert, introvert, style

Process:

1. Tell participants that the purpose of this activity is to recognize their unique communication styles and how styles are influenced by the kind of people they are.
2. Distribute the *Communication Style* activity pages. Tell participants that the activity will help determine if a person is an extrovert or an introvert. Remind participants that there are no right or wrong answers and that being an introvert is no better than being an extrovert and vice versa.
3. After participants have totaled their responses, explain that the differences between an introvert and an extrovert are as follows:

Extrovert

A person who is an extrovert frequently:
   a. finds it easy to talk to other people
   b. enjoys talking and spending time with people
   c. enjoys parties and being around many people
   d. likes a variety of daily activities
   e. acts before thinking in certain situations
   f. likes the world of people

Introvert

A person who is an introvert frequently:
- a. does not like to talk to people
- b. enjoys being alone
- c. enjoys being with people, but may find it tiring to do so
- d. likes working on one thing for a long time
- e. thinks before acting in certain situations
- f. likes the world of ideas

4. Ask participants if they agree that the definitions of introvert/extrovert fit with the results from the activity pages. Share your own activity page results with them. Then ask participants to share their results and to determine if they are primarily an introvert, an extrovert, or have qualities of both.

5. Distribute magazines and instruct each participant to find and cut out pictures of five people who *appear* to be introverts and five who *appear* to be extroverts. Display the pictures on a bulletin board or a large piece of paper that has been divided into the two categories. Ask participants to explain why each of their pictures is representative of an extrovert or an introvert.

6. Conclude the activity by discussing how being an extrovert/introvert may affect group interaction. What will the introverts bring to group interaction? How will extroverts help interaction? Emphasize the strengths of both. What roles might participants take in the group depending on whether they are introverts or extroverts?

Ideas for this activity were adapted from McElmurry and Bisignano (1985).

Developing a Group Concept: Recognizing Communication Differences

COMMUNICATION STYLE

Directions: The following statements will help you decide if you are an introvert or an extrovert. Check (✔) the statement that best describes how you *usually* act or feel. There are no right or wrong answers.

1. When I am with friends, I usually
   ___ a. start the conversation.
   ___ b. wait for someone else to talk first.

2. When I am by myself, I usually
   ___ a. miss other people.
   ___ b. enjoy my time alone.

3. Unplanned parties with friends are usually
   ___ a. fun.
   ___ b. annoying.

4. In my group of friends, I usually
   ___ a. know the latest news.
   ___ b. get behind on the latest news.

5. When I relax, I usually like to
   ___ a. get together with friends.
   ___ b. be alone.

© 1992 Thinking Publications
Duplication permitted for educational use only.

Social Communication

6. I like to have

   ____ a. a lot of friends.

   ____ b. a few good friends.

7. During lunch, I usually eat with

   ____ a. several friends.

   ____ b. one good friend.

8. At a party, I usually feel

   ____ a. comfortable.

   ____ b. nervous.

9. I am

   ____ a. easy to get to know.

   ____ b. careful about making new friends.

10. At parties, I

    ____ a. like to be one of the last people to leave.

    ____ b. like to leave after a short period of time.

Total number of statements marked *a* _____

Total number of statements marked *b* _____

If you checked more *a* statements, you tend to be an extrovert.

If you checked more *b* statements, you tend to be an introvert.

Activity 9—Developing a Group Concept
Establishing Group Trust (HS)

Language Purpose:

1. To define the concept of *trust*
2. To rate trust levels to determine whom to tell what information
3. To arrange events on a communication trust scale

Self-Esteem Focus:

To achieve a greater degree of openness within the group

Materials:

paper

Vocabulary:

acquaintance, confidential, continuum, order, pantomime, rank, trust

Process:

1. Write the following list where all participants can see it before assembling in a group:
   a. Give a two-minute talk about your life.
   b. Imitate a dog barking.
   c. Do a silent pantomime of trying on a hat.
   d. Walk across the room with a book balanced on your head.
   e. Recite a nursery rhyme.
2. Explain to participants that today's activity will revolve around a discussion of trust. Ask them why trust is important. What happens when people don't trust each other? Tell them you would like them to read the list you have written. They are to rank the items from 1 to 5, with 5 being the item they would least like to do in front of the group. Each person should do this ranking individually on paper.
3. Defer questions about whether these activities will actually be performed until after the ranking has been finished.
4. Note where everyone can see, the number of participants who rank each option as number 5, 4, 3, 2, and 1.
5. Explain that the activities will not be performed and that the list was a way to get people to think about how it would feel to perform in front of the group. Ask the following questions:

Social Communication

    a. How did it feel to think you were going to be asked to perform?

    b. Did some tasks seem more embarrassing to do than others?

    c. How did your level of trust in this group affect how you felt?

    d. What is your level of trust in this group? Do you feel comfortable? Why or why not?

    e. How is trust built?

    f. What behaviors might lower the group trust level (e.g., laughing at others' mistakes, not listening to each other, talking about group members outside the group, etc.)?

6. Draw the following scale where everyone can see it. Explain that it represents a continuum of how comfortable people are about sharing personal information.

Communication Trust Scale

Trust Level Ranking	1	2	3	4	5	6
Telling Comfort Level	Tell Everyone	Tell a Stranger	Tell an Acquaintance	Tell a Friend	Tell Family/Best Friend	Tell No One

Ask if everyone generally agrees that personal information is most comfortably shared with a best friend or a family member. Does everyone agree with the continuum of the scale (i.e., it would probably be easier to tell your best friend something personal than it would be to tell a stranger)? If participants do not agree, change the scale to reflect the opinions of the group.

7. Based on group discussion, ask participants to place the group on the scale. How would they rank the trust level within the group?

8. Brainstorm events that human beings may experience (e.g., becoming engaged, getting arrested, falling in love, etc.). Try to elicit a wide variety of experiences so that participants can rank a whole range of events using the communication trust scale.

9. As a group, rank the events that were brainstormed. For example, some experiences are so personal that you would tell only your best friend or a trusted family member. That event would be ranked as a 5. Information that you could tell a friend is ranked as a 4, etc.

10. Ask participants to write down two personal things that have happened to them. Participants should then place these events on the scale at the appropriate place, depending upon whom they would tell. Assure them that they will not have to disclose anything they choose not to.

11. Ask the following questions after participants have ranked their personal items:

    a. Where did you place your two items on the scale?

    b. Why wouldn't you want some events to be known by everyone?

    c. Would you trust group members with information about your personal items? Why or why not?

    d. Is there information that you would trust with no one? How does that feel?

    e. What can we do to increase trust levels? (E.g., don't use put-downs, respect each other, keep what is said by group members confidential, talk about yourself as you are comfortable doing so, etc.)

12. Conclude the activity with a discussion about the group's trust level. Is there still information that is too personal to be talked about in the group? Is it possible that participants will become more trusting? How? Why? What happens when people don't trust each other? Is it always good to be trusting? Why or why not? How does confidentiality affect trust?

Social Communication

Activity 10—Developing a Group Concept
Trusting Others

Language Purpose:

1. To explore how to communicate trust
2. To rate the trust of another person

Self-Esteem Focus:

To develop the concept of trust in a group situation

Materials:

blindfolds, *Trusting Others* activity page

Vocabulary:

dependent, external, interdependence, internal, reassure, trust

Process:

(Note: Before the group session, decide where you would like to have this activity take place and make the necessary arrangements.)

1. Ask participants why it is important to have or develop trust relationships within a group, or help them discuss ideas about trust from the previous activity. Brainstorm ideas about the advantages of trusting relationships (e.g., friendships can deepen, problems can be solved, etc.).

2. Explain to participants that this activity necessitates that people trust each other. Elaborate on this idea by assuring them that this activity is to be taken very seriously.

3. Divide group members into pairs.

4. Explain that one person in the pair is to be blindfolded while the other leads them around by giving verbal directions such as "go left," "stop," "turn right, then take three small steps," etc. (At your discretion, participants can go outside the room for more space, or stay inside, doing the trust walk with fewer pairs at a time.) Briefly discuss what the leader can do to make the blindfolded person more comfortable. (For example, the leader can describe where the pair is going, alert the blindfolded partner to changes, reassure the blindfolded partner, etc.).

5. Remind participants that they are to be back at the starting point in 5 to 10 minutes. The roles will then be reversed, with the previously blindfolded individual leading the other partner. The leader is to maintain physical contact with the blindfolded participant at all times.

6. Tell participants to be aware of external sounds and internal feelings as they participate in this activity.

7. If you want to expand this activity to include a writing task, distribute the *Trusting Others* activity page when all pairs have completed the blindfold activity. Be sure participants understand all items and how to use the scale. Have participants exchange completed activity pages with their partners when they are finished. Answers may be compared and discussed.

8. Conclude the activity with a discussion comparing the reactions of the partners. Did both partners feel equally "safe" on the walk? Why or why not? Did a partner's level of providing help change depending on how that person was treated when blindfolded? If so, how? How did it feel to be dependent? How can interdependence help group interaction?

Some ideas in this activity were adapted from Coleman (1980).

Social Communication

◇— TRUSTING OTHERS —◇

Directions: Rate each of the following items on a scale of 1 to 5: 1 = Never, 2 = Almost Never, 3 = Sometimes, 4 = Almost Always, 5 = Always.

While Blindfolded:	Never		Sometimes		Always
1. Did you feel safe?	1	2	3	4	5
2. Did you know where you were?	1	2	3	4	5
3. Did you trust your leader?	1	2	3	4	5
4. Did you feel comfortable?	1	2	3	4	5
5. Did you feel dependent?	1	2	3	4	5

While Leading:	Never		Sometimes		Always
1. Did you feel responsible for your partner?	1	2	3	4	5
2. Was your partner comfortable?	1	2	3	4	5
3. Were you confident?	1	2	3	4	5
4. Did your partner cooperate?	1	2	3	4	5
5. Did you calm your partner?	1	2	3	4	5

If you had this activity to do over again, what would you change and why?

Has this exercise helped build trust with your partner? Why or why not?

Section 2: Communicating with Others

In this section, participants learn about clear, straightforward, empathetic communication. Topics such as constructive criticism, nonverbal communication, active listening, and assertiveness are introduced with the idea that they will be developed and refined as the group progresses. *Learning the concepts in this section is crucial for group success.*

As participants investigate communication style and effectiveness, they assess and discuss their own shortcomings and strengths. They explore the process of communication and discover the payoffs of knowing how communication works.

As in all activities in *Social Communication: Activities for Improving Peer Interactions and Self-Esteem,* the communication focus is on discourse. The activities are designed to provide the content for discussion.

Activities in this section include:

		Page
1.	How Do I Communicate?	62
2.	Constructive Criticism	66
3.	Differing Visual Perceptions	68
4.	Relaying Spoken Information	70
5.	Nonverbal Communication	73
6.	Active Listening	76
7.	Empathizing (HS)	81
8.	Being Assertive	85
9.	Following Directives and Commands	90
10.	Getting Along with Others	92

Social Communication

Activity 1—Communicating with Others
How Do I Communicate?

Language Purpose:

1. To assess communication skills
2. To analyze communication behaviors

Self-Esteem Focus:

To explore the role of communication in relating with others and the effect of communication on self-concept

Materials:

Personal Communicator Inventory activity pages

Vocabulary:

authority, compromise, dominate, frequency, message, negotiate, prejudice, rating, valuable

Process:

(Note: There are no right or wrong answers in this exercise. Participants should be encouraged to answer questions honestly. It would be very helpful for you to fill out a *Personal Communicator Inventory* and to share the information with the group to aid in the opening discussion. You may choose to make this activity two days in length by completing process steps 1 through 3 the first day, then collecting and reading each *Personal Communicator Inventory* and completing the discussion portion of the activity the second day.)

1. Ask participants why it is important for them to understand how they communicate with others. Does it matter how they communicate as long as communication is taking place?

2. Explain that in this activity, participants will rate the frequency with which they each perform various communication skills and the feelings associated with communicating.

3. Distribute the *Personal Communicator Inventory* activity pages. Explain that this is a brief exploration of each participant's communication skills and behaviors. Participants are to read each question and to assess their skills. They are then to circle the number that describes them best. Read and paraphrase any questions causing confusion.

4. Review all questions that participants gave a 1 or a 3 rating. If some participants are not comfortable sharing their ratings with the group,

try to note their responses privately and incorporate those questions in your discussion. The questions rated 1 and 3 spark discussion and thus aid the participants in exploring why they almost always or almost never behave in a particular way. For example, if the question, "Do I maintain eye contact when listening?" is discussed, the facilitator could ask the group why a person might not maintain eye contact when listening, when eye contact might be difficult, and why it is necessary for the listener to maintain good eye contact. Of vital importance are maintaining trust in the group and not singling out one participant as being wrong in the answer given. Group discussions should not take on a punitive air when disclosing personal communication skill information.

5. Conclude the activity with a discussion about the importance of adequate communication skills. Did the participants learn anything about themselves and their communication skills?

Some ideas in this activity were adapted from Goldstein et al. (1980).

Social Communication

☑ Personal Communicator INVENTORY

Directions: The following questions will be helpful in assessing your communication. Be honest in your responses. Draw a circle around the number that describes you best. (1 = Almost Never; 2 = Sometimes; 3 = Almost Always)

1	2	3	1. Am I afraid to be wrong?
1	2	3	2. Do I ask questions when I don't understand something?
1	2	3	3. Do I ask questions just to get attention?
1	2	3	4. Do I speak loudly enough to be heard?
1	2	3	5. Do I speak more loudly than is necessary?
1	2	3	6. Do I speak just to fill in time?
1	2	3	7. Do I listen when others are speaking?
1	2	3	8. Do I maintain eye contact when speaking?
1	2	3	9. Do I maintain eye contact when listening?
1	2	3	10. Do I dominate conversations?
1	2	3	11. Is my message easily understood?
1	2	3	12. Do I understand others' verbal messages?
1	2	3	13. Do I stick to the topic?
1	2	3	14. Do others have difficulty following my topic changes?

© 1992 Thinking Publications
Duplication permitted for educational use only.

Communicating with Others: How Do I Communicate?

1	2	3	15.	Can I compromise with people my own age?
1	2	3	16.	Are my ideas better than others'?
1	2	3	17.	Am I truthful?
1	2	3	18.	Am I able to negotiate with adults or authority figures?
1	2	3	19.	Do I give in to others too easily?
1	2	3	20.	Do I confuse others when I talk with them?
1	2	3	21.	Do I state my opinion when speaking with adults or authority figures?
1	2	3	22.	Do I express my feelings to others?
1	2	3	23.	Do I tell others when they are annoying me?
1	2	3	24.	Do I have strong prejudices?
1	2	3	25.	Do I feel I am a valuable person?

© 1992 Thinking Publications
Duplication permitted for educational use only.

Social Communication

Activity 2—Communicating with Others
Constructive Criticism

Language Purpose:

1. To compare and contrast *put-downs* and *constructive criticism*
2. To consider alternative communication messages

Self-Esteem Focus:

To increase awareness of put-downs and the effect they have on communicative situations and self-concept

Materials:

none

Vocabulary:

constructive, criticism, impact, intent, message, negative, positive, put-down

Process:

1. Instruct participants that the purpose of this activity is to help them recognize the difference between constructive criticism and put-downs. They will also explore the effect each type of communication has on the listener.
2. Ask participants why it is important to understand the communicative intent of messages. What impact can messages have on how participants see themselves?
3. Brainstorm a definition for *constructive* (or helpful) *criticism*. For example:

    constructive criticism—criticism designed to help another; telling someone how they can improve something

4. Explain that *put-downs* are negative statements made by others which can hinder or stop good communication. Examples of put-downs include:

    "Boy, was that dumb."

    "You look like you just got out of bed."

    "That was a stupid thing to say."

5. Brainstorm other put-downs and write them where all participants can see them.

6. Explain that for criticism to be constructive, it must have three basic elements. It must:

   a. say something positive;

   b. state what the problem is;

   c. suggest a solution to the problem.

   Example:

   "I understand what you're saying, but I disagree. I'd like to tell you my opinion..."

7. Change the put-downs listed to constructive criticism containing the three elements listed above. Write the constructive criticism after the put-down.

   Example:

   (Put-down) "This work is dumb."

   (Constructive Criticism) "I like this class, but I don't like this activity. Could I do it another way?"

8. Conclude this session with a discussion about communication. What does a put-down do to communication? How do participants feel when someone puts them down? Which kind of criticism can keep communication going? What purpose is served by put-downs? Why are put-downs used? Should participants worry about other people's feelings? Why or why not?

Some ideas in this activity were adapted from Brewner, McMahon, Paris, and Roche (1987).

Social Communication

Activity 3—Communicating with Others
Differing Visual Perceptions

Language Purpose:

1. To recognize that changes occur in visual and spoken messages
2. To compare and contrast different visual images

Self-Esteem Focus:

To develop an awareness of how differing perceptions can affect interpersonal communication

Materials:

pictures taken from magazines or other sources (Simple line drawings would be best.)

Vocabulary:

aware, communication, perception, verbal

Process:

1. Ask participants why learning about perceptions is important. Ask whether checking their own perceptions is important or not. What does perception have to do with communication? If any participants don't know, assure them this activity will explore that question.
2. Instruct participants that the purpose of this activity is to make them aware of how different perceptions can totally change original information and thus affect communication about that information.
3. Ask for four volunteers to demonstrate changing perceptions.
4. Instruct three of the volunteers to leave the room. The fourth stays in the room and is shown a picture. When the picture is removed from view, the volunteer copies the picture from memory onto a piece of paper. Pictures can vary in complexity depending on the group's ability.
5. Ask volunteer #1 to return to the room. This group member is shown volunteer #4's picture and copies it from memory onto a piece of paper.
6. Ask volunteer #2 to return. Show this volunteer only #1's picture. Volunteer #2 then copies it from memory onto a piece of paper.
7. Ask volunteer #3 to return. Show this volunteer #2's picture. Volunteer #3 then copies it from memory.

Communicating with Others: Differing Visual Perceptions

8. Compare volunteer #3's drawing with the original picture. Ask participants for ideas about changes in the pictures. Expand on their ideas by explaining that the differences noted are due to the volunteers each changing (by adding to or leaving out particular portions) the picture slightly. The changes are based on what the person doing the drawing perceived as important. (Artistic talent plays a minor role, but that topic is not important to this discussion.)

9. Compare all drawings. Look for a progression. Ask the volunteers to talk about why there are differences among the drawings and/or why they changed the drawing the way they did.

10. Conclude the activity with a discussion of how the drawing exercise relates to life situations. Ask if any of the group members have been in a situation where perceptions of the facts differed even though all participants had experienced the same event. Explain that differences in perception often occur in a stressful situation (e.g., an auto accident or an argument with relatives or a significant other). How can problems resulting from differing perceptions be resolved? When is it important to make sure perceptions are the same? What happens when perceptions differ? Reexamine the question, "What does perception have to do with communication?"

Social Communication

Activity 4—Communicating with Others
Relaying Spoken Information

Language Purpose:

1. To repeat significant information
2. To differentiate between significant and insignificant information
3. To understand the concept of *accuracy*

Self-Esteem Focus:

To develop the idea that accurate communication can foster healthy interpersonal interaction

Materials:

Relaying Spoken Information activity page

Vocabulary:

accuracy, distort, gossip, intact, relay, repetition, significant, verbal

Process:

1. Review information from Section 2, Activity 3—"Differing Visual Perceptions" or explain to participants that information sometimes gets changed as it goes from one person to another. Ask if they have had such experiences. Ask why learning about changes in spoken messages is important. What effect can changing spoken information have on communication?

2. Ask for six volunteers. (Use fewer volunteers if your group does not have that many members.) Explain that each will be sharing information with another volunteer when he or she returns. Give each volunteer a number from 1 through 6 and send them all out of the room.

3. Give each remaining group member an activity page. Read the accident report aloud and explain to the remaining participants that you will call in the first volunteer and read the report. The first volunteer will then call in the second volunteer and will retell the report to the best of her or his memory. Then the second will call in the third, and so on until all have been called in to hear the report from the previous volunteer. (Record all the repetitions, if desired.)

4. As each volunteer reports to the next, the rest of the group should note any changes in the new version from the previous version on the activity page provided. (For participants who have difficulty taking notes, a recorded version can be played at the conclusion of the exercise and differences can then be discussed.)

5. Immediately after the last volunteer has repeated the report to the group, read the original report once more.

6. Discuss the differences noted by the group for each individual repetition, and especially those in the final repetition versus the original report. Were the changes significant? Was the basic report still intact? Would fewer details have helped to make the repetitions more accurate? Why? What effect would more details have had on accuracy? Why? What could the volunteers have done to help remember the information in the report? What tools or strategies might they have used?

7. Ask participants to brainstorm and list situations that require messages to be remembered and repeated. (Examples might include telephone messages, explaining rules of a game, etc.) If gossip does not appear on the list, introduce it as a situation in which information can be distorted (or remind them of the discussion from Activity 3—"Differing Visual Perceptions" when participants compared drawings and discussed the distortions that occurred).

8. Conclude the activity with a discussion about possible changes in the participants' awareness of how and why to repeat spoken information accurately. Is it always appropriate to convey all spoken information accurately? When might it not be appropriate (e.g., when the information would be hurtful to another, when too many unnecessary details are given, etc.)? Why should people be accurate when they retell stories or events? What difference does it make if a few details get changed? Can that change hurt/help anyone? How? How does accuracy affect communication? Is accuracy really important? Why?

Additional Activity:

Group members may want to continue this exercise. Adapt the activity by using different circumstances (e.g., conveying telephone messages, relaying gossip, giving directions, etc.).

Some ideas in this activity were adapted from Bormaster and Treat (1982).

Social Communication

Relaying Spoken Information

Please listen carefully. I have to leave immediately for the hospital. I have just called the police from the principal's office. Wait here and report the accident to them. I was standing on the south side of the street in front of the school when I saw a girl who was wearing a multi-colored pullover sweater, jeans, and black sneakers step into the crosswalk on the north side of the street. She didn't even look up. A blue '92 Jeep Cherokee traveling west swerved, barely missing her. She must have panicked because she just stood motionless in the street. That was when the '91 brown Dodge pickup traveling east hit her. The pickup didn't even slow down. I managed to get part of the license number. The first letter was J and the last three numbers were 738. Don't forget to tell them everything.

Directions: Write any changes in the repetitions in the spaces provided.

First repetition:

Second repetition:

Third repetition:

Fourth repetition:

Fifth repetition:

Sixth repetition:

Activity 5—Communicating with Others
Nonverbal Communication

Language Purpose:

1. To recognize the impact of nonverbal communication on interpersonal interaction
2. To describe nonverbal behaviors

Self-Esteem Focus:

To develop an understanding that feelings can be expressed nonverbally as well as verbally

Materials:

Nonverbal Communication activity page

Vocabulary:

expression, facial, gesture, inhibit, nonverbal, tone, verbal

Process:

(Note: It is not in the scope of this text to provide an indepth study of nonverbal communication. See Schwartz and McKinley [1984] for detailed suggestions.)

1. Ask group members to define *nonverbal communication*. Discuss the difference between verbal and nonverbal communication. Ask why knowing about nonverbal communication is important. What kind of information might people be sending or missing if they aren't aware of nonverbal communication?

2. Expand upon participants' ideas by explaining that nonverbal communication consists of body language (body positioning), facial expressions, gestures, and tone of voice. Give a few examples of each as you present them. If you have another way of categorizing nonverbal communication, use that system.

3. Brainstorm as many examples as possible for each type of nonverbal communication and write the examples where all participants can see them. Items might include:

Social Communication

Body Language	Facial Expressions	Gestures	Tone of Voice
Turning your back on someone	Smiling	Holding your nose	Yelling
Slouching in chair	Frowning	Raising and lowering your shoulders	Whining
Folding your arms across your chest	Rolling your eyes	Playing with your hair	Whispering
Leaning against a wall	Puckering your lips	Extending your hand	Laughing

4. Explain that feelings are frequently expressed nonverbally. Brainstorm a list of feelings and some of the nonverbal behaviors that go with them. Ask participants, for example, to identify what they do when they are nervous, sad, or angry.

5. Distribute the *Nonverbal Communication* activity page and have participants complete it.

6. Ask participants to share examples.

7. Discuss the impact of nonverbal communication within a group. How can people inhibit or stop communication with inappropriate nonverbal behaviors? How can people encourage communication using appropriate nonverbal behaviors? How can participants guess other group members' feelings even if no one is talking? What are the most important nonverbal behaviors for encouraging group discussion? Why?

Additional Activities:

If time permits, include supplemental activities such as these:

1. View a movie or TV program with the sound off. Analyze nonverbal behaviors that are observed.

2. Play charades.

3. Role play situations using nonverbal communication.

Communicating with Others: Nonverbal Communication

NONVERBAL COMMUNICATION

Directions: List a nonverbal behavior for every category below:

Feeling	Body Language	Gesture	Facial Expression	Tone of Voice
1. happy	walking tall	clapping	smiling	pleasant
2. excited				
3. angry				
4. sad				
5. terrified				
6. proud				
7. bored				
8. disgusted				
9. disappointed				
10. depressed				

© 1992 Thinking Publications
Duplication permitted for educational use only.

Social Communication

Activity 6—Communicating with Others
Active Listening

Language Purpose:

1. To concentrate attention on a speaker
2. To define the concept of *active listening*
3. To practice active listening skills

Self-Esteem Focus:

To develop an awareness of how active listening can facilitate interpersonal communication

Materials:

Active Listening Quiz activity page

Vocabulary:

attend, encouragement, mood, passive, reflection, sincere

Process:

(Note: Skills learned in this activity should be developed and refined as participants progress through all activities. This activity may need two sessions because of the importance of the subject and the time needed to role play.)

1. Inform participants that this activity is about being a good listener. Ask what happens when people don't have good listening skills.
2. Ask participants to define the word *hear* and then the word *listen*. Explain that people frequently think they have the same meaning. Clarify this idea by explaining that *hearing* means to receive sound through the ears. *Listening* refers to understanding what has been heard. *Listening* means to pay attention, or to tune in. Ask participants why it is important to listen well.
3. Introduce the concept of *active listening*. Explain that in *active listening* the listener tries to understand what the speaker is saying and feeling. Listening, therefore, is not a passive activity. Discuss what that means.
4. Explain that active listening has three basic parts: attention, encouragement, and reflection.

Part One: Attention

a. Define the idea of *attending*. Explain that keeping your mind closely on something or someone is attending. Attending also includes:

   i. nonverbal communication: looking at or facing the speaker; and

   ii. keeping quiet while the speaker is talking.

b. Ask participants what happens in a conversation when the speaker thinks the listener isn't listening. How does the speaker feel? What can cause a listener not to listen? What does faking listening do to a conversation?

c. Ask a participant to role play a conversation with you in which poor attending skills are used. You should play the role of the poor listener. When the conversation is over, ask the participant to discuss how the situation felt.

Part Two: Encouragement

a. Explain that sometimes people want to talk but feel uncomfortable, shy, or embarrassed. They sometimes need encouragement. Ask how a listener might encourage a speaker.

b. Expand participants' ideas by discussing the following:

   i. *Asking questions*—How does asking questions encourage conversation? What kind of questions could be asked? How could asking too many questions or questions that are too personal discourage or stop conversation?

   ii. *Using brief phrases*—Give a few examples, then brainstorm more examples like:

I see.	Then what happened?
Mm-hmm.	Go on.
Tell me more.	Oh.
Right.	Really?

   How do these phrases encourage conversation? What happens when these phrases are used, but not sincerely?

   iii. *Being quiet*—In addition to asking questions and using phrases, the listener can also just be silent while letting the speaker know that the conversation is being followed. How might the listener do that? Discuss again the importance of nonverbal communication (e.g., head nods, eye contact, appropriate facial expressions).

c. Ask for two volunteers to role play a conversation in which encouragement skills are practiced. When the conversation is over, ask the role players to discuss how the situation felt.

Social Communication

Part III: Reflection

a. Ask participants what comes to mind when they think of the word *reflection* (mirror). Ask what reflection has to do with listening.

b. Expand on participants' discussion contributions by sharing the following ideas about reflective listening:

   i. The listener restates what the speaker has said to understand the message better (e.g., "You said you were out of school for two days").

   ii. The listener helps the speaker to understand feelings (e.g., "That sounds very sad"). People learn to do this by tuning into others' moods.

c. Divide the group into pairs. Have participants role play a conversation using good reflective listening skills. Instruct them to take turns being the speaker and the listener. Ask pairs to tell the large group how their conversations progressed.

d. Conclude this part of the discussion by asking why someone would want to learn to be an active listener. Why is active listening important for group members to learn?

5. If appropriate for participants' language levels and/or goals, distribute the *Active Listening Quiz*. Allow 5 to 10 minutes to complete the quiz.

6. Break the group into pairs again. Assign a role play situation such as those below to each person. The speaker role plays the situation and the listener practices active listening skills. After a few minutes, instruct participants to change roles and begin with a new situation. Ideally, each participant would have the opportunity to role play several situations. (Write these situations on cards for participants to read, if desired.)

Role Play Situations:

a. You are nervous because you have been missing too much school.

b. Your parent/spouse is upset because you have been staying out late too many nights during the week.

c. You are worried that you won't have enough money to make your car payment this month.

d. You are concerned about the fact that your best friend has been drinking too much.

e. You are nervous about dating someone for the first time.

7. Conclude the activity by explaining that active listening skills take practice. Tell participants that they will be perfecting these skills as the group continues to interact. Ask participants how it felt to have someone really listen to them. How did listeners feel? Who felt awkward? Comfortable? Why?

Some of the ideas in this activity were adapted from Bolton (1979).

Social Communication

Active Listening Quiz

Directions: Answer the following questions:

1. How is hearing different from listening?

2. What does *active* mean?

3. What are the three parts of active listening?

4. What are two things you could say to encourage a speaker to go on talking?

5. On a scale from 1 to 5 (with 5 being "very good"), how would you rate your active listening skills? _____ Why?

Activity 7—Communicating with Others
Empathizing (HS)

Language Purpose:

1. To define *empathy* and *sympathy*
2. To formulate empathic messages in response to life situations

Self-Esteem Focus:

To develop an understanding of the concept of empathy and how it can impact interpersonal communication

Materials:

Life Messages activity pages

Vocabulary:

acknowledgment, convey, empathy, sensitivity, sincere, sympathy

Process:

(Note: Before the session, copy the *Life Messages* activity pages and cut along the lines.)

1. Explain that the purpose of this activity is to define *empathy* and *sympathy* and to practice using empathic messages.

2. Explain that *empathy* has to do with sensitivity to others and taking another's point of view. Make sure participants understand the concept of *another's point of view*.

3. Explain that *empathy* means trying to understand or experience how another person is feeling. Write the following sayings where everyone can see them: *Crawl into another person's skin. See the world through another's eyes. Walk in another person's shoes.*

4. Describe the difference between empathy and sympathy:

    empathy—feeling with another person (e.g., "Looks like you're feeling sad today.")

    sympathy—feeling sorry for another person (e.g., "You poor guy.")

5. Remind participants that empathic messages must contain two elements:

    a. Acknowledgment of the person's feelings or emotional reactions (e.g., "I can tell you're really upset.")

Social Communication

    b. Understanding of the situation that brought on the reaction (e.g., "You must have loved your grandmother a lot.")

    Example:

    Situation: A friend says, "My grandmother died last night."

    Empathic response: "I can tell you're upset. You must have loved your grandmother a lot."

    Sympathetic Response: "I'm sorry she died."

    Both are appropriate responses, but the empathic response lets the other person know you are feeling with them, not for them. Ask participants to give examples of each type of response.

6. Divide the group into two teams of equal size. Have group members number themselves. Participant #1 from team A sensitively reads a Life Message to Participant #1 from team B. (Brainstorming life messages with the group to make them more appropriate for the members' situations may be helpful.) Participant #1 from team B responds with a sincere, empathic message (not a sympathetic message). If the response is appropriate, team B is awarded one point. Play continues with team B participant #2 reading a Life Message to team A participant #2 and so on. The team with the most points at the end of play wins, though all participants will be winners by learning to use empathic messages.

7. Discuss how empathy can be useful in the group situation. Help participants explore how they could be empathic in the group.

8. Conclude the activity with a discussion about empathy. What message is conveyed through empathy that is missing in sympathy? Which type of message would participants rather receive? Why? Which type of message is easier to share? Why?

Some ideas in this activity were adapted from Bolton (1979).

Communicating with Others: Empathizing

Life Messages

Directions: Copy this page and the next one, then cut apart the messages along the lines. Blank spaces are provided for life messages brainstormed by the group.

I just lost the best job I ever had.	I get really nervous when I have to talk to adults.
I just broke up with my girlfriend/boyfriend.	I waited in line six hours and and when I got to the ticket window, they said the concert was already sold out!
Somebody dented my brand new car!	I took my girlfriend out to lunch and discovered I didn't have any money to pay for it.
Mr. Jones just flunked me! Now I'm going to have to take his class again.	My parents won't let me get any "hot" clothes. They're so behind the times.
My boyfriend hasn't spoken to me for two days.	My parents are splitting up.
Somebody stole my radio!	I ran out of gas on the way to work.
I bent over in biology and my pants ripped.	I have to take a blood test and I'm terrified of needles.

© 1992 Thinking Publications
Duplication permitted for educational use only.

Social Communication

This uniform I have to wear to work looks stupid.	My parents don't understand me.
My dog died last night.	I took a "hot" date out for dinner last night and spilled spaghetti in my lap.
I didn't get paid last week so I don't have any money.	The blind date my brother set me up with was a disaster.

Activity 8—Communicating with Others
Being Assertive

Language Purpose:

1. To compare communication styles for similarities and differences
2. To assess assertive communication of each group member
3. To be clear and precise in language so the listener understands

Self-Esteem Focus:

To introduce the idea that assertiveness can positively influence group interaction

Materials:

Assertiveness Assessment, Assertiveness activity page

Vocabulary:

aggressive, assertive, interpersonal, passive, right, violate

Process:

(Note: Depending on the level and ability of group participants, it may be helpful to do this activity in two sessions. If the content is particularly challenging, break for discussion after process step 5.)

1. Remind participants that the focus of Activity 6—"Active Listening" was to understand how someone else was feeling and what he or she was saying. Explain that the current topic, assertiveness, has to do with expressing personal feelings and rights.
2. Ask participants why knowing the difference between expressing oneself and helping others to express themselves is important.
3. Explain that this activity is about how to communicate feelings, needs, wants, and opinions clearly. Briefly brainstorm examples of each to ensure that participants know the difference. For example:

Feelings	*Needs*	*Wants*	*Opinions*
I'm angry.	I need more sleep.	I want you to be quiet.	It's too noisy in here.
I'm worried.	I need to graduate.	I want to pass this class.	I think school is boring.

85

Social Communication

4. Distribute the *Assertiveness Assessment*. Allow time for it to be completed.

5. Discuss participants' responses and explain that all are meant to be false. Any response marked "True" may indicate that a person is not taking proper care of himself or herself. Give participants time to discuss their comments.

6. Expand the definition of *assertiveness* to include the idea that it means expressing ourselves in a way that indicates self-respect. It does not mean putting down others. It means taking care of oneself and standing up for one's rights without violating the rights of others.

7. Explain that basic interpersonal communication behavior can be separated into three styles:

   a. *aggressive style*—bullying, fighting, threatening, and generally disregarding other people's feelings

   b. *passive style*—letting yourself get pushed around, not standing up for yourself, and generally doing what you are told to do regardless of how you feel

   c. *assertive style*—standing up for yourself, expressing your feelings, and not letting others take advantage of you

   Discuss the possible advantages and disadvantages of each style.

(Note: *Style* was discussed in Section 1, Activity 8—"Recognizing Communication Differences Among Group Members" as *introvert-extrovert*. Make participants aware that *style* can refer to several types of communication behaviors.)

8. Write this list of assertive behaviors where everyone can see them:

   Assertive Behaviors
   1. Use direct eye contact.
   2. Speak in a clear, strong voice.
   3. Face the person to whom you are talking.
   4. Start conversations.
   5. Practice saying no.
   6. Express how you feel without being overly emotional.
   7. Tell people what you want.
   8. Ask for help.
   9. Treat people with respect.
   10. Use *I* messages—instead of saying, "You make me angry," say, "I am angry."

Add your own ideas. Discuss each item, explaining and getting feedback from participants about the importance of each.

Communicating with Others: Being Assertive

9. Distribute the *Assertiveness* activity page. Have participants complete the page and compare responses. Then ask two volunteers to role play one of the scenarios from the *Assertiveness* activity page. They should role play one of the responses provided (or create a new response) for the scenario. If participants are hesitant about role playing, play one of the roles yourself or write scripts for the characters to follow. As a group, have participants judge scenarios as aggressive, assertive, or passive. Additional scenarios from the *Assertiveness* activity page can be role played by the same or different volunteers. Group participants may also create scenarios for each other (e.g., "Someone calls you on the phone and asks if you will buy a magazine to support a special cause"); observers of the role play should judge the scenarios as aggressive, assertive, or passive.

10. Discuss responses and talk about why some people are not assertive. Include ideas such as:

    a. They never learned how to be assertive. They don't have the skills.

    b. They learned that they should put the needs of others before their own needs.

    c. They learned that saying no or standing up for yourself is not friendly or nice.

11. Conclude the activity by discussing which communication style will work best for the group. What will happen if people act aggressively or passively in the group? What should participants do when that happens during a group activity? Does the group need any guidelines for handling aggressive or passive communication? What are they?

Social Communication

Assertiveness Assessment

Directions: Write T (True) or F (False) beside each item.

_____ 1. People don't want to hear that you feel bad, so keep it to yourself.

_____ 2. It is always selfish to put your needs before the needs of others.

_____ 3. You should always respect the views of others, especially if they are in a position of authority.

_____ 4. It is wrong or shameful to make mistakes.

_____ 5. You should never interrupt people.

_____ 6. You should always have a good reason for what you feel and do.

_____ 7. When someone is in trouble, you should always help.

_____ 8. You should never make people mad at you.

_____ 9. If someone asks you a question, you should always try to answer it.

Communicating with Others: Being Assertive

ASSERTIVENESS

Directions: Following each situation are three responses. Decide if each response is aggressive (AG), assertive (AS), or passive (PA).

1. You have a lot of homework and your mother asks you to mow the lawn.

   _____ Why can't you get someone else to do it? Can't you see how much homework I have to do?

   _____ I have a lot of homework to do tonight, and I'd rather mow the lawn tomorrow afternoon.

   _____ OK, Mom.

2. You are talking to your girlfriend and you suddenly realize that you will be late for class. She wants to keep talking.

   _____ I really need to go soon.

   _____ You're making me late for class.

   _____ I know you want to talk more, but I have to go now.

3. Someone you don't want to go out with asks you to go to a movie.

   _____ I'm busy that night.

   _____ I don't want to go out with you.

   _____ Thanks for asking, but I'd rather not.

4. You want to take an art class and your friend is making fun of your artistic interests.

   _____ Shut up.

   _____ Yeah, you're right.

   _____ I really want to take this class. Please stop giving me a hard time.

5. Your parents want you to go with them to dinner at the home of a neighbor who you do not like.

   _____ I don't like being with those people, and I prefer to stay home.

   _____ All right, if you want me to.

   _____ I won't go. I hate those people.

Social Communication

Activity 9—Communicating with Others
Following Directives and Commands

Language Purpose:

1. To develop an understanding of the motives behind directives
2. To increase ability to deal effectively with directives and the feelings associated with them

Self-Esteem Focus:

To increase awareness of the impact of directives on self-concept

Materials:

none

Vocabulary:

command, directive, impact, interpersonal, motive, reaction

Process:

1. Explore the definitions of *command* and *directive* and ask participants what other words have similar meanings (e.g., order, demand, request).
2. Ask participants what comes to mind when they think about someone giving them a command or a directive. Why is it important to learn about reactions to directives? Is it necessary to understand the motives behind directives? Why or why not?
3. Explain to participants that the purpose of this activity is to examine how they react to directives and why directives are sometimes necessary.
4. Brainstorm a list of 10 people in participants' lives who give directives (e.g., parents, police officers, bosses, etc.).
5. Beside each, list at least one directive that person might give.
6. Divide participants into pairs. Each pair takes a turn acting out directives from those listed. One participant plays the part of the person from process step 4 who is giving the directive, and the other participant plays himself or herself. The other participant pairs are observers, commenting on the reaction to the directive given.
7. Brainstorm a list of possible motives for the directives acted out in process step 6. Following the format below, write the information where everyone can see it:

Communicating with Others: Following Directives and Commands

Person	Directive	Reaction	Motive
Roommate	Clean your part of the room	Anger	Wants it to look good
			Health risk
			Company coming over

8. Have the same pairs of participants act out the situations again as they did during process step 6. Did the situations change after knowing the motives behind the directives? Why or why not?

9. Conclude the activity with a discussion of directives and their impact on our lives. Is it possible to get beyond the reaction and look at the reason for the directive? Do the participants give directives? Why? To whom? Who receives more directives—children or teenagers? Teenagers or adults? Why? Does everyone receive directives from someone? Are there alternatives to giving directives? How can directives be given so the listener doesn't feel negative about them? Is that always possible? How does it feel to be getting a lot of directives? What do directives do to interpersonal communication? What are alternatives to giving directives? How does giving directives relate to assertive behavior? Are directives assertive, aggressive, or both?

Social Communication

Activity 10—Communicating with Others
Getting Along with Others

Language Purpose:

1. To discuss the concept of *compromise* in communication situations
2. To consider alternative solutions to problem situations

Self-Esteem Focus:

To increase awareness of choices in problem situations in relationships

Materials:

Getting Along with Others activity pages

Vocabulary:

choice, communicate, complicate, compromise, explore

Process:

1. Ask participants why learning how to get along with others is important. Are choices about how participants communicate made in relationships? How?
2. Instruct participants that the purpose of this activity is to explore choices in problem situations with others and to learn to communicate their needs and desires in those situations.
3. Ask participants what is required for a compromise to be successful. List ideas where everyone can see them.

    Examples: Must be agreeable to both parties.

    Should solve the problem.

    Should be reasonable.

4. Explain that in the past few years the term *win-win* has become popular. *Win-win* means that both parties in a situation decide what is important to them and what they would be willing to do without. With both parties willing to compromise, chances of both being satisfied with the result are greater. This prevents a win-lose situation, in which one party is pleased at the expense of the other person.
5. Explain that compromising involves being aware of both parties' feelings and the ability to communicate openly and honestly without hurting the other person. This explanation is simplified. The act of compromising can be a complicated process.

Communicating with Others: Getting Along with Others

6. Distribute the *Getting Along with Others* activity pages and have participants complete them. Provide as much assistance as necessary. The activity can be completed orally rather than in writing, if you prefer. Compare and contrast win-win and win-lose solutions.

7. When students have completed the activity, list the different solutions where everyone can see them. Ask participants how many different possible solutions there are to each situation. Have participants give each other feedback on their responses.

8. Conclude the activity with a discussion about problems and choices. What is the difference between a win-win solution and a win-lose solution? Can there always be a compromise? Why or why not? What can a person do if the other party refuses to compromise?

(Note: An alternative to completing the activity pages presented in process step 6 would be to cut the activity situations apart and have pairs of participants act out win-lose situations. Different pairings could act out various win-lose outcomes. The large group could then brainstorm win-win solutions and choose one win-win solution to be acted out. If this option is chosen, process step 7 could be omitted, with step 8 concluding the activity.)

Social Communication

Getting Along with Others

Directions: Read the problems. Give an example of each kind of solution.

Example: Your date wants to go to a movie. You'd rather go dancing. You've gone where your date wanted to go the past three weeks. You'd like to decide what to do this time.

    Win-win solution: Suggest going to the movie and then dancing afterward.

    Win-lose solution: Insist on going dancing and refuse to go to the movie.

1. You want to go to a party. Your parent says you have to be in at 10 p.m. You want to stay until 11:30 p.m. You feel your parent is overly protective.

    Win-win solution: _____

    Win-lose solution: _____

2. Your brother wants to borrow your favorite tape for his party to which you're not invited. The last time he borrowed a tape, he ruined it and didn't replace it when asked. You're very careful with your things.

    Win-win solution: _____

    Win-lose solution: _____

3. Your girlfriend with whom you eat lunch every day always wants pizza. You have eaten pizza every day this week. You would like to have something different for lunch today.

    Win-win solution: _____

    Win-lose solution: _____

Communicating with Others: Getting Along with Others

4. You want a new computer game, but you have no money. You are afraid to ask your parents for money because they think you spend too much time at the computer.

   Win-win solution: _____

   Win-lose solution: _____

5. Your best friend, whom you drive to school every day, borrowed $20 from you. You need the money now. Every time you've asked about it, your friend has laughed and said he'll give it to you later.

   Win-win solution: _____

   Win-lose solution: _____

Section 3: Understanding Oneself

Now that group participants have established a degree of rapport, trust, and openness, they are ready to begin the process of understanding themselves. The self-exploration of the activities in this section begins by asking participants to think about themselves. There is little emphasis at this time on change or options for change. The ideas of alternatives and choices are addressed more directly in following sections. The road toward self-exploration is a gradual one that must be handled with care and sensitivity.

Similar to activities in other sections, activities in *Understanding Oneself* vary in content quantity to provide sufficient information without overtaxing participants' capabilities. It is important to encourage participants to take the time to think about themselves before completing assignments.

As in all activities in *Social Communication: Activities for Improving Peer Interactions and Self-Esteem,* the communication focus is on discourse. The activities are designed to provide the content for discussion.

Activities in this section include:

		Page
1.	Who Am I? (C)	98
2.	What Am I Thankful For?	102
3.	Understanding Emotional Reactions (C)	104
4.	Examining Obligations and Options	109
5.	Understanding Procrastination	112
6.	Understanding Stress	116
7.	Assessing Stress (C) (HS)	120
8.	Self-Evaluation	125
9.	Respect	129
10.	An Ideal Day	132

Social Communication

Activity 1–Understanding Oneself
Who Am I?(C)

Language Purpose:

1. To analyze meanings of labels
2. To look for cause-and-effect relationships between events and experiences

Self-Esteem Focus:

To develop an awareness of how labels (whether accurate or false) contribute to self-concept

Materials:

Who Am I? activity pages

Vocabulary:

label, negative, positive, power

Process:

1. Explain to the group members that they will be examining how others view them and how they view themselves. In this activity, participants will select labels which described them as children in elementary school and labels which describe them now. Discuss the similarities between a label and a name.

2. Ask participants why it is important to learn about labels. Responses may include:

    "So you don't call anyone a name."

    "So you don't hurt anyone's feelings."

3. Ask participants if they have ever been called a name that made them feel uncomfortable, like "stupid" or "dummy." Ask them to give examples of name-calling (fatso, geek, etc.). Ask for ideas about why people call each other names.

4. Distribute the *Who Am I?* activity pages. *Read all labels and explain any labels that are unclear to participants.* Brainstorm additional labels to add to the list. As you go through the list, differentiate between labels that are positive and those that are negative. Tell participants to complete only the top half of the first activity page at this time.

5. Ask group members to recall when they were younger. Direct them to circle all the labels which described them as children. These could be labels placed on them by others or feelings they have about themselves from that time.

6. Ask participants to share a few of the childhood labels they circled.

7. Then direct group members to underline all the labels which describe them now. These again could be labels others attribute to them or how they feel about themselves now. Tell them to include both positive and negative labels.

8. Ask participants to compare a few of the current labels they circled. Compile a list of frequently identified labels and write them where everyone can see them. Are most of the commonly identified labels positive or negative?

9. To complete the activity pages, request that participants look over the labels circled and underlined. Tell them to write answers to the questions. (If preferable, questions can be answered orally.) Discuss the questions before and after participants complete them to ensure that they fully understand the concepts.

10. Conclude the discussion by asking questions such as: Why did we originally decide that it was important to learn about labels? What power do labels have in our lives? The person receiving a label can choose to accept or reject it. Labels participants put on themselves are extremely important. These labels can determine how the past and the future are viewed. Discuss why people may be labeled differently in different situations.

Social Communication

Who Am I?

Directions: Read all of the following labels. Circle the labels that were given to you when you were younger. Underline the labels that describe you now. Some of these labels might be the same, some may be different.

stupid	brat	nerd
dumb	obnoxious	jock
nice	nurturing	whiner
sweet	giving	weirdo
caring	considerate	ignorant
dependable	eager	wonderful
self-centered	jerk	hyper
cute	clumsy	geek
quiet	worthless	smart
responsible	funny	silly
shy	serious	calm
hardworking	devoted	special
fantastic	rambunctious	terrific
coward	spoiled	bully

STOP!

Directions: When you have completed the top part of this activity page, write answers to the following questions:

1. What are the differences between the labels you circled and the labels you underlined?

Understanding Oneself: Who Am I?

2. Are the labels you marked accurate in your opinion? _____
   Why or why not?

3. Did you mark more positive or negative labels? _____
   Why?

4. How can a label affect your behavior?

5. Were any of the labels you marked labels that you gave yourself? _____
   If so, which ones?

6. As a child, did you see yourself as other people did? _____
   Explain your answer.

7. Do you see yourself as other people do now? _____
   Explain your answer.

Social Communication

Activity 2—Understanding Oneself
What Am I Thankful For?

Language Purpose:

1. To find categories to which experiences belong
2. To formulate an idea about another person

Self-Esteem Focus:

To differentiate personal opinions about oneself from public opinions

Materials:

paper

Vocabulary:

accomplishment, characteristic, personality, possession, significant, trait

Process:

1. Explain that the topic of conversation for this activity is based on things in life for which we are thankful. Ask why this topic is important to discuss.

2. Brainstorm examples for the following categories:
    a. accomplishments (making it to the 10th grade, getting a job, buying a car, etc.)
    b. physical characteristics (tall, slim, black hair, etc.)
    c. personality traits (outgoing, shy, secretive, etc.)
    d. possessions (car, horse, compact disc player, etc.)
    e. significant people/relationships (parents, friends, girlfriend or boyfriend, teacher, etc.)

3. Ask group members to think of one or two things for which they are thankful. (These could include material possessions, personal accomplishments, physical characteristics, personality traits, or significant people/relationships.) Discuss similarities and differences between participants' responses. Distribute one piece of blank paper to each participant. Tell each group member to write his or her name at the bottom of the sheet of paper.

4. Tell participants that they are now going to write ideas for each other about what they should be thankful for. Collect the papers and redistribute them so that each participant has a chance to write about every other

Understanding Oneself: What Am I Thankful For?

group member. Remind participants of the categories discussed in process step 2. Tell participants to write one or two ideas for each group member.

5. Tell group members to begin writing at the top of the page, and upon finishing, fold the paper forward so that the next person cannot see what has been written. (See diagram at the bottom of this page.)

6. Pass the papers around so that all participants have written a comment for every other participant. When all members have finished writing, pass the paper back to the person whose name is at the bottom of the sheet.

7. Instruct participants to read silently what has been written about them. Ask how they feel after reading about what was written about them.

8. Conclude with a discussion about what was written as opposed to what each participant shared in process step 3. Were there any differences? Were the written comments accurate? Why or why not? Were there some things listed that participants had not thought of before? Was it easy or difficult to think about things to write about others? Why? How did participants feel when they read what others said about them?

Top folded down to conceal written message

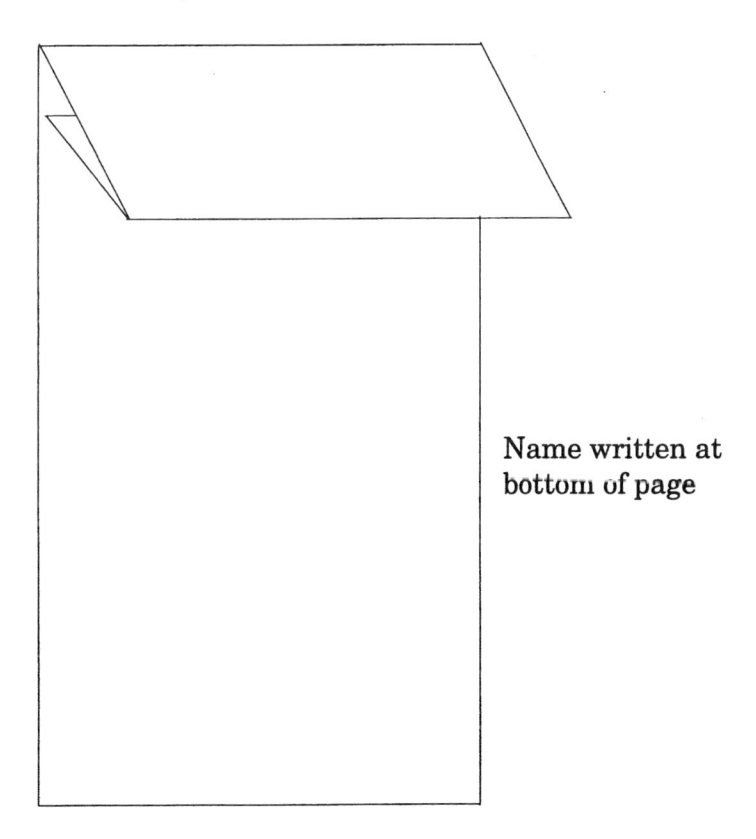

Name written at bottom of page

Some ideas in this activity were adapted from Rice (1986).

103

Social Communication

Activity 3—Understanding Oneself
Understanding Emotional Reactions (C)

Language Purpose:

1. To differentiate emotions and emotional reactions
2. To recognize relationships between emotions and reactions to emotions

Self-Esteem Focus:

To increase awareness of emotional reactions to different situations

Materials:

Emotions activity page, *Emotional Reactions* activity pages

Vocabulary:

acceptable, emotion, feeling, norm, physical, reaction, sensation

Process:

1. Give participants a formal definition of *emotion,* such as:

    emotion—any strong feeling, such as joy, love, hate, or sorrow, that usually arises without thinking

2. Ask participants why they think learning about emotions is important.
3. Brainstorm examples of emotions and write them where all participants can see them.
4. Ask participants how emotions are usually expressed (e.g., words or actions). Engage participants in a brief discussion about the difficulty or ease of expressing emotions. Is it a good idea to express emotions? Why or why not?
5. Provide a definition of *sensation*:

    sensation—a feeling that comes from the senses of the body

    Go back to the emotions list and differentiate "sensations" from "emotions." Physical sensations include sick, tired, cold, hungry, sexually aroused, etc. If any sensation words were included in the emotions list, ask participants to identify them. Place the sensation words in a new list, discussing why some words are "emotion" words and some are "sensation" words.

6. Distribute the *Emotions* activity page. Remind participants that they are thinking of examples, not definitions. Have them complete the page.

Understanding Oneself: Understanding Emotional Reactions

7. Ask for volunteers to share what they have written and compare responses. Ask participants which emotions are the easiest and hardest to express and why (e.g., some people find it easier to express anger than to express sadness).

8. Explain to participants that they will now be discussing their typical emotional reactions to different situations. In this way, they will become more aware of their reactions and the fact that they have choices in their methods of reaction. Choices may be appropriate or inappropriate.

9. Ask participants to think about and give examples of a situation they've been in and reacted to differently on different days. What influences these variations in reactions?

10. Distribute the *Emotional Reactions* activity pages. Ask the group members to complete the sentence starters.

11. Allow participants to compare their completed sentences with others in the group without being judgmental about differences. If an unacceptable response is given, point out that it is very different from the norm.

12. Ask why there are similarities, if any. Discuss socially acceptable emotional reactions as they relate to the answers given. Did the participants find out anything about themselves?

13. Conclude with a discussion of social norms and emotional reactions. Do social norms dictate our reactions? What happens if a person behaves/reacts in a socially unacceptable fashion (e.g., an adult screaming at a child or a couple locked in an intimate embrace in a public place)? What makes certain emotional reactions socially acceptable or unacceptable? Are norms changing (e.g., men learning to cry, women becoming more outspoken)? What are some acceptable ways of expressing strong emotions (e.g., write, draw, talk to friends, etc.)? How can verbalizing feelings help to control emotional reactions? Is it possible to choose how we will feel in different situations and/or how we will express those feelings? For example, if someone puts you down, do you have to feel hurt or angry about it? Why or why not?

Social Communication

Emotions

Directions: Give an example of a situation in which a person may choose to feel each emotion. Do not give a definition.

Example:

　Correct response: amazed—You see a spaceship land in your back yard.
　Incorrect response: amazed—To be very surprised

1. angry _____

2. content _____

3. disappointed _____

4. disgusted _____

5. embarrassed _____

6. excited _____

7. furious _____

8. guilty _____

9. happy _____

10. jealous _____

11. proud _____

12. sad _____

13. scared _____

14. surprised _____

Understanding Oneself: Understanding Emotional Reactions

Emotional Reactions

Directions: Complete the sentence starters below.

Example:

When I feel afraid, I get very quiet.

1. When I feel afraid, I _____.

2. When I'm happy, I like to _____.

3. When I dislike someone, I _____.

4. When I feel good, I _____.

5. When I am frustrated, I _____.

6. When I love someone, I _____.

7. When I'm with someone I like, I feel _____.

8. When I am embarrassed, I _____.

9. When I am worried, I _____.

10. When I feel angry, I usually _____.

11. When I feel guilty, I _____.

12. When I'm disappointed, I _____.

13. When I'm excited, I _____.

14. When I'm upset, I _____.

15. When I feel totally content, I _____.

© 1992 Thinking Publications
Duplication permitted for educational use only.

Social Communication

The easiest sentence to complete was number _____.
Why do you think it was the easiest for you?

The hardest sentence to complete was number _____.
Why do you think it was the hardest for you?

Activity 4—Understanding Oneself
Examining Obligations and Options

Language Purpose:

1. To compare and contrast obligations and options
2. To consider different alternatives

Self-Esteem Focus:

To recognize that obligations can create pressure in life

Materials:

Examining Obligations activity page

Vocabulary:

choose, desire, duty, mandate, obligation, option, pressure, visible, wish

Process:

1. Define *obligation* and *option* through discussion, or provide these definitions:

    obligation—something you feel you should do because it is your duty

    option—the right or act of choosing

    Compare and contrast the two definitions.

2. Ask participants why it is important to learn about obligations. Responses may include: "It's good to do what you're supposed to do." "People get mad at you if you don't do your duties."

3. Brainstorm a few obligations (e.g., go to work, cook, go to meetings, call a friend back, etc.).

4. Distribute the *Examining Obligations* activity page to all group members. Ask participants to fold the page along the dotted line so that only the "Obligations" portion is visible.

5. Instruct them to write the things they feel pressured to do in the "Obligations" column. Allow a few minutes for this portion of the exercise.

6. Divide the group into pairs.

7. Explain that many times when people feel obligated to do something they say, "I have to…" Tell participants to use the phrase "I have to…" as a sentence starter before each item they listed in the left-hand column

109

Social Communication

and see how it makes them feel. One person in the pair starts by reading his or her list aloud to the other partner using the "I have to..." sentence starter. When that person finishes, the other member of the pair shares his or her list using the same sentence starter.

8. Compare and contrast "I choose to" and "I have to." Repeat the exercise in process step 7 using "I choose to..." as a sentence starter. How did participants feel when saying, "I choose to"?

9. Then ask participants to move only those things they wish to do from the "Obligations" list to the "Options" list. They should avoid moving those things they do not desire to do or that others want them to do, and move only those things they honestly wish to do.

10. Compare the two lists. Has this activity caused participants to reexamine their activities? Are there still some things they don't choose to do, but feel pressured to do? If so, what? How do they feel when they think they *have to* do something as opposed to *choosing to* do something? Is there a difference? Why do people do things they frequently don't want to do? What would happen if they didn't?

11. Continue the activity with a discussion about why people feel pressure to do certain things. Where does the pressure come from? Is pressure useful? Why or why not? How much pressure comes from the participants themselves? How much comes from others? Is there a difference?

12. Conclude the activity with a discussion about options. Ask participants how feeling that they have options reduces pressure or changes how they feel about doing things that have to be done. Why is the idea of having options important? Ask how having options can affect how they feel about themselves and others. What happens when people don't understand the difference between what they choose to do and what they feel obligated to do?

Understanding Oneself: Examining Obligations and Options

EXAMINING OBLIGATIONS

Directions: Fold the paper in half lengthwise so that only the "Obligations" portion is visible. Write all the things you feel pressured to do in the "Obligations" column. Then listen for further instructions.

Obligations (Things you feel pressured to do)	**Options** (Things you choose to do)
1. _____	1. _____
2. _____	2. _____
3. _____	3. _____
4. _____	4. _____
5. _____	5. _____
6. _____	6. _____
7. _____	7. _____
8. _____	8. _____
9. _____	9. _____
10. _____	10. _____
11. _____	11. _____
12. _____	12. _____
13. _____	13. _____
14. _____	14. _____
15. _____	15. _____

© 1992 **Thinking Publications**
Duplication permitted for educational use only.

Social Communication

Activity 5—Understanding Oneself
Understanding Procrastination

Language Purpose:

1. To define the concepts of *procrastination* and *excuses*
2. To identify the relationships among delaying tactics, procrastination, and consequences in daily activities

Self-Esteem Focus:

To analyze the relationship between procrastination and self-concept

Materials:

Dealing with Procrastination activity page

Vocabulary:

acknowledge, confront, consequence, delay, excuse, favorable, procrastinate, rank, tactics, tolerable

Process:

1. Ask participants to brainstorm a definition for *procrastination*. For continuity, give participants a formal definition of *procrastinate,* such as:

    procrastinate—to delay or put off decisions or actions

    Write the definition for all to see.

2. Discuss with participants the importance of learning about procrastination. How can knowing about procrastination help in everyday life?

3. Ask participants if they ever delay doing things. Brainstorm and list excuses for not doing the following activities/jobs/chores (or use your own examples):

    a. Homework or research paper (e.g., I'll do it tomorrow).

    b. Housework or yard work (e.g., The day is too nice to waste by doing work).

    c. Asking for a date or telling a significant other you're unhappy (e.g., She'd never say yes; she'd get angry).

4. Explain that there are at least four common reasons for procrastinating. (You can also use your own reasons or brainstorm reasons with the group.) They include:

    a. We don't want to do something.

    b. We're afraid we won't "do it right."

Understanding Oneself: Understanding Procrastination

      c. We have two choices and choose the more favorable before the less favorable one.

      d. We think the task is difficult. (Sometimes we say a task is stupid or dumb because we believe it is too hard.)

5. Beside each excuse from process step 3, put an a, b, c, or d to indicate the reason for procrastinating from process step 4.

6. Distribute the *Dealing with Procrastination* activity page. Ask participants to go through the following steps, giving them time to complete each one before proceeding to the next:

      a. List five activities you need to do but would rather not do.

      b. Rank those five items by placing a 5 by the one you least want to do and a 1 by the item that is the most tolerable.

      c. Write the consequences (what will happen) if you don't do these five things.

7. Ask for volunteers to share their information and comment on the significance of the consequences.

8. Engage participants in a discussion of what happens when people don't do what they need to do (e.g., they get anxious, they get in trouble, they are not successful, etc.).

9. Have participants brainstorm plans of action (ways to prevent procrastinating) and be sure to include the following:

      a. Reward yourself for accomplishment of the task (e.g., I'll listen to my new tape after I finish).

      b. Set a deadline for accomplishment (e.g., I will finish this assignment by 7:45 p.m.).

      c. Recognize an excuse as being just that: an excuse (e.g., I have to watch this TV program. I could tape it and begin the job now; telling myself that I have to watch it is an excuse).

      d. Set a definite time for working on the task (e.g., I'll start working on the project in 10 minutes).

      e. Acknowledge when you are thinking about procrastinating and confront those thoughts (e.g., I'd rather do anything, even clean out the garage; I must be pretty desperate to avoid this project because I'm willing to do a nasty job rather than begin on the project).

10. Remind participants that procrastination delays solving problems but does not alleviate the problems. By recognizing procrastination and delaying tactics when they occur, participants can choose to tackle their problems on their own terms instead of falling victim to resulting consequences.

Social Communication

11. Conclude the activity by asking these questions: What purpose is served by procrastinating? Why do we make excuses? How does it make you feel about yourself if you continually procrastinate and make excuses? How do others feel about you?

Some ideas in this activity were adapted from Bailey (1984).

Understanding Oneself: Understanding Procrastination

Dealing With PROCRASTINATION

Directions: Listen to the instructions given to you and fill in the blanks.

Activities	Rank	Consequences
1.	____	
2.	____	
3.	____	
4.	____	
5.	____	

Social Communication

Activity 6—Understanding Oneself
Understanding Stress

Language Purpose:

1. To define *stress*
2. To look for relationships between stressful events and reactions
3. To express an opinion about stress

Self-Esteem Focus:

To examine positive methods of dealing with stress

Materials:

Stress activity pages

Vocabulary:

anxiety, cope, demand, nervous, premature, pressure, stress, stressors

Process:

(Note: This activity and the next are designed to be done as a unit.)

1. Ask participants to define the term *stress*. Accept a wide range of possible definitions and point out that people may have differing definitions.
2. Ask participants why they think it is important to learn more about stress or why it may be critical to their well-being. Responses might include these: "It's good to know when you are uptight. You might do something you're sorry for later. It makes you nervous." Explain that long-term effects of stress may include ulcers, premature aging, headaches, etc.
3. Offer a formal definition of *stress*, such as:

    stress—a response of the body to pressures or demands placed on it; it is frequently thought to be emotionally or physically uncomfortable.

    Expand this idea by asking questions such as these: Where else have you heard the word *pressure*? What happens when you shake a can of soda? How is that kind of pressure like the pressure a person might feel? Who might make demands of you? What are some demands made of you now?
4. Explain that stress causes physical reactions in our bodies. For example, during stressful situations, the muscles tighten, adrenaline is released into the bloodstream, the stomach tightens and secretes acid, and breathing becomes quick and shallow.

Understanding Oneself: Understanding Stress

5. Explain that some of these physical responses evolved ages ago to help us fight off predators or run away if we needed to. We no longer have that lifestyle, however. Ask participants to compare that lifestyle with our modern lifestyle.

6. Ask participants to brainstorm stressful events in their lives. Explain that these events are called *stressors*. When brainstorming stressful events (stressors), participants should include personal stressors such as being in a hurry and not having enough money. They can also include environmental stressors such as noise and smog. List the stressors where everyone can see them.

7. Explain that people need to be aware of stress and how they react to it. Ask participants to discuss ways they react to stress. How does stress make them feel?

8. Distribute the *Stress* activity pages. Review the example on the first activity page and include one or two more examples. Emphasize the difference between how one reacts to stress (e.g., fear, anger, depression, anxiety) and how one deals with stress (e.g., sleep, fight, argue, eat, drink alcohol). Have participants complete the first page.

9. Pair participants who have listed a similar stressor. Have them complete the second half of the *Stress* activity pages together. Ask for volunteers to share their responses with the whole group.

10. Ask participants if they know any positive ways of dealing with stress. Add your ideas about coping with stress and discuss such strategies as relaxation, biofeedback, relaxed breathing, exercise, communicating one's feelings, etc. Be sure to define terms that are unfamiliar.

11. Divide participants into small groups. Refer to the list of stressful events generated during process step 6. Ask each group to identify two causes of stress. Then ask them to generate three possible positive coping strategies from information they have learned or from their imaginations (e.g., exercise, relaxation).

12. Conclude the activity with a discussion comparing positive and negative ways of dealing with stress (e.g., working out and eating healthy versus drinking and drug use). Ask how negative ways of dealing with stress may cause more stress. How can people incorporate positive methods of dealing with stress in their lives? Is this always easy to do?

Social Communication

STRESS

Directions: Fill in the blanks below. Then answer the questions on the next page with a partner.

Things that are stressful to me:	How my body reacts to the situation:	How I deal/cope with my stress:
Example: Too much work to do	I get nervous.	I overeat.
1.		
2.		
3.		
4.		
5.		

Understanding Oneself: Understanding Stress

Find someone who has listed something stressful that is similar to one of your items. Compare your answers. Answer the questions below.

A. Do you react the same? _____ Yes _____ No

If not, explain the different reactions:

B. Do you deal with the stressful situation in the same way?

_____ Yes _____ No

If not, explain the different methods:

C. Which was the better way, your way or the way your partner reacted?
_____ Why?

Social Communication

Activity 7—Understanding Oneself
Assessing Stress (C) (HS)

Language Purpose:

1. To recognize life situations that are stressful
2. To assess one's stress level

Self-Esteem Focus:

To differentiate between different types of stress and their relationship to self-concept

Materials:

Stress Test, Personal Sources of Stress activity page

Vocabulary:

event, ongoing, significant

Process:

(Note: Depending on how much discussion is generated, this activity may be extended to two sessions.)

1. Take a few minutes to review the discussion from the previous activity. Start by asking participants why they decided it was important to learn about stress. Ask if any questions have arisen since the last discussion.

2. Explain that today the discussion will differentiate two types of stress:

    a. stress that is ongoing or experienced every day or frequently (e.g., daily hassles, traffic jams, getting to school on time, getting homework done)

    b. stress that is produced by an event (e.g., death in the family, moving to a new city, getting suspended from school)

   Ask participants to add their examples for each type of stress.

3. Ask which type of stress was discussed primarily in the previous activity. The answers will most likely be related to ongoing stress.

4. Distribute the *Stress Test*. Explain vocabulary terms if necessary. Tell participants that the *Stress Test* is for their reference only. Since some of the items are very personal, assure them that you will not be collecting the tests. Instruct participants not to leave the test lying around for others to see. Suggest they take the test home or destroy it. If reading is a problem, read the test to participants or pre-record the test on tape.

Understanding Oneself: Assessing Stress

5. After the scores have been added, write the following scale where everyone can see it.

Stress Test Scale

150 and above	Major stress problem. Seek help to reduce your stress now.
90–149	Significant stress problem. Your life is stressful.
50–89	Minor stress problems. Where can you do better?
0–49	No significant problem with stress.

Tell participants to use this scale cautiously. Scores may indicate that someone is having a stressful year but is dealing well with difficult situations. Scores may also indicate that particular individuals might need help. Discuss what participants might do or who they could talk to if their scores are disturbing or worrisome (e.g., ask to talk with you in private, talk to a parent or counselor, etc.). If they are alarmed by a test score, they should seek immediate guidance from an appropriate resource.

6. Examine the *Stress Test* and have participants label each happening as ongoing stress or event stress. Point out that positive situations can also produce stress. Ask for examples of when participants have experienced positive stress.

7. Distribute the *Personal Sources of Stress* activity page and have participants complete it.

8. Generate discussion by encouraging participants to tell which type of stress (event stress or ongoing stress) is more common in their lives. Is there a similarity in responses? Do most people experience more event stress or more ongoing stress? Why?

9. Conclude the activity by asking participants to recall different ways of dealing with stress from the previous activity. Are there particular methods that could be applied to particular situations? Ask participants to give each other feedback and suggestions about how an individual's stress can be dealt with. Remind them of positive ways to cope with stress (e.g., exercise, diet). Ask participants to list professionals who deal with stress reduction therapies. If necessary, help complete their list with such examples as psychologists, counselors, psychiatrists, etc. Define these professional roles for participants, if necessary.

Social Communication

STRESS test

Directions: Read each item or listen while the following items are read. If the situation happened to you in the last year, circle the number to the right. When you have finished the list, add up the circled points.

(Note: Some of these items are very personal. This test will only be seen by you. It will not be collected. Take it with you when you leave or throw it away.)

Situation **Points**

1. A parent died 10
2. Became pregnant or became a father 9
3. Beaten by a parent 9
4. Sent to jail or a reform school 9
5. A close family member or friend died 9
6. Caught doing drugs 9
7. Physically attacked or raped 8
8. Parents got divorced 8
9. A pet died 8
10. Caught a sexually transmitted disease 8
11. Broke up with someone special 7
12. Sudden change in income 7
13. Started or stopped doing drugs 7
14. Got fired 7
15. Personal property lost or stolen 7
16. Moved to a new city 7
17. Fell in love 7
18. Got a new job 7
19. Constant fighting at home 7
20. Moved out on your own 7
21. Owed someone a large sum of money 7
22. Felt you were unattractive 6
23. Pressured to have sex 6

© 1992 Thinking Publications
Duplication permitted for educational use only.

Understanding Oneself: Assessing Stress

24. Started to drink alcohol 6
25. Got suspended from school 6
26. Graduated from high school 6
27. Had an important job interview 6
28. Gained too much weight 6
29. Worried about war or environmental problems 6
30. Teacher or boss did not like your work 6
31. Got poor grades or evaluation 6
32. Took a pet to the vet 5
33. Responsible for too many decisions at home 5
34. Got a traffic ticket 5
35. Started to date..5
36. Had difficulty with acne 5
37. Had a major disagreement with a neighbor 5
38. Took final exams...5
39. Had to wear braces or glasses 5
40. Had a birthday 4
41. Began the school year 4
42. Pressured to do what your friends do 4
43. Christmas 4
44. Got a car for the first time...4
45. Made the team or a tryout..4
46. Had a major change in how or when sleep occurs..................4
47. Changed eating habits..4
48. Got a new, close friend 3
49. Went on vacation...3
50. Got a minor illness...3

Total _____

Some ideas in this activity were adapted from Holmes and Rahe (1979); Jacobs, Turk, and Horn (1989); Jaffee and Scott (1984); and Restak (1984). (Note: Stress usually happens in two situations: [1] at home with parents, friends, or loved ones, and [2] at school or work with teachers, employers, or friends.)

Social Communication

Personal Sources of Stress

Directions: List events that happened in the past two months at school or work and at home or in your personal life that caused you stress. Then list ongoing stressors at school or work and at home or in your personal life.

	School/Work	**Home/Personal**
Event Stress	*Example:* Got fired 1. 2. 3.	*Example:* New baby born 1. 2. 3.
Ongoing Stress	*Example:* Constant disagreement with coworker 1. 2. 3.	*Example:* Never enough money 1. 2. 3.

Activity 8—Understanding Oneself
Self-Evaluation

Language Purpose:

1. To examine information about oneself
2. To describe human qualities
3. To classify qualities as positive or negative

Self-Esteem Focus:

To develop a beginning awareness of what is important in life

Materials:

Self-Evaluation activity pages

Vocabulary:

feature, ideal, quality, reality, state

Process:

1. Explain that this activity was designed to help people begin thinking about who they are and what they want. Ask participants what can happen to people who don't know what they want. Why is knowing what one wants important?

2. Define the word *quality:*

    quality—a feature that makes a person what she or he is

    Brainstorm qualities people might have (e.g., honest, loving, angry, friendly). Be sure participants understand that qualities can be both positive and negative.

3. Distribute the *Self-Evaluation* activity pages. Instruct the participants to stop after item 4.

4. Discuss items 1 through 4 on the activity pages. Include ideas such as:
    a. Was it easier to think of positive or negative qualities? Why might that be?
    b. In item 1, were participants too hard on themselves?
    c. In item 2, does the group see the participant in this way?
    d. Are there similarities within the group in the qualities that participants listed in item 3?

Social Communication

      e. What were the similarities and differences between what participants listed in item 4?
5. Instruct participants to complete item 5 on the activity page.
6. Ask participants to share their inheritance fantasies. How would it feel to have $10,000 for a while? Ask how it would feel to be told they had to give most of it away. Ask participants to comment on each other's responses.
7. Explain whether there was any relationship or similarity between answers given in items 4 and 5. When given the opportunity, did individuals go for their ideals?
8. Conclude with a discussion by asking if thinking about one's ideals helps to make them a reality. How can knowing your positive and/or negative qualities be helpful? Ask why it is important to know what your ideals are. What could a person do to make an ideal into a reality?

Understanding Oneself: Self-Evaluation

Self-Evaluation

Directions: Answer the following questions as completely as possible.

1. What kind of person are you? List five positive and five negative qualities you possess.

   Positive Qualities   **Negative Qualities**

   1. _____   1. _____

   2. _____   2. _____

   3. _____   3. _____

   4. _____   4. _____

   5. _____   5. _____

2. How would the person who knows you best describe you?

3. What kind of person do you want to be? List five qualities that tell about your ideal self.

   1. _____

   2. _____

   3. _____

   4. _____

   5. _____

Social Communication

4. What do you want? List three things you want in each category:

   Material possessions (Examples: boat, ranch, car)

   1. _____
   2. _____
   3. _____

   Physical state or appearance (Examples: good health, long life, black hair, thin body)

   1. _____
   2. _____
   3. _____

   Mental state of mind (Examples: happy, excited, satisfied)

   1. _____
   2. _____
   3. _____

   Relationships (Examples: good friends, wife/husband, children)

   1. _____
   2. _____
   3. _____

   STOP!

5. How would you spend $10,000 that a wealthy relative has left you? The will says that you can only spend $1,000 on yourself. The remaining $9,000 must be given away. What would you do with your share? What would you do with the $9,000 you must give away?

Activity 9—Understanding Oneself
Respect

Language Purpose:

1. To recognize qualities in oneself and others
2. To look for relationships between one's perceptions of oneself and one's perceptions of others
3. To take sufficient time to think through a response

Self-Esteem Focus:

To develop an understanding of how significant others affect self-concept

Materials:

paper, *Respect* activity page, various magazines

Vocabulary:

admire, perception, realistic, respect

Process:

1. Ask participants to give examples of different situations where they have heard the word *respect* used. Explain that this activity helps people to think about who they respect and admire and why. Ask why learning about who we respect is important. What might it tell us about ourselves?
2. Instruct participants to vertically list the numbers 1 through 10 on a piece of paper. The activity then proceeds in this manner:
   a. Next to number 1, write the name of the person you would most prefer to be like.
   b. Next to number 10, write the name of the person you would least prefer to be like.
   c. Place your name between the two where you feel it is most appropriate. If you are similar to the number 1 person, your name may go in the number 2 or number 3 position, but if you aren't very similar to the number 1 person, your name may go at the number 5 or number 6, etc. position.
3. Distribute the *Respect* activity page. Participants should complete the activity using the information above.

129

4. Have participants share a few things that they don't like about themselves that they either can or cannot change. Are there similarities in responses among participants? Can any conclusions be drawn from similarities?

5. Ask participants to give feedback about whether they agree with other group members' perceptions of themselves. Also ask participants to give each other ideas about how they could change things they don't like about themselves.

6. Continue the activity by having participants analyze their lists completed during process step 2. Discussion could revolve around:

    a. Whose names were number 1 and number 10? Why?

    b. Where did you put your name? Were you too hard on yourself?

    c. Do you agree that most things you don't like about yourself can be changed?

7. Distribute the magazines. Explain to participants that they are to find a picture of a person they may want to be like. Tell them to take their time and narrow their choices to one picture. Allow 10 minutes to complete this segment.

8. Ask participants to share their choices with the group. Engage participants in a discussion about why they chose particular pictures by asking questions like:

    a. What caused you to choose this picture?

    b. Do you think you are like the person in the picture now? Why or why not?

    c. If you are not like that person at this time, how can you change to become similar?

9. After each participant has talked, conclude the activity by asking participants to give feedback about how they see each person in relationship to the picture that person selected. Discussion may revolve around ideas such as:

    a. Is the person already like the example that he or she chose? If so, how?

    b. Is the quality the person is attracted to a realistic one to attain? Why or why not?

Some ideas in this activity were adapted from Smuin (1978).

Understanding Oneself: Respect

RESPECT

Directions: Complete the tasks and questions below. Give yourself a few minutes to think first.

1. List three qualities of the person whose name you chose as number 1:

   a. _____

   b. _____

   c. _____

2. List three faults of the person whose name you chose as number 10:

   a. _____

   b. _____

   c. _____

3. Are you like either of those people? How?

4. List five things you don't like about yourself. Put a check mark (✓) by those things that you could not change even with hard work.

   a. _____ ( )

   b. _____ ( )

   c. _____ ( )

   d. _____ ( )

   e. _____ ( )

Social Communication

Activity 10—Understanding Oneself
An Ideal Day

Language Purpose:

1. To describe details of an ideal day
2. To plan a time schedule for an ideal day
3. To evaluate the effect of fantasies on reality

Self-Esteem Focus:

To develop an understanding that fantasizing can lead to self-exploration

Materials:

An Ideal Day activity page, *Ideal Day Plan* activity pages

Vocabulary:

fantasize, fantasy, ideal, realistic, reality, reflective

Process:

1. Ask participants what comes to mind when they think of the word *fantasy* and how learning about fantasies could be important to reality.
2. Contrast *fantasy* with *fantasize*. Ask for possible synonyms for *fantasize* (e.g., daydream, imagine, pretend).
3. Explain that this activity involves fantasizing about one's ideal day. This day is not to be a vacation day, but a regular day as participants would love it to be. As participants think about their day, encourage them to think about it in the present tense and in detail, from getting up in the morning to going to bed at night.
4. Encourage their thinking process by giving the following examples:
    a. What is the first thing you do when you wake up?
    b. What do you have for breakfast? Do you make it yourself?
    c. Do you take a hot bath or a cold shower, or maybe not bathe?
    d. What kind of clothes do you put on?
    e. How do you spend the morning? The afternoon? The evening?
    f. At each time of the day, are you indoors or outdoors, busy or quiet, alone or with others?
5. Suggest that as participants go through the hours of their fantasy day, they keep three helpful questions in mind:

Understanding Oneself: An Ideal Day

    a. What are they doing—what kind of work or play?

    b. Where are they—in what place, city, situation?

    c. Who do they spend time with? These could be real people or people they would like to be surrounded by.

6. Start the actual fantasy with something like the following:

   You've just awakened in the morning. You feel great. The weather is perfect. You have the whole day ahead of you to do whatever you want.

7. Instruct participants to take about five minutes to think about their day before they start writing.

8. Distribute all activity pages. After examining the details of their day, instruct participants to plan a 24-hour written schedule of their day. When appropriate, hours may be combined (e.g., 11 p.m.–6 a.m.: sleep). Allow about 20 minutes for them to complete this process.

9. Go over the activity pages. Give everyone a chance to discuss their ideal day and to discuss how one's ideal day may be reflective of one's personality, needs, and sense of self. For example, a quiet, introspective person *may* choose to spend more time alone than a talkative, outgoing person. What conclusions can people draw about themselves from their ideal day? Examples might include:

    a. I'd rather live in the city than the country.

    b. I like to spend most of my time with people.

    c. I'm a night person.

    d. I'd like to live on my own.

    e. I'd rather be working than doing nothing.

10. Have participants think about and explain what they have to do or change to make their ideal day a reality (e.g., finish school, earn money, move near an ocean, etc.). Ask group members to give each other suggestions. Are these changes realistic?

11. Conclude the activity with a discussion of the importance of fantasies. Are fantasies important? Why or why not? Can fantasies affect reality? How? Did you learn anything new about yourself from fantasizing about your ideal day? What did you learn about others in the group from their fantasies?

Social Communication

An Ideal Day

Directions: Describe the details of your ideal day. Write answers to the following questions as you would like your day to be:

1. What is the first thing you do when you wake up?

2. What do you have for breakfast?

3. Who makes your breakfast?

4. Do you take a bath or a shower, or maybe not bathe?

5. What kind of clothes do you put on?

6. How do you spend the morning?

7. How do you spend the afternoon?

8. How do you spend the evening?

Understanding Oneself: An Ideal Day

Ideal Day PLAN

Directions: Fill in the blanks for each time period as you would like them to be.

	What are you doing?	Are you indoors or outdoors?	Are you alone or with others?	How are you feeling?
midnight–2 a.m.				
2 a.m.–4 a.m.				
4 a.m.–6 a.m.				
6 a.m.–8 a.m.				
8 a.m.–10 a.m.				
10 a.m.–noon				

Social Communication

	What are you doing?	**Are you indoors or outdoors?**	**Are you alone or with others?**	**How are you feeling?**
noon–2 p.m.				
2 p.m.–4 p.m.				
4 p.m.–6 p.m.				
6 p.m.–8 p.m.				
8 p.m.–10 p.m.				
10 p.m.–midnight				

Section 4: Exploring Self-Concept

In this section, participants continue to synthesize ideas about themselves as they explore the idea of self-concept. Activities in this section require that participants integrate ideas about their histories, likes, dislikes, perceptions, and fantasies, and begin to formulate a picture of their self-concept. Figuring importantly into self-concept are discussions about topics such as self-talk, positive thinking, and values.

After defining the idea of self-concept, participants are then ready to explore self-esteem, which is addressed directly in Section 5.

As in all activities in *Social Communication: Activities for Improving Peer Interactions and Self-Esteem,* the communication focus is on discourse. The activities are designed to provide the content for discussion.

Activities in this section include:

		Page
1.	Defining Self-Concept	138
2.	Identifying Attributes of People	141
3.	Exploring Personality (C)	143
4.	Personal Descriptors	146
5.	Analyzing Self-Talk	150
6.	Positive Thinking	152
7.	Affirmations	154
8.	Personal Values (C)	157
9.	Developing Goals	160
10.	Writing an Autobiography	165

Social Communication

Activity 1—Exploring Self-Concept
Defining Self-Concept

Language Purpose:

1. To define *self-concept*
2. To identify how self-concept develops
3. To assess self-concept

Self-Esteem Focus:

To increase understanding of how self-concept influences attitudes

Materials:

Self-Concept Questionnaire

Vocabulary:

attitude, belief, competent, inadequacy, insult, personality, questionnaire, risk, significant, unworthy

Process:

1. Write a definition for *self-concept* where everyone can see it:

    self-concept—beliefs and attitudes we have developed about ourselves from birth; how individuals describe themselves

    Ask participants where else they have heard the words *beliefs* and *attitude*.

2. Ask participants why it is important to learn about self-concept. What can be learned from finding out how self-concept develops?

3. Distribute the *Self-Concept Questionnaire* as a baseline measure. Assure participants that these will not be graded. The questionnaire is for the participants' information only and will be used as a basis for discussion about self-concept.

4. Read and discuss the statements on the questionnaire. Explain vocabulary terms if necessary. The answers and explanations are as follows:

    1) *False*—One's self-concept is helped or hurt by the opinions and beliefs of significant others, but basically it is one's beliefs and attitudes about oneself.

    2) *True*—Some psychologists say that 80 percent of a person's present personality was formed by the age of six. Others estimate that personality develops by age two. We are not born with a self-concept. It is learned.

Exploring Self-Concept: Defining Self-Concept

    3) *False*—Because self-concept is learned, it can be changed—sometimes through our own efforts, other times through the efforts of significant people in our lives.

    4) *True*—If we believe that a person's attitudes and opinions are important, negative comments or attitudes can reinforce feelings of inadequacy, stupidity, or unworthiness.

    5) *True*—If you believe you cannot do math, chances are you will not like it, and, therefore, will not do well in that subject. This is known as a *self-fulfilling prophecy*. What you think will determine whether you succeed or even try.

    6) *False*—Your self-concept is the basis for your interaction in the world. It affects your relationships, your job, your goals for the future. Some people have been taught that they are not important. They often put others before themselves. This can reflect a poor self-concept.

    7) *False*—A person who continually insults you, criticizes you, or verbally abuses you can bring you to see only the negative parts of yourself. On the other hand, a person who treats you as a competent, loving, valuable person can help you realize and concentrate on those parts of your personality.

    8) *True*—When an important person in your life trusts you, it encourages you to trust yourself. On the other hand, if someone questions you or your actions all the time, it makes you feel upset or angry.

    9) *False*—When you are angry, sad, or depressed, many times it seems that things go wrong. When you are pleased, proud, or feel good about yourself, you are better able to deal with things that go wrong and people enjoy being around you.

   10) *True*—When you have a positive attitude, you are more willing to try new things, to take risks. This is not to say that bad things don't happen to people who feel good about themselves, but research has shown that achievement increases with a good self-concept.

5. Conclude the activity with a discussion about how participants think their self-concepts developed. Do group members agree with the importance of self-concept as stated in this activity? Did group members learn anything new about themselves? If so, what?

Additional Activity:

Repeat the *Self-Concept Questionnaire* in a few months to see if attitudes about self-concept have changed.

Social Communication

SELF-CONCEPT QUESTIONNAIRE

Directions: Read the statements. Circle **T** if the statement is true, **F** if the statement is false, and **DK** if you don't know.

T   F   DK   1. *Self-concept* is the beliefs and attitudes others have about us.

T   F   DK   2. How you feel about yourself is learned.

T   F   DK   3. You cannot change your feelings about yourself.

T   F   DK   4. Other people's negative comments can affect how you feel about yourself.

T   F   DK   5. Your attitude about yourself can affect your life goals.

T   F   DK   6. What you believe about yourself is not important.

T   F   DK   7. Other people's opinions of you have no effect on you.

T   F   DK   8. A person who trusts you can change your feelings about yourself.

T   F   DK   9. Your attitude has no effect on your behavior.

T   F   DK   10. A positive attitude can help you succeed.

Activity 2—Exploring Self-Concept
Identifying Attributes of People

Language Purpose:

1. To name attributes in other people
2. To discuss similarities in attributes of admired people
3. To discuss how positive attributes can be developed

Self-Esteem Focus:

To increase understanding of attributes admired in others

Materials:

none

Vocabulary:

attribute, contradiction, lack, quality, relevance

Process:

1. Ask participants to explain the term *attribute* in their own words. Ask why it is important to study the attributes or qualities of other people. What relevance does this have for a person's self-concept?
2. Have participants brainstorm and list qualities people possess, such as honesty, dependability, or jealousy. Listed qualities do not need to be considered positive attributes. If necessary, review information about qualities discussed in Section 3, Activity 8—"Self-Evaluation."
3. Explain to participants that this activity will not only reveal qualities possessed by those they admire, but it will also reveal qualities that are important to group members.
4. Ask participants to write down the names of four people they admire. These people can be friends, celebrities, family members, or others in the participants' environments.
5. Tell group members to leave space below each name for answering the following questions:
   a. What relationship, if any, does the person named have with you?
   b. Why did you select this person?
   c. What qualities or attributes do you admire most in this person? List at least three.

Social Communication

>***Example:*** Bo Jackson
> 1. No relationship, celebrity sports figure
> 2. Plays both professional baseball and football and is on commercials
> 3. Smart, sense of humor, versatile athlete and person

Participants are to answer the questions for each name listed.

6. Ask participants to look for similarities among the qualities or attributes listed for the four individuals. What are they?
7. Conclude the activity with a discussion. What do attributes of other people have to do with one's self-concept? Are there any contradictions in the attributes listed? Do participants think it is true that people admire qualities in others that they themselves lack? Why or why not? Do participants possess some of the same attributes that they listed for others? How can group members develop attributes they admire, but don't have?

Exploring Self-Concept: Exploring Personality

Activity 3—Exploring Self-Concept
Exploring Personality (C)

Language Purpose:

1. To define the concept of *personality*
2. To examine a personal sense of identity
3. To formulate an idea of one's personality

Self-Esteem Focus:

To develop an awareness of what makes a person unique

Materials:

Personality Questionnaire

Vocabulary

behavior, characteristics, personality, questionnaire, unique

Process:

(Note: Ideally, this is a writing assignment. Since the questions require some thought, allow adequate time to process the information. If writing is too demanding for participants, questions can be read to them and responses given orally. Responses will be needed to complete Activity 10—"Writing an Autobiography.")

1. Explain that the topic of this activity is personality awareness. Ask participants what *personality* means to them. List the ideas where everyone can see them. Using this list and a dictionary, compose a definition of *personality,* such as:

    personality—the qualities, characteristics, and behaviors that make one person unique from another

2. Ask participants why learning about personality may be important to their own lives. Responses may include:

    "It's good to know how you are special."

    "It helps to have a good personality."

3. Tell participants that you will be distributing a questionnaire. Instruct participants to take their time and think about each question before answering. Explain that the questions were designed to help people examine different parts of their personalities. Distribute a *Personality Questionnaire* to each person.

4. When participants have completed the questionnaire, ask them if they learned something new about themselves. Engage participants in a brief discussion about their thoughts and discoveries.

5. Explain that now participants are to look at their questionnaire responses and then do the following activity:

   a. Number a piece of paper from 1 to 20.

   b. Think about the question, "Who am I?"

   c. Write as many answers as possible (at least 10) to the question, "Who am I?" List roles (son, brother, student), words that reflect activities (dancer, runner), qualities (helpful, funny), feelings (a happy person, a worrier), etc.

6. After lists are completed, explain that personality is made up of many different parts. No single definition or answer makes a whole personality, and the whole of a person's personality is much more than the answers on participants' papers. There may, however, be parts that influence personality more than others. What might those be?

7. Now ask participants to rank their responses, thinking about which response is most important to them and the most expressive of who they really are.

8. Ask participants to write a one-sentence description of their own personalities. This description should be based on the information discussed in this activity.

9. Conclude the activity by asking for volunteers to read their own personality descriptions. Do people see each other as they see themselves? What are the differences? Are people too hard on themselves? Have they left out important parts of their personalities that others see? Has the definition of *personality* changed for anyone from the beginning of the activity? How? How are participants unique from one another?

Exploring Self-Concept: Exploring Personality

Personality Questionnaire

1. What are you concerned about or worried about at this time?

2. What are the major goals you would like to achieve in your life?

3. What has been the best experience of your life?

4. What is the biggest problem in your life at this time?

5. What is the thing that you do the best?

6. What would you like to stop doing?

7. What would you like to learn how to do?

8. What is the most important change that you expect to make in the next 10 years?

9. Which is more important to you, a well-paying job or a job you really like?

10. Do you want to have children? Why or why not?

Social Communication

Activity 4—Exploring Self-Concept
Personal Descriptors

Language Purpose:

1. To restate self-concept in terms of different descriptors
2. To compare individual and group descriptors

Self-Esteem Focus:

To expand the idea of self-concept development

Materials:

Personal Descriptors activity pages

Vocabulary:

descriptor, sub-item

Process:

(Note: Participants should save their completed *Personal Descriptors* activity pages for Activity 10—"Writing an Autobiography.")

1. Ask participants why it is important to be aware of how others see us as opposed to the way we see ourselves. Is there sometimes a difference? What accounts for the difference?
2. Explain that group members will be describing themselves as well as others in the group. Explain that the words used to describe participants are called *descriptors*.
3. Brainstorm and list names of categories such as food, animals, colors, etc. (List categories that have many sub-items.)
4. Instruct participants to think about themselves (their overall personalities, physical characteristics, talents, qualities, etc.).
5. Distribute the *Personal Descriptors* activity pages. Remind participants that they need to be sensitive to each other's feelings as they proceed through this activity.
6. Ask participants to copy all categories from the board onto their activity pages in the column labeled "Category." To the right of each category on the first page, tell participants to write sub-items that best describe themselves and explanations of why those items were selected.

Example:	Category	Sub-item	Explanation
	animals	cheetah	because I'm a fast runner

7. Instruct participants to form groups of two or three persons and to complete the second page of the *Personal Descriptors* activity. Tell each participant to read a category and select a sub-item to describe each of the other members of their small group. Participants should explain their responses to each other and write down on their own activity pages descriptors they want to remember. The process continues until all persons in the small group have heard descriptors about themselves for every category from members of their small group and have written down those descriptors to be remembered.

8. Ask group members to keep their activity pages and to think about them after the session. Participants can examine not only how they see themselves, but how others see them. There may not be enough time during the session for participants to fully appreciate what others have said about them.

9. Conclude the activity with a discussion. Was it difficult for participants to describe themselves and others with terms not normally used for this purpose? Why or why not? Were the descriptors of small-group members accurate? Were small-group descriptors different from the participants' descriptors of themselves? Did they learn anything about how others see them? If so, what?

Social Communication

Personal Descriptors

Directions: List categories generated during discussion in the column labeled "Category." Fill in the other blanks in this section.

Personal Descriptors:

Category	Sub-item	Explanation
Example: colors	yellow	a warm person, sunny personality
1.		
2.		
3.		
4.		
5.		

Exploring Self-Concept: Personal Descriptors

Directions: List categories generated during discussion in the column labeled "Category." Listen to how others in your small group describe you. Write down the responses you want to remember.

Others' Descriptions of You:

Category	Sub-item	Explanation
1.		
2.		
3.		
4.		
5.		

Social Communication

Activity 5—Exploring Self-Concept
Analyzing Self-Talk

Language Purpose:

1. To define the concept of *self-talk*
2. To differentiate positive and negative self-talk messages
3. To generate positive self-talk messages

Self-Esteem Focus:

To increase awareness of self-talk and its impact on self-concept

Materials:

3-by-5-inch note cards

Vocabulary:

disgusted, empower, negative, positive, powerless, script

Process:

1. Instruct the participants that the purpose of this activity is to make them aware of messages they give themselves about themselves (i.e., *self-talk*) and the effect these messages have on behavior, stress level, emotions, and self-concept. Review the definitions of these concepts. Of the estimated 50,000 self-talk messages we give ourselves each day, on average, 80 percent are negative and 20 percent are positive (Helmstetter, 1987).

2. Ask participants what impact the messages we tell ourselves can have on self-concept. Why is it important to learn about self-talk messages?

3. Explain that *self-talk* is another term for what we say to ourselves in response to a situation or event. The many thoughts that go through our minds all day long are *self-talk*.

4. Remind group members that self-talk messages are not only negative, but can be positive. Negative self-talk in response to one situation can leave one feeling sad, disgusted, and powerless in similar situations. Positive self-talk, on the other hand, can leave one feeling happy, empowered, proud, encouraged, and in control in similar situations.

    Examples: "That was a dumb thing to do." (Negative)
    "I really learned a lot from that mistake." (Positive)

Exploring Self-Concept: Analyzing Self-Talk

5. Brainstorm other examples of positive and negative self-talk messages.
6. Divide the participants into small groups. (Four is an ideal small-group size, but a smaller group size will not affect the outcome of the activity.)
7. Distribute 10 note cards (3-by-5-inch) to each small group.
8. Explain to participants that they will be writing short scripts. The scripts should contain:
    a. A situation or event (e.g., losing a $20 bill)
    b. A self-talk message (e.g., "You never can keep track of anything.")
    c. A description of resulting feelings (e.g., angry, disappointed, lack of trust in yourself)
    d. An ongoing reaction (e.g., "Don't trust me" attitude; "I'll probably just disappoint you.")
9. Instruct small-group members to write five scripts (some positive and some negative), being sure to include the four elements described. Possible scripts might include being turned down for a date, failing a class, getting a speeding ticket, getting an "A" on a test, getting a new job, etc. If participants have difficulty generating scripts, provide the above "starter" situations and require participants to generate the remaining three elements.
10. Conclude the activity by sharing scripts between groups and discussing the situations. How could participants change a negative self-talk message to make it have less of an effect? Are they affected by each situation equally? Why or why not? How aware are participants of their own self-talk? How could they tune into it more? How can they get better at using more positive self-talk?

Some ideas in this activity were adapted from Helmstetter (1987).

Social Communication

Activity 6—Exploring Self-Concept
Positive Thinking

Language Purpose:

1. To define and discuss the concept of *positive thinking*
2. To name positive and negative aspects of situations
3. To formulate positive statements about situations

Self-Esteem Focus:

To increase awareness and understanding of how positive thinking can affect a person's view of situations

Materials:

None

Vocabulary:

defense, positive, prophecy, negative, superior

Process:

1. Write a definition for *positive thinking* where everyone can see it, such as:

    positive thinking—looking for the "good" in every situation

2. Ask participants why it is important to think positively. What advantages are there to this type of thinking? If appropriate, refer participants to discussions about positive self-talk from the previous activity.

3. Explain that, as human beings, we are sometimes inclined to see negatives before positives.

    Example: You are involved in a car accident. Your family or significant other may seem to be more concerned with the damage to the car than with your well-being (negative). It will cost a lot to repair the damage, insurance rates will probably go up, and you won't have transportation for a time (negative). At least you were not seriously injured (positive).

4. Test the theory of negatives outweighing positives by asking participants to brainstorm a list of negative thoughts related to flying on an airplane, owning a pet, or any situation you name. Next, have them list positive thoughts about the same situation. The negative list will probably be longer than the positive list.

Exploring Self-Concept: Positive Thinking

Example: Negative thinking about flying on an airplane...
a. it can crash
b. the bathrooms are too small
c. it's noisy
d. seats are too cramped
e. you can't get up when you want
f. the food is terrible
g. babies cry and don't let you rest

Positive thinking about flying on an airplane...
a. it's a faster way to get where you are going
b. attendants wait on you
c. it's safer than a car
d. it has oxygen masks

5. Ask participants the following questions:
   a. Was it easier to come up with positive or negative thoughts?
   b. As a large group, were there more positive or negative responses?
   c. Why do people think more often of the negative aspects of a situation than the positive aspects of a situation? Discuss these possibilities in detail, making sure that participants understand these concepts: defense against disappointment, ability to feel superior in relation to another person, habit, learned reaction.

6. Have participants brainstorm positive self-talk messages about the following situations (an example is given for each situation):

Situation	*Positive Thinking*
It's raining outside...	but the plants need water.
My mom drives me crazy...	but she is always there when I need her.
I'm hungry...	but I'm losing weight.
My boss makes me nervous...	but I've learned a lot from this job.

7. Conclude the activity with a discussion about positive thinking. Is positive thinking always realistic? Can it change the way participants view others or themselves? What effect does negative thinking have on them? What effect does positive thinking have on them? What relationship is there between positive thinking and self-talk? What does positive thinking have to do with a self-fulfilling prophecy?

Some ideas in this activity were adapted from Bormaster and Treat (1982).

Social Communication

Activity 7—Exploring Self-Concept
Affirmations

Language Purpose:

1. To define the concept of *affirmation*
2. To use simple sentences to express ideas clearly and concisely

Self-Esteem Focus:

To increase awareness of positive aspects of people and positive thinking

Materials:

large ball of string

Vocabulary:

affirm, affirmation, assert, attitude, communication, compliment, connected, deprecate, positive, unity

Process:

1. Discuss the definition of the word *affirm*, such as:

    affirm—to say positively or firmly; to maintain to be true; to assert to be so; to compliment

    Why is it important to affirm or compliment the different qualities (behavior, physical characteristics, etc.) of those around us (e.g., to say, "You are a good friend." "You are very kind")? Frequently, the word *affirmation* is used when one is saying something positive about oneself, and *compliment* is used when saying something positive about another person. How do people feel when they have affirmed themselves or been complimented by others? Explain that *affirm* and *compliment* mean the same thing in this activity.

2. Remind participants that most of us have a nearly continuous stream of self-talk going on in our minds. This self-talk is very important. Sometimes it is negative and worn out, which doesn't help us. One way of changing negative thoughts to positive thoughts is through affirmations. Ask participants how giving themselves or others affirmations can change negative thinking.

3. Explain to the participants that they will be giving and receiving affirmations or compliments. This activity is designed to make each person aware of the positive aspects of their lives and the lives of those around them.

Exploring Self-Concept: Affirmations

4. Brainstorm positive sentences that could be used to describe members of the group. Examples might include:

    You have beautiful eyes.

    You are a very giving person.

    You always seem happy.

5. Ask participants to stand in a circle.
6. Remind them that affirmations can include positive comments about physical characteristics, attitudes, personality traits, etc. The object of the exercise is to share with another person in the group something positive about that person.
7. Hold the end of the ball of string and toss the ball to another person in the group. Say something positive about that person. The catcher, while holding the string, then tosses it to another person in the group and affirms that person. A string pattern should begin to form.
8. Continue tossing the string until everyone in the group has said something positive and has received an affirmation. A web should form.
9. Instruct participants to lower the web to the floor carefully. If appropriate for the group, the pattern can then either be drawn or mounted on the wall to be a symbol of group connectedness and unity.
10. As the group leader, write several examples of affirmations for yourself where all participants can see them (e.g., "I am a valuable, considerate person"). Explain guidelines for writing affirmations:
    a. Write affirmations in the present tense.
    b. Write affirmations in a positive way.
    c. Make them short.
    d. Choose those that feel comfortable.
    e. Try to believe that they are already true.

    Ask participants to write five affirmations for themselves. These affirmations are private and will not be shared with others. You should review them to assure that the self-statements are positive and self-enhancing.
11. Encourage participants to keep the affirmations and read them frequently, reminding them that what they tell their minds can affect their behavior, attitude, and self-concept.
12. Conclude with a discussion comparing feelings before and after the activity. How did it feel to say something positive about another person? How did participants feel when someone said something good about them? What response came to mind? Was it positive or self-deprecating? Did this activity unite the group members? Why or why not? What is the relationship between affirmations and positive thinking? Affirmations

and self-talk? How can affirmations be used throughout the day? How can affirmations influence success? How can affirmations get people through difficult times?

Some ideas in this activity were adapted from Jacobs et al. (1988).

Additional Activity:

Keep a journal of affirmations that participants add to all year long.

Activity 8—Exploring Self-Concept
Personal Values (C)

Project PASS
(Preparing Autism Specialists)
Special Education
University of Oregon

Language Purpose:

1. To define the concept of *values*
2. To discuss relationships between experiences and values
3. To organize values in order of importance

Self-Esteem Focus:

To show how values can affect self-concept

Materials:

Values Ranking activity page

Vocabulary:

principle, quality, worthwhile

Process:

(Note: Participants should save their completed *Values Ranking* activity page for Activity 10—"Writing an Autobiography.")

1. Ask participants what comes to mind when they think of the word *value*. Responses may include:

    "Something that's expensive or important."

    "It's worth a certain amount."

    Explain that in this activity participants will be discussing *a value* (or *values*) as it pertains to what people think is important in their lives.

2. Give a formal definition of *a value*, such as:

    a value—a principle or quality considered worthwhile or desirable

    Ask where they have used or heard the word *quality* (*Section 3: Understanding Oneself*).

3. Ask participants what might happen if people aren't aware of or sure of what they value. Why is it important to learn about what participants value or consider worthwhile?

4. Brainstorm a list of values. Use examples from the *Values Ranking* activity page, if necessary.

Social Communication

5. Explain that what we value is based on many different experiences. These experiences influence our values and affect our decisions and direction in life. Brainstorm a list of what has influenced participants' values. Examples are:

parents	books	politics
brothers/sisters	work	military
friends	family history	school
TV	music	movies

6. Next, brainstorm possible values that might be learned from some of the above areas. For example:

   school: punctuality is important, show up every day

   TV: violence is justifiable, you have to be attractive to be successful

   parents: stay out of trouble, finish school

7. Distribute the *Values Ranking* activity page and have participants complete it. Explain any unfamiliar vocabulary terms.

8. When everyone has completed the activity page, tally the results and display them where everyone can see how much similarity there is in participants' responses. What does this group value most/least? Why? Where were these values learned? How do participants' individual values differ from the group's, or do they differ?

9. Conclude the activity by asking participants how one's values could change. Has anyone in the group experienced a change in values? How does it feel to know someone whose values are different from one's own values? Can people with different values be friends? Why or why not?

Exploring Self-Concept: Personal Values

Values Ranking

Directions: Arrange the values in order of importance to you. Read each sentence carefully. Place a 1 next to the value that is most important to you. Place a 15 next to the value that is least important. Take your time.

_____ Being a cheerful person is important to me.

_____ Cleanliness is important to me.

_____ Attractiveness is important to me.

_____ Having independence is important to me.

_____ Being a friendly person is important to me.

_____ Being brave is important to me.

_____ Being honest is important to me.

_____ Being assertive is important to me.

_____ Being religious is important to me.

_____ Being a loving person is important to me.

_____ Having good health is important to me.

_____ Having strength is important to me.

_____ Being adventurous is important to me.

_____ Loyalty is important to me.

_____ Being educated is important to me.

Social Communication

Activity 9—Exploring Self-Concept
Developing Goals

Language Purpose:

1. To define the concepts of *goal* and *objective*
2. To create objectives to meet a goal
3. To create a plan, with needed steps, to reach a personal goal

Self-Esteem Focus:

To develop an awareness of how to make personal changes by setting goals

Materials:

Goal Plan activity pages

Vocabulary:

goal, objective, realistic, reward, specific, success, vague

Process:

(Note: Participants should save their completed *Goal Plan* activity pages for Activity 10—"Writing an Autobiography.")

1. Ask participants what comes to mind when they think of the word *goal*. Point out different contexts where *goal* is used, such as "goal post," "goal line," "goalie," etc. Ask why learning about goals and establishing them are important to success.
2. Explain that our dreams, the things we want for ourselves, and changes we want to make in our lives can be our goals.
3. Brainstorm a list of goals that someone the participants' age might have. Write the goals where everyone can see them.
4. Ask participants to identify goals from this list that could be reached within one month.
5. Explain that once people decide where they want to go, and they have explored where they are now, they are ready to set goals. Effective goals should follow these guidelines:
   a. *Reachable*—Your goals must be within your abilities. If you are 18 years old and your height is 5 feet 2 inches, being tall is not a reachable goal for you.
   b. *Believable*—You must believe that you can reach your goal.

Exploring Self-Concept: Developing Goals

   c. *Clear*—Your goal should be well thought out, with realistic steps for reaching it. The goal of "getting a good job" is too vague. It needs to be more specific, like "getting a job as a welder."
   d. *Controllable*—Your goal should be within your control. For example, if your goal is to date a particular person who does not want to date you, your goal is not within your control. An acceptable goal in this situation would be to *ask* someone out. *Asking the person to go out with you* is within your control.
   e. *Measurable*—Usually goals are easier to reach if you can see your progress along the way.
6. Expand on the concept of *goals* by explaining that goals state how you intend to change over a period of time. To make those changes, a plan of action is needed. A plan includes steps known as *objectives* (or short-term goals). *Objectives* are the steps that will help to accomplish the goal.

   To illustrate this, tell participants to think about the goal of buying a car. Have participants brainstorm possible objectives that would help to reach this goal. Tell participants to think about the following areas and write an objective for each related to buying a car:

   a. information
   b. materials
   c. people
   d. money

Examples:

Information
   1. Find information about the type of car I want.
   2. Get information about how much the car costs.

Materials
   1. Read car magazines.
   2. Read consumer magazines.

People
   1. Ask a friend to help choose the car.
   2. Ask a friend to lend me the down payment.

Money
   1. Decide how much money I will need.
   2. Apply for a car loan.

Explain to participants that planning objectives to reach a goal means getting more information about what is needed to reach the goal. Thinking about these four areas will help them decide what is needed.

161

Social Communication

7. Tell participants that it is also helpful to know where they are at this time in relation to their goals and to think about giving themselves a reward when they reach a goal.

8. Distribute the *Goal Plan* activity pages. If participants have difficulty projecting a goal for six months or one year, change a *Goal Plan* activity page to read *One-Month Goal Plan*.

9. When completed, ask participants to share their six-month or one-year goal plans with the group. Encourage participants to give each other feedback about the five guidelines discussed during process step 5. Did participants follow the guidelines? Did participants write objectives that considered information, materials, people, and money needed?

10. Conclude the activity with a discussion about the reality of carrying out goals. Are participants going to follow through with their plans?

Some ideas in this activity were adapted from Canfield and Wells (1976) and Farmer and Farmer (1989).

Exploring Self-Concept: Developing Goals

GOAL Plan

Directions: Think of a goal that you would like to reach within the next six months. Create your plan by completing the other sections of the chart. Repeat the activity by planning a one-year goal.

Example:

Goal	Where I Am Now	Objectives	My Reward
To try out for an athletic team	Not on any team	1. Find out how to try out. 2. Find out when tryouts are going to be held. 3. Find out how good other players are. 4. Talk to the coach to find out what he expects. 5. Find out how much uniforms are going to cost.	Buy a new football

Six-Month Goal Plan:

Goal	Where I Am Now	Objectives	My Reward

© 1992 Thinking Publications
Duplication permitted for educational use only.

Social Communication

One-Year Goal Plan:

Goal	Where I Am Now	Objectives	My Reward

Activity 10—Exploring Self-Concept
Writing an Autobiography

Language Purpose:

1. To synthesize self-concept information
2. To organize information into an autobiography

Self-Esteem Focus:

To form a complete view of the participant's self-concept

Materials:

Personality Questionnaire, Personal Descriptors activity pages, *Values Ranking* activity page, and *Goal Plan* activity pages completed during previous activities in this section; *Autobiography Instruction Sheet* found in this activity

Vocabulary:

advantage, anxiety, autobiography, background, disadvantage, personal, synthesize

Process:

(Note: If handwriting is too taxing for particular participants, instruct them to record their autobiographies or enter the information on a word processor.)

1. Explain to participants that the purpose of this activity is to bring together or synthesize information from the previous activities in this section with the individual's background information. This information will form a complete, written record of the participant's self-concept.

2. Ask participants why it is important to synthesize their ideas and findings about self-concept.

3. Ask group members to reread the *Personality Questionnaire, Personal Descriptors, Values Ranking,* and *Goal Plan* activity pages and begin to think about themselves.

4. Distribute the *Autobiography Instruction Sheet*. Read it aloud to the participants. Explain that the instructions are guidelines for writing their autobiographies. The time line for completion of this activity and the length of the autobiography should be determined for each group. With participants who are more capable writers, the autobiography could be a minimum of five pages and require three class sessions for completion. (If additional time is needed, the activity would be completed as homework.) Participants who have difficulty writing could write fewer pages, dictate the autobiography to another person, record it, or use a word processor to write it.

5. Conclude the activity by answering any questions the participants have about self-concept. Did the participants learn anything about themselves and their self-concepts? Was the assignment overwhelming at first? How was anxiety dealt with? Did participants learn anything about others in the group? Encourage participants to read each other's autobiographies, if they are comfortable doing so.

Exploring Self-Concept: Writing an Autobiography

Autobiography Instruction Sheet

1. *First Section*—Describe yourself. Give your name, age, and birthplace. Describe your physical self and your personality using vocabulary terms from the previous group activities. List each of your immediate family members and describe their personalities.

2. *Second Section*—Write about your past. Write about your significant memories—those which you personally remember or stories you have been told. Be sure to include the feelings associated with these memories. Begin with your earliest significant memory and continue from there.

3. *Third Section*—Write about your present. Write about your current abilities, talents, and interests. Include only the things that you feel, or others feel, you do well. Use positive self-talk messages and affirmations rather than negative comments or self put-downs.

4. *Fourth Section*—Write about your values. Write about both the advantages and disadvantages of being you. Write about your likes and dislikes. These are *your* opinions, not the opinions of others.

5. *Fifth Section*—Write about your personal goals. Will you change anything you described about yourself in the fourth section? By when? What steps will you take? How will the change affect your life in the future?

Section 5: Defining Self-Esteem

In this section, participants differentiate between self-concept and self-esteem and begin to create an image of their positive feelings of self-worth and self-confidence. Activities encourage participants to analyze their level of self-esteem and to speculate about why their self-esteem is where it is.

Activities in this section are based primarily on the model of self-esteem discussed in the Introduction on page 1. Expanded discussions of important self-esteem principles are incorporated into the activities. Particular emphasis is on designing concrete plans for improving self-esteem.

As in all activities in *Social Communication: Activities for Improving Peer Interactions and Self-Esteem,* the communication focus is on discourse. The activities are designed to provide the content for discussion.

Activities in this section include:

		Page
1.	Analyzing the Concept of Self-Esteem	170
2.	Personal Time Line	173
3.	Identifying Personal Strengths	176
4.	Responsibility Collage	178
5.	Body Image and Self-Esteem (C)	180
6.	Identifying Low Self-Esteem (C)	184
7.	Creative Visualization	188
8.	Enhancing Self-Esteem	190
9.	Developing Self-Esteem	194
10.	Self-Esteem Collage	198

Social Communication

Activity 1—Defining Self-Esteem
Analyzing the Concept of Self-Esteem

Language Purpose:

1. To define *self-esteem*
2. To look for relationships among experiences

Self-Esteem Focus:

To differentiate between self-concept and self-esteem

Materials:

none

Vocabulary:

accountable, appreciate, character, compassion, evaluation, impression, reflection, self-esteem

Process:

(Note: Ideas in this activity are very important. If necessary, spend time during the succeeding sessions to review and clarify vocabulary and concepts.)

1. Review the definition of *self-concept*. Next ask participants to define *self-esteem*. Help participants distinguish between self-concept (our overall picture of who and what we are, which can be positive or negative) and self-esteem (our sense of self-worth; pride in oneself). This is an important distinction.

2. Expand the ideas to a more formal discussion of *self-esteem*, including ideas such as:

    a. self-esteem means appreciating the self-worth of oneself and others
    b. self-esteem means being responsible and accountable for oneself
    c. self-esteem means being socially responsible
    d. self-esteem means living by our values
    e. self-esteem is based on our experiences, impressions, and evaluations
    f. self-esteem refers to how positive and confident we feel about what we do
    g. self-esteem affects all areas of life
    h. self-esteem is necessary for a feeling of well-being

    Discuss each idea briefly; key ideas are discussed again in process step 4.

Defining Self-Esteem: Analyzing the Concept of Self-Esteem

3. Since self-esteem affects all "areas of life," ask participants to brainstorm some of these "areas of life." Brainstorm as many areas as possible. The list could include:

    a. family
    b. friendships
    c. school
    d. job
    e. hobbies/leisure time
    f. sex
    g. religion, spirituality
    h. environment

    After the "areas of life" have been listed, discuss how self-esteem affects all areas on the list.

4. Explain that self-esteem includes *having character, being accountable,* and *acting responsibly toward others.*

    a. Ask participants what they think *having character* means. Where/when have they heard the word *character* used before? Explain that *having character* can be seen as a reflection of the values by which one lives. Values such as honesty, courage, and compassion are values that reflect one's character.

    b. Ask participants to define *being accountable*. Expand their definitions by telling the group that *to be accountable* means to accept responsibility for one's own actions and to accept consequences of one's behavior. *Being accountable* means doing what you say you are going to do. It is based on inner values, not outside influences.

        i. Go back to process step 3 and ask participants to explain how being accountable could be associated to the items they listed as areas of life affected by self-esteem (e.g., environment—recycling; sex—practicing safe sex).

        ii. Divide participants into pairs. Tell pairs to choose one of the areas of life for a role play. Role plays can focus on being accountable or lacking accountability (e.g., initiating a recycling project at home versus throwing trash out the car window). Give participants five minutes to plan their role plays. Role plays need only last for two or three turns. Circulate among the pairs, giving them assistance as needed. If necessary, give them ideas about what possible conversations might include.

    Examples:

    Participant #1: Do you want to go to a movie tonight?
    Participant #2: I can't. I have to finish my English paper.
    Participant #1: It's not due for three days.
    Participant #2: I know. I'm busy the next two nights.
    Participant #1: Wow—are *you* planning ahead!

Social Communication

>   Participant #1: This TV show is really stupid.
>
>   Participant #2: Why don't you do something else?
>
>   Participant #1: I don't want to.
>
>   Participant #2: You like biking. It's a great day outside. Why don't you get out of here?
>
>   Participant #1: I'd rather waste time.

      iii. Have participants perform the role plays and discuss any ideas that surfaced.

  c. Ask participants to define *acting responsibly toward others*. Explain that the primary way of acting responsibly is to give others our attention, understanding, and care. Ask if participants have additional ideas.

5. Conclude the activity with a discussion of how people develop high self-esteem. Why do some have it and some don't? How do childhood experiences affect self-esteem? What does the statement "You can't love another person until you love yourself" mean? Do participants agree with this statement? Why or why not?

Activity 2—Defining Self-Esteem
Personal Time Line

Language Purpose:

1. To simultaneously organize experiences by different characteristics
2. To use relevant information and ignore irrelevant information
3. To compare experiences for similarities and differences

Self-Esteem Focus:

To develop an understanding of how past experiences can affect self-concept and self-esteem

Materials:

legal-sized paper (or any long paper), pencil (or erasable pen)

Vocabulary:

graph, horizontal, plot, vertical

Process:

(Note: This activity may require two sessions.)

1. Explain that in this activity, participants will examine personal experiences that make up individual lives and that to do so will involve looking back at the past. Ask participants how important they feel it is to examine past experiences. How do past experiences affect the present and future?

2. Explain that participants will be looking at past experiences by creating a personal time line. Explain that it will be a graph. After distributing the paper, have participants orient the paper so the longest side is parallel with their desks or tables, and then proceed with the following instructions:

    a. Draw a vertical line along the left-hand side of the paper, about 1 inch from the edge. Starting at the bottom of the page and going to the top, write the numbers 0 through 10 (equally spaced) in the margin. This line represents good and bad experiences and the feelings associated with them. Have participants label this vertical line "Feelings" on their graphs. The number 10 is the best experience ever. The number 0 is the worst possible experience.

    b. Draw a horizontal line along the bottom of the paper, about 1 inch from the bottom edge. Starting at the far left and going across the

Social Communication

bottom, write the numbers 0 through your current age (equally spaced). (If participants are over 30, they could number by 5.) This line represents how long a participant has lived. Tell participants to label this horizontal line "Age" on their graphs.

3. Tell participants to put down their pencils. Tell them to take a minute to think about the very first thing they can remember as a child—their first memory. Was the memory good or bad? How good was it? How bad? Along the vertical "Feeling" line, what number would this memory have? Zero through 4 represent negative experiences, 5 is neutral or OK, and 6 through 10 are good experiences. Plot this experience on the graph by placing an X where the "Age" and "Feeling" lines intersect.

4. Direct participants to complete their time lines, plotting as many major experiences as possible on the graph. It may be necessary to stimulate thinking by suggesting common experiences such as the birth of a sibling, starting school, major illnesses, trips, moves to new places, adventures with friends, getting a first pet, etc. All experiences should be coded so that participants can remember what they plotted on their graphs. Invite participants to include even very personal or difficult experiences on their graphs, and then code those experiences so that only the person who draws the graph will know what it means. (Suggest they use initials, e.g., getting arrested = A.) The last point plotted on the graph should be how participants are feeling at this time considering all they have experienced.

5. After participants have plotted all experiences, instruct them to draw lines to connect the Xs on their graphs. The resulting line graph represents the emotional progression of their lives. See the sample time line below:

Sample Time Line:

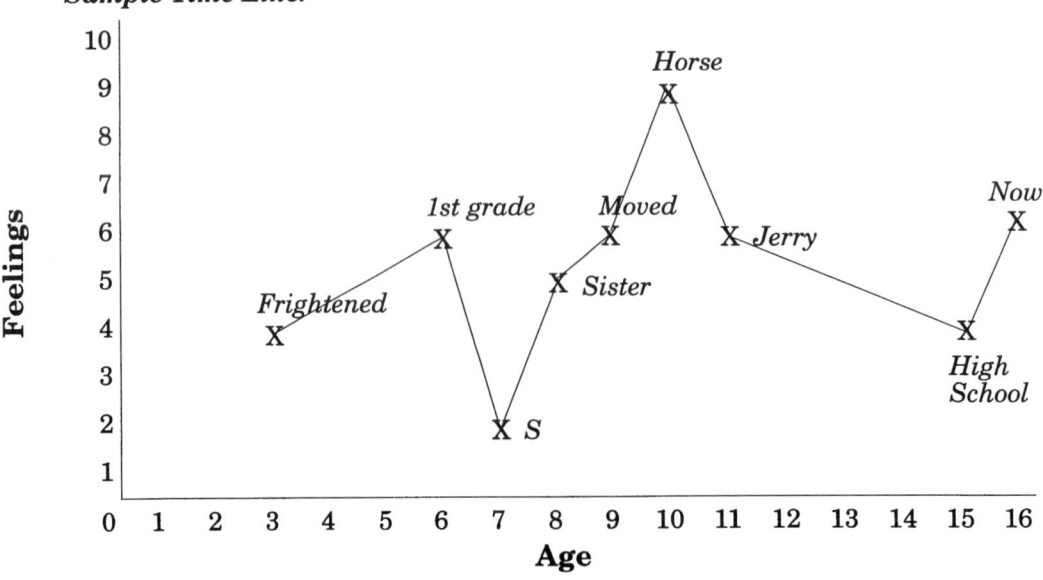

Defining Self-Esteem: Personal Time Line

6. Request that participants show their graphs to the group with an explanation of what the high and low points represent. Tell participants they can omit any experiences that are too personal to discuss.

7. Conclude the activity by again asking how past experiences can affect the present and future. How many experiences that shaped the line graphs resulted from choices others made for them? How do past experiences affect self-esteem? Which experiences resulted in high self-esteem and positive self-concept? Which experiences made participants feel inadequate, hurt, or embarrassed? Although all graphs were different, were there any similarities in experiences among participants?

Social Communication

Activity 3—Defining Self-Esteem
Identifying Personal Strengths

Language Purpose:

1. To identify personal strengths within a group
2. To relate individual strengths to group strength

Self-Esteem Focus:

To increase self-esteem by identifying strengths participants bring to a group

Materials:

writing paper, pencil

Vocabulary:

shameful

Process:

(Note: Some participants will have considerably more interpersonal strengths than others. Be sure to help participants who are less able to identify their potentials.)

1. Explain that in this activity, participants will be investigating the strengths they contribute to the group. Ask why it is important to have feelings of high self-esteem in a group. What might happen, or how would participants feel, if they didn't have high self-esteem but felt others did?

2. Explain that part of self-esteem is being realistic about both strengths and weaknesses. Ask why or how knowing one's weak areas could contribute to feelings of self-worth. Are weaknesses shameful? Is anyone without them?

3. Brainstorm a list of strengths different people might bring to a group that make it function and communicate successfully. For example:

good listening skills	creativity
assertiveness	sense of humor
positive thinking	caring attitude

4. Tell participants to draw a circle about the size of a grapefruit on a piece of writing paper. Inside that circle, tell them to draw another circle the size of a lemon. Give these instructions:

   a. *In the smaller circle, write the greatest strength you contribute to the group. What is the most important thing you bring to the group?*

Take a few minutes to think about your response. (Give suggestions to those who are having difficulty thinking of a strength.)

b. *Next, list three or four other strengths that you bring to the group in the outside ring. Take your time.* (Give individual help as needed.)

c. *Next, outside of the circles, list strengths that you don't think you have, but that the group needs to function successfully. If you can think of group members who have those strengths, write their names by the strengths you have listed.*

5. Ask participants to report their strengths and the strengths that the group needs. Write all the strengths where everyone can see them. Also write participants' names and one strength per participant. Identify the strengths, necessary for group success, that no one is contributing to the group.

6. Conclude the activity with a discussion about what can be done if the group listed strengths necessary to group success, but there are no participants who have those strengths. Can strengths be developed? How? What will happen to group interaction if they aren't developed? What does this activity say about the relationship of group strength to individual strengths? How do participants who have high self-esteem contribute to a group?

Social Communication

Activity 4—Defining Self-Esteem
Responsibility Collage

Language Purpose:

1. To examine areas of responsibility
2. To formulate an idea of how to take responsibility
3. To create a symbolic representation of responsibility

Self-Esteem Focus:

To identify and acknowledge responsibility as it relates to self-esteem

Materials:

magazines, scissors, paper, glue

Vocabulary:

collage, empower, freedom, power, responsibility, symbolism

Process:

1. Ask participants why it is important to identify and examine parts of their lives for which they have responsibility. What are some of those areas of responsibility?
2. Remind participants that part of the definition of *self-esteem* is taking responsibility and being responsible for oneself. By recognizing we have responsibilities and by being responsible for ourselves, we become independent. With independence comes power and freedom. When we are not responsible for ourselves, we become dependent on others for our happiness, self-worth, and self-concept. We lose our power and freedom. If others do not respond in the way we desire, our self-esteem is affected. Ask what it means to "give responsibility for our happiness" to another person. What are some relationships in which people commonly think another person can or will make them happy (e.g., boyfriend/girlfriend, husband/wife)? Can a relationship make a person happy? Why or why not?
3. Ask participants to consider the relationships they are presently involved in (e.g., family, teacher, boss, friends, significant other). Who is responsible for the participant's happiness in each relationship (the participant, the other person, or both)? Why?
4. Brainstorm with the group some common responsibilities in each relationship (e.g., family: sharing in housecleaning; friends: listening;

Defining Self-Esteem: Responsibility Collage

teacher: completing assignments; significant other: comforting; boss: doing the job you're paid to do).

5. Ask participants to think of 5 to 10 more responsibilities per relationship that they feel they are fulfilling at the present time. Explain that fulfilling these responsibilities will empower them and will have a positive effect on their self-esteem.

6. Explain to the group that the next part of the activity involves symbolism (the use of a picture or sign that stands for something else). Tell participants they will be creating collages using pictures as symbols to represent responsibilities. Have participants brainstorm symbols to represent the responsibilities mentioned in process step 4:

   Examples:
   Family—sharing in housecleaning: picture of a cleaning product
   Friends—listening: side view of a head showing an ear
   Teacher—completing assignments: picture of a book
   Significant other—comforting: picture of a couple embracing
   Boss—doing the job you're paid to do: picture of a person working at a task

7. Distribute magazines, glue, scissors, and paper. Tell participants to select magazine pictures symbolizing the relationships and responsibilities from process step 5. When selected and cut out, the pictures should be arranged on paper and glued to form a collage of responsibilities they fulfill in relationships. The pictures should depict responsibilities that empower them and add positively to their self-esteem. If preferable, or if participants are having difficulty finding appropriate pictures, encourage them to draw pictures.

8. Ask participants to volunteer to explain their collages to the group. As group facilitator, you may want to be the first to share your collage.

9. Conclude the session by discussing responsibility. Is there a situation in which one person takes on too much responsibility? How does it feel to be too responsible? Why do people take on too much responsibility? How does it feel to be in a relationship when your partner is not responsible?

Social Communication

Activity 5—Defining Self-Esteem
Body Image and Self-Esteem (C)

Language Purpose:

1. To discuss how body image is formulated
2. To recognize the difference between aspects of physical appearance that can be changed and those that can't be changed
3. To formulate an idea of positive body image

Self-Esteem Focus:

To develop an awareness that physical appearance can affect self-esteem

Materials:

Body Image Checklist

Vocabulary:

feature, image, social, valid, value

Process:

(Note: You may find that many individuals within the group have poor body image. If that is the case, you will need to plan additional follow-up sessions. Participants may need more information about taking care of themselves and more time to develop good feelings about themselves. This activity could conceivably be extended into a larger unit to study how people can feel good about their bodies. Many of the values in process step 4 are Caucasian in orientation because they represent stereotyped values reflected by the mass media. After participants complete Section 9, Activity 4—"Defining Stereotyping," you may want to go back to this activity and discuss it in terms of racial stereotyping.)

1. Explain that this activity is based on how people feel about their bodies and how those feelings can affect self-esteem. Ask participants how they think body image and self-esteem are related. How can thinking positively or negatively about one's body affect self-esteem? Responses may include:

    "If you like your body, you feel good."

    "You have to have a nice body or people will laugh at you behind your back."

2. Incorporate the responses into a brief discussion about how important bodies are. Brainstorm all the ways that people benefit from their bodies. For example, bodies:

Defining Self-Esteem: Body Image and Self-Esteem

taste food	carry us around
create language	experience pleasure
express feelings	hear music

3. To stimulate thought, ask some rhetorical questions such as:
   a. What comes to mind when you think about your body?
   b. Do you like it?
   c. How do you want it to look and feel?
   d. Do you have a plan for it?
   e. Do you take care of it?

4. Explain that how and what people think about their bodies is called *body image*. Much of what people feel about their bodies comes from social values. Review the definition of *values* with participants. (See Section 4, Activity 8—"Personal Values.") Ask them to define *social values*. Brainstorm values they have learned about physical appearance and health. Emphasize the idea that people do not always have the same values. Remind participants that values can come from movies, television, parents, church, peers, etc. Include values such as:
   a. Being thin is attractive.
   b. Being strong is healthy.
   c. Being slim is healthy.
   d. Being tall is attractive.
   e. Being blond is attractive.
   f. Being tall, blond, and thin is the best.
   g. Females who have small feet are attractive.
   h. Females who have big breasts are attractive.
   i. Males who are muscular are attractive.
   j. Having thick hair is attractive.
   k. Having full lips is attractive.

   Remind participants that these values may not be true or valid, but they are values within our society. Some of these values may even be dangerous if we strive for them (e.g., causing anorexia nervosa or bulimia, or unnecessary cosmetic surgery).

5. Engage participants in a discussion about which of the values listed are valid to them. Ask them to think about which of the above values they personally believe in. Of the values participants believe in, which would they consider changing about themselves? Which physical features about themselves are necessary to accept? Is it easy for participants to accept that some physical features can't be changed?

Social Communication

6. Ask participants how body image pertains to self-concept. (Body image is one part of self-concept.) Can body image be separated from self-concept? Why or why not?

7. Distribute the *Body Image Checklist*. Discuss any unfamiliar vocabulary terms with participants.

8. After participants complete the checklist, tell them that the checklist represents things that can be changed. Tell them that a question with a "no" response probably indicates a change that could be made. Ask if anyone would like to tell the group about an item marked "no." Ask participants to share information with each other. For example, how can a person who doesn't know about muscle tone learn about it? If no one in the group knows about muscle tone, how can they find out?

9. Conclude the activity by again asking how body image can affect self-esteem. What can someone who is short and dark-haired do if his or her image of "attractive" is tall and blond? What would participants tell such a person? What affirmations could the person use during self-talk? How can taking care of one's body and taking responsibility for it improve self-esteem?

Additional Activity

Suggest that participants set goals and objectives for their bodies (e.g., exercise, weight loss, nutrition). Use the *Goal Plan* activity page in Section 4, Activity 9—"Developing Goals," if desired.

Defining Self-Esteem: Body Image and Self-Esteem

☑ BODY IMAGE CHECKLIST

Directions: Read each question. Indicate with a (✓) if your answer is yes or no.

	Yes	No
1. Are you in good physical condition?	____	____
2. Do you try to eat only foods that are good for you?	____	____
3. Do you know which foods are good for you?	____	____
4. Do you have good stamina and endurance?	____	____
5. Do you have good muscle tone and strength?	____	____
6. Do you get enough sleep?	____	____
7. Do you have a lot of energy?	____	____
8. Do you feel graceful and/or coordinated?	____	____
9. Do you think your body is beautiful?	____	____
10. Would someone else think your body is beautiful?	____	____

Which of the above questions is the most important to you? _____ Why?

© 1992 Thinking Publications
Duplication permitted for educational use only.

Social Communication

Activity 6—Defining Self-Esteem
Identifying Low Self-Esteem (C)

Language Purpose:

1. To describe components comprising self-esteem development
2. To define *low self-esteem*
3. To assess low self-esteem

Self-Esteem Focus:

To develop an understanding of the difference between low and high self-esteem

Materials:

Self-Esteem Evaluation

Vocabulary:

circumstance, factor, identity, satisfy, spontaneity, unique

Process:

(Note: The *Self-Esteem Evaluation* can be read to those participants with reading difficulties.)

1. Tell participants that this activity focuses on *low self-esteem*. Ask them to define the concept. Ask them why it is important to identify factors associated with low self-esteem. What do you have to know about high self-esteem in order to understand low self-esteem?
2. Distribute the *Self-Esteem Evaluation*. After participants have finished, explain that you will be discussing the results at the end of the activity.
3. Explain that a healthy sense of self-esteem develops in people (hopefully in childhood) when their emotional needs have been satisfied. High self-esteem can be achieved when people experience positive feelings in three particular areas. They are:
   a. *Identity:* the sense that people know who they are. People feel good when they understand they are unique and that they are respected for that uniqueness. For example, questions may arise such as: Why am I so tall? What does it mean to be black? What really makes me happy? What does it mean to be a girl?
   b. *Connectedness:* the close feeling one gets when in relationships with others. People need a sense of belonging and good feelings about the relationships they have. Concerns in this area may be: What do I

Defining Self-Esteem: Identifying Low Self-Esteem

think of my friends and family? What are my values? How do I make new friends? How do I keep the relationships I have?

c. *Power:* a sense of control over one's own life. People need to feel that they have the ability to influence others and circumstances. Questions that may arise are: Can I achieve my goals? Can I convince my friend to change his mind? Can I make things happen for myself?

If time permits, brainstorm more questions people might have in each area. Explain that asking these questions is a natural part of developing high self-esteem.

4. Explain that participants will examine each of the above areas to see how people might act if their needs aren't satisfied. In each area, brainstorm possibilities such as:

   a. Identity
      - always do what they are told
      - take little pride in appearance
      - resist being the center of attention
      - speak negatively about themselves
      - lack spontaneity, are often bored
      - show little imagination

   b. Connectedness
      - unable to communicate easily
      - act shy or withdrawn, have few friends
      - experience being disliked by peers
      - act uncomfortable around adults or always want their attention
      - always arguing with parents
      - act uncomfortable when touched or touching

   c. Power
      - avoid taking responsibility
      - act helpless frequently
      - act stubborn
      - always want their own way
      - may have limited skills
      - lack emotional self-control

After brainstorming as many examples as possible, take some time to discuss particular behaviors. For example: Why would someone who has a power problem act stubbornly?

185

Social Communication

5. Have each participant study the *Self-Esteem Evaluation*. Explain that items 1 through 5 generally apply to "connectedness." Items 6 through 10 apply to "power." Items 11 through 15 apply to "identity." Ask participants to share which behaviors they checked as those they most want to improve. Tally the number of items checked in each area for the entire group. Do most participants want to improve items in the areas of connectedness, power, or identity?

6. Conclude the activity with a discussion of how people can improve their self-esteem. If a person knows he or she has a problem with connectedness, identity, or power, what can that person do about it? How can people in this group help each other out?

Defining Self-Esteem: Identifying Low Self-Esteem

Self-Esteem Evaluation

Directions: How do you rate yourself in each of these situations? In the left column, write one of the numbers 1 to 4 to describe how in charge you are of your actions and behaviors.

1 = I am out of control in this situation; I am not in charge.
2 = I depend on others for direction in this situation.
3 = I am in charge of myself some of the time in this situation.
4 = I am in charge of myself in this situation.

_____ 1. Making new friends

_____ 2. Knowing what to say to people

_____ 3. Being part of a group

_____ 4. Getting along with others

_____ 5. Feeling comfortable with other people

_____ 6. Getting myself up in the morning

_____ 7. Getting to school or work on time

_____ 8. Convincing other people

_____ 9. Organizing my time

_____ 10. Developing goals

_____ 11. Expressing my feelings

_____ 12. Taking care of my body

_____ 13. Standing up for myself

_____ 14. Limiting the amount of television I watch

_____ 15. Knowing what I want to change about myself

Which number did you write most often: 1, 2, 3, or 4? _____

Place a check mark (✓) next to the two behaviors that you would most like to improve.

Social Communication

Activity 7—Defining Self-Esteem
Creative Visualization

Language Purpose:

1. To define *creative visualization*
2. To comprehend information and follow directions

Self-Esteem Focus:

To develop visualization as a strategy for enhancing self-esteem

Materials:

none

Vocabulary:

creative, discipline, outcome, process, rehearse, visualize

Process:

(Note: The process involved in this activity is beneficial to use on a regular basis.)

1. Explain to participants that this activity is about how to improve self-esteem by visualizing positive outcomes. Ask them to define *visualize*. Expand on their definition by including ideas such as:

    visualize—to form a mental picture or image; to imagine; to mentally rehearse; to see with the mind

2. Explain that by visualizing, people can bring about a change in how they see themselves. Through this creative process, people use their imaginations to create a clear picture of something they want to happen or change. An important part of visualization is imagining the desired changes and, while visualizing, feeling how it would be if the changes had already been made.

3. Expand on the idea of visualization by brainstorming possible outcomes people may want to effect. Ideas may include:

    a. performing in a sport in a relaxed and successful manner
    b. being successful on a test
    c. asking a friend out on a date
    d. losing weight
    e. talking to a parent with confidence
    f. being relaxed at an interview

4. Explain to participants that you are now going to take them through the process of visualization. The process will probably take about 5 to 10 minutes.

   Step 1: Decide on a specific area, feeling, or event that you want to change. (Possible ideas may have surfaced from the previous activity.)

   Step 2: Relax. Close your eyes. Breathe deeply three or four times.

   Step 3: Focus on your breathing. Count to 10 each time you exhale. Relax.

   Step 4: Imagine yourself at a very special, quiet place—on a beach, in the mountains, near a waterfall, in a beautiful room. Choose a place and think about it for a minute. Relax.

   Step 5: Imagine yourself improving or achieving whatever it is that you want to improve or achieve. Think about how it feels to be getting what you want.

5. Ask participants for feedback about their experiences. Were they able to actually visualize changes?

6. Explain that for visualization to work, people have to believe that they can make changes. Using one's mind to overcome fears and improve self-esteem takes practice, a positive attitude, and discipline. To achieve what they want, participants should practice the process of visualization several times a day.

7. If appropriate for your group, repeat the visualization process.

8. Conclude the activity by discussing the outcome of negative visualization. What happens when people tell themselves that they can't do something? How can people be aware of negative visualization? How is it like negative self-talk (see Section 4, Activity 5—"Analyzing Self-Talk")? How can people change negative self-talk by using visualization? How can creative, positive visualization affect self-esteem?

Ideas for this activity were influenced by Duco (1986) and Knepflar and Laguaite (1991).

Social Communication

Activity 8—Defining Self-Esteem
Enhancing Self-Esteem

Language Purpose:

1. To define the concept of *self-care*
2. To discuss the relationship between daily self-care and self-esteem
3. To create a plan for improving self-care

Self-Esteem Focus:

To enhance self-esteem through self-care

Materials:

Enhancing Self-Esteem activity pages

Vocabulary:

enhance, maintain, risk, wellness

Process:

1. Ask participants why it is important to enhance their self-esteem. Does self-esteem always remain at the same level? Why or why not? Ask participants why self-esteem, once raised, can fall back to a lower level. What are some things that can lower self-esteem?

2. Explain to the group that today's activity will focus on self-care. By taking care of oneself, a level of overall wellness can be maintained, making highs and lows in self-esteem less extreme. Ask participants to define *wellness* and *self-care* in their own words.

3. Brainstorm some self-care activities. Self-care activities can include things we do to maintain good health (e.g., practicing good nutrition, getting enough sleep), good communication (e.g., being listened to by friends, using assertiveness), good relationships (e.g., having a significant other, learning from support groups), and good work habits (e.g., being more productive, managing time well to decrease stress). Take ample time for this section of the activity to ensure that participants understand the examples in each category. Draw from concepts in previous activities, such as listening actively, reducing stress, maintaining a positive body image, etc.

4. Remind participants that they have choices in all areas of life. To maintain self-esteem, it may be necessary to take risks, to try new things, and to practice self-care. Ask them what *risk taking* means. Why is it

Defining Self-Esteem: Enhancing Self-Esteem

important? What are some examples of risk taking that could enhance self-esteem? Answers may include becoming a vegetarian, refusing to drink alcohol even though your friends drink, asking a new friend to a movie, etc.

5. Distribute the *Enhancing Self-Esteem* activity pages.

6. Tell participants to complete the activity pages and then divide into pairs. The paired participants should share information from their activity pages with each other. Is there a self-care activity that a participant would like as a goal, but is unable to put into practice? By sharing information with another participant, new choices may be presented.

7. Conclude the activity with a discussion. What happens to behavior, stress level, and self-esteem when self-care is ignored? Is it necessary to address all areas listed? Why or why not? Who is responsible for self-care? Why don't some people take care of themselves? Is there any way to encourage or help people who aren't aware of self-care ideas?

Social Communication

Enhancing Self-Esteem

Directions: List examples of self-care activities under each heading and answer the questions.

Self-care activity	How does the activity maintain self-esteem?	Is this activity a future goal area?
Health		
A. Practicing good nutrition	I feel better physically.	yes
B.		
C.		
D.		
Communication		
A. Using assertiveness	I have more personal power.	yes
B.		
C.		
D.		

Defining Self-Esteem: Enhancing Self-Esteem

Self-care activity	How does the activity maintain self-esteem?	Is this activity a future goal area?
Relationships		
A. Learning from support groups	I affirm myself more often.	yes
B.		
C.		
D.		
Work habits		
A. Being more productive	I affirm that I'm successful at managing my time.	yes
B.		
C.		
D.		

Social Communication

Activity 9—Defining Self-Esteem
Developing Self-Esteem

Language Purpose:

1. To discuss suggestions for improving self-esteem
2. To plan a long-range self-esteem goal

Self-Esteem Focus:

To facilitate development of self-esteem

Materials:

Self-Esteem activity pages

Vocabulary:

accountable, appreciate, character, nurture, resentment, restore, risk

Process:

(Note: This activity is based on important concepts found in Section 4, Activity 9—"Developing Goals.")

1. Remind participants that each of them has a personal definition of what self-esteem is. Ask participants to give their personal definitions of self-esteem. You may want to integrate these definitions and past information into a group definition such as:

    self-esteem—appreciating one's own worth; having character; being accountable and responsible for oneself; acting responsibly toward others

2. Explain that this activity focuses on developing and nurturing self-esteem. Growth is always possible; anyone can change. A sense of self-esteem can be restored, developed, or nurtured. Ask participants to define *nurture*.

3. Discuss the following suggestions for improving self-esteem, and elicit examples and ideas from previous activities as you proceed. Allow participants to generate as many examples as possible of each suggestion for improving self-esteem before contributing examples.

    a. *Accept yourself.* (E.g., be honest with yourself. Accept your strengths and weaknesses. Be realistic about what you can and can't do. Don't feel you have to compare yourself to other people. Appreciate that you are unique.)

Defining Self-Esteem: Developing Self-Esteem

    b. *Express your feelings.* (E.g., learn to listen to your body and your mind about how you are feeling. Try to give labels to your feelings. Learn how and when to express feelings. Remember that feelings are clues to one's sense of well-being.)

    c. *Have realistic expectations.* (E.g., set goals that are attainable. Don't expect too little or too much of yourself. If you are trying to live up to someone else's expectations, be sure they are also your expectations.)

    d. *Take risks.* (E.g., explore unknown areas that may seem a little frightening. Don't always play it safe. Realize that change can be frightening even when it is change that you want. Try new things.)

    e. *Trust yourself and others.* (E.g., trust that when you accept yourself, express your feelings, set realistic expectations, and take risks, you are taking good care of yourself, which is something to be proud of. Trusting others helps them to be trustworthy. Be sure the people you trust are trustworthy.)

    f. *Forgive yourself and others.* (E.g., don't be overly critical. Let go of resentment. Realize that making mistakes is how people learn and grow.)

    g. *Appreciate your mind.* (E.g., learn to think positively. Identify destructive ways of thinking. Use affirmations. Learn to distinguish between thoughts that are healthy and those that are not.)

    h. *Appreciate your body.* (E.g., learn to like your body. Do not be ashamed of it. Take care of it. Learn what is healthy and what is not. Enjoy your physical senses.)

Expand on this section of the activity by duplicating items *a* through *h*. Cut the suggestions apart and place them in a pile. Have each participant draw one suggestion and ask another participant a corresponding question directed at "how to" follow the suggestion. (E.g., how do you accept yourself? How do you express your feelings?)

4. Remind participants of how they developed goals in Section 4, Activity 9—"Developing Goals." Review the process of how to plan a goal.

5. Distribute the *Self-Esteem* activity pages. Explain any unfamiliar vocabulary terms to participants.

6. Have participants complete the activity pages. Then, ask volunteers to describe their self-esteem goals. Ask participants to give feedback about how particular goals could be achieved.

7. Conclude the activity with a discussion of self-esteem. What have participants learned? At this point, has any participant achieved change in the area of self-esteem? Can participants identify low self-esteem in others?

Some ideas in this activity were adapted from the California Task Force to Promote Self-Esteem and Personal and Social Responsibility (1990).

Social Communication

SELF-ESTEEM

Directions: Choose one of the following suggestions to focus on to develop higher self-esteem. Then set a long-range goal for yourself.

Accept yourself.	*Trust yourself and others.*
Express your feelings.	*Forgive yourself and others.*
Have realistic expectations.	*Appreciate your mind.*
Take risks.	*Appreciate your body.*

Example:	**Your Self-Esteem Goal:**
Suggestion: Express your feelings	*Suggestion:*
Long-range goal: To express myself at home	*Long-range goal:*
Objectives to help you get there: 1. *Information:* Read about anger.	*Objectives to help you get there:* 1. *Information:*
2. *Materials:* Get book from library.	2. *Materials:*

Defining Self-Esteem: Developing Self-Esteem

3. *People:*

Ask the school counselor for ideas about talking to my parents.

3. *People:*

4. *Money:*

No money needed.

4. *Money:*

Things that stand in your way:

Fear
Parents aren't home much.

Things that stand in your way:

Social Communication

Activity 10—Defining Self-Esteem
Self-Esteem Collage

Language Purpose:

1. To describe positive aspects of yourself and other people
2. To comprehend positive feedback from other people

Self-Esteem Focus:

To give participants the opportunity to enhance the self-esteem of others

Materials:

magazines, butcher paper, glue

Vocabulary:

bombard, feedback

Process:

1. This activity focuses on getting positive feedback from other people. Ask participants to define *bombard* and tell you if they have heard the word used in other situations.
2. Ask participants why it may be helpful to get positive information or feedback from others. What might such feedback do to one's self-esteem?
3. Divide the group into pairs. Ask partners to trace one another's outlines on pieces of paper that are long enough for each student to lie down on. If you believe participants are too old, sophisticated, or self-conscious to trace each other's outlines, allow each person to sketch a life-size outline on the paper.
4. Have participants cut out their own outlines. Tell them to draw a vertical line down the middle of the outline. Distribute magazines and glue and tell them to fill the left side of the form with pictures or words that reflect their own positive feelings about themselves. Remind them of all the information they have learned about positive self-concept and self-esteem. They should try to include at least 8 to 10 items on the left side of the form. Caution participants that magazines often reflect values promoted by society; they are to be finding pictures or words that reflect their own positive feelings about themselves. If they are unsuccessful finding the items they want in magazines, encourage participants to draw or write in their own ideas. Allow approximately 20 minutes for this process.

5. When participants have completed the left side, they are to leave their forms and bombard another participant's human form outline with positive feedback. On the right side of another person's form, each participant should glue one picture or headline reflecting a positive aspect of that person. Ideally, both sides of each human form should have the same number of items. If the group size is small, ask each participant to glue two or three items on the right side of the form for each of the other participants. Participants can also draw pictures, write words, or use a combination of drawings, cutouts, and words. Allow about 20 minutes for this portion of the activity.

6. Display all the human forms. Focusing on one person at a time, the group should tell that person what all the items represent. The person being bombarded should remain silent until everyone in the group has finished.

7. Ask participants to compare the left and right sides of the form. Was one side more positive than the other? Invite participants to ask questions of each other, if they want.

8. Conclude the activity with a discussion about how it felt to be bombarded with positive information. Did it affect self-esteem? If so, how?

Section 6: Decision Making and Problem Solving

Now that participants have investigated the principles of self-esteem and assessed their own self-concept, they are ready to understand how self-esteem affects making decisions and solving problems. Activities begin at a general level where problem-solving strategies are learned. Once the foundation has been established, participants are required to use the strategies in various problem situations.

Also included in this section are activities on conflict management and resolution. Participants use their problem-solving skills to discuss appropriate outcomes to difficult situations.

As in all activities in *Social Communication: Activities for Improving Peer Interactions and Self-Esteem,* the communication focus is on discourse. The activities are designed to provide the content for discussion.

Activities in this section include:

		Page
1.	Learning About Decisions	202
2.	Priorities (C)	205
3.	Time Management	208
4.	Examining a Problem-Solving Strategy	211
5.	Problems for Solving	216
6.	Writing a Letter to an Advice Column (HS)	219
7.	Examining Conflict (C)	221
8.	Conflict Management (C)	224
9.	Relationship Problem Solving	227
10.	Reaching Consensus: Moon Base Situation (C) (HS)	229

Social Communication

Activity 1—Decision Making and Problem Solving
Learning About Decisions

Language Purpose:

1. To differentiate among types of decisions
2. To compare and contrast individual and group decisions

Self-Esteem Focus:

To develop an awareness that how decisions are made can be influenced by and have an impact upon self-concept

Materials:

none

Vocabulary:

con, consensus, impose, majority, method, minority, poll, pro

Process:

1. Tell participants that this topic involves how individual and group decisions are made. Ask what happens when people have difficulty making decisions.
2. Explain that everyone makes decisions. Discuss what motivates individuals to make decisions. Do people make decisions differently? Why? How? How much does a person's history affect the decision-making process?
3. Brainstorm decisions that people commonly face, such as:
   a. getting married
   b. going to school
   c. going on a diet
   d. buying a new car
   e. experimenting with drug
   f. telling the truth
   g. choosing what to eat
   h. going to college
   i. having sex
   j. doing homework
   k. going out on a date

Decision Making and Problem Solving: Learning About Decisions

    l. playing a video game

    m. joining a team

    n. deciding to go to a dance

    o. selecting what to wear

4. Brainstorm types of decisions that people face. Limit the types to four or five and code them. Here is an example:

		Code:
a.	Decisions that you make every day without thinking	A
b.	Decisions that take some thought before making	B
c.	Decisions that need time and research before making	C
d.	Decisions that others make for you	D

Code the responses from process step 3 according to what type of decision is involved. Discuss differences of opinion and what accounts for those differences.

5. Explain to participants that, like individuals, groups are also making decisions all the time. Ask participants how individual and group decision making are similar and different. Brainstorm a short list of decisions made by this group (e.g., who sits where, group rules, etc.).

6. Explain that it is important to observe how decisions are made in a group. Some people try to impose their ideas on others. Other people want all members to participate or share in the decisions that are being made.

7. Explain that there are several different methods by which groups can make decisions. They include:

    a. Leaving decisions to one person

    b. Leaving decisions to one person who checks to see if everyone agrees with the decision

    c. Majority-minority voting

    d. Polling ("Let's see what everyone thinks.")

    e. Reaching consensus (everyone comes to an agreement; everyone participates in the discussion)

If appropriate for your group, discuss the pros and cons of each method.

8. Choose one or two examples from process step 3. With the group, briefly apply the examples to each method of making decisions from process step 7. Choose examples that are appropriate for your group members to discuss. For example, *buying a new car* may not be a relevant topic for middle school participants. *Having sex* may not be a comfortable topic to discuss in this activity. Discuss how each method of making decisions felt.

9. Conclude the activity with a discussion about how the group makes decisions. Is the method satisfactory? Why or why not? Do any changes need to be made? If appropriate, ask if the group's decision-making method has changed since participants first got together. How does self-esteem affect the decision-making process? Does it affect the individual and group process in the same way? How?

Decision Making and Problem Solving: Priorities

Activity 2—Decision Making and Problem Solving
Priorities (C)

Language Purpose:

1. To define the concept of *prioritize*
2. To apply the concept of *priorities* to a situation
3. To rank value items as priorities

Self-Esteem Focus:

To develop the idea that what is prioritized can affect self-esteem

Materials:

Priorities activity page

Vocabulary:

evacuation, generality, monetary, priority, rank, urgency, visualize

Process:

1. Ask for a volunteer to give a definition of *prioritize*. Expand on the definition by adding ideas such as:

    prioritize—to order by importance or urgency; placing appropriate items first in position to get done

2. Ask participants to tell about current priorities in their lives. What is the most important situation, problem, or goal at this time? Ask why those items are priorities. How did they get to be priorities? Ask participants why it is important to know what is a priority and what isn't.

3. Tell participants that there are many types of priorities. Explain that in this activity they will explore how prioritizing choices of material possessions can better help them understand themselves.

4. Read the following situation to the group:

    It's a rainy afternoon and an emergency message has just been broadcast in your area. The broadcast states that due to the extremely heavy thundershowers, severe flooding is expected within the next one to two hours. It is expected that your home will be totally under water. Evacuation is ordered. You have 20 minutes in which to gather 10 items to take with you in your car. Which 10 items will you save?

205

5. Distribute the *Priorities* activity page. Instruct participants to visualize going through each room in their houses. Have them write down the items they would take.
6. Tell group members to rank the items, using numbers 1 to 10, in order of importance (i.e., 1 being the most important). To the right of the ranking, instruct participants to write a brief explanation of the personal importance of each item. Be specific in the explanation (e.g., instead of "sentimental value" put "given to me by my grandmother before she died").
7. Ask participants to share their top two or three items, giving explanations of why they are the most important.
8. Conclude the activity with a discussion. Did participants learn anything about themselves? If so, what? Did participants learn anything about others in the group? What did participants learn about people from examining what is valuable to them? Were all priority items the most valuable in terms of monetary worth? If appropriate for your group, continue the discussion by asking the following questions: How can understanding what we value help us to understand what we think of ourselves? What category was the most important to participants (family items, personal awards, equipment, etc.)? Can any generalities be made about these categories? Do participants like the way they prioritized things? Why or why not?

Decision Making and Problem Solving: Priorities

PRIORITIES

Directions: In the left-hand column, list items you would take with you. When you have listed all 10 items, use numbers 1 to 10 to rank them according to how important they are to you. (Number 1 is most important.) Then write why each item is important to you.

Item to be taken:	Rank	Why it is important:
Example: Family portrait	1	It is my favorite picture.
1.		
2.		
3.		
4.		
5.		
6.		
7.		
8.		
9.		
10.		

© 1992 Thinking Publications
Duplication permitted for educational use only.

Social Communication

Activity 3—Decision Making and Problem Solving
Time Management

Language Purpose:

1. To discuss *time-management* concepts
2. To assess time management on a typical day
3. To evaluate time-management abilities

Self-Esteem Focus:

To assess how time management can affect self-esteem

Materials:

Time Management activity page

Vocabulary:

alternative, efficient, estimate, fatigue, impact, inventory, listless, management, overwhelm, stress, symptom

Process:

1. Ask participants what comes to mind when they think of *time management*. Ask what problems can occur when one does not manage time efficiently.
2. Explain that time can be thought of as an endless chain of decisions that can slowly change the shape of one's life. Inappropriate decisions produce frustration, lowered self-esteem, and stress. They can result in six symptoms of poor time management:
   a. rushing
   b. always going back and forth between unpleasant alternatives
   c. having feelings of fatigue or listlessness
   d. frequently missing deadlines
   e. not having enough time for rest or personal relationships
   f. feeling overwhelmed by details, and always having to do what you don't want to do

   Discuss each example and ask participants if they ever feel similarly or know someone who does.
3. Explain that the next part of this activity helps participants see how and where they spend time and energy in their lives.

Decision Making and Problem Solving: Time Management

4. Distribute the *Time Management* activity page. Be sure participants understand that there are no right or wrong answers, only differences in how people spend their time. Explain that the circle represents one day. The circle or "pie" is divided into four parts, each representing six hours. Draw your "pie" where everyone can see it and demonstrate how you would estimate your day (seven hours sleeping, eight hours working, three hours eating, etc.). The estimates need not be exact, but they should add up to 24 hours.

5. Ask participants to complete their own 24-hour inventories and share them with other participants.

6. Engage participants in a discussion about how satisfied they are with how they spend their time. Questions might include:
   a. Do you get enough sleep?
   b. Do you have enough time for homework and/or chores?
   c. Do you have enough alone time or too much alone time? Why?
   d. Is there enough time in the day to have fun? Why or why not?
   e. Is there anything about your day you would like to change? How can you change it?
   f. How does your day compare to other participants' days?

7. Discuss the "Rules for Making Time":
   a. Learn to say no. Unless the person has authority, say no to people who want you to do things you don't have time to do.
   b. Don't rush. What does "haste makes waste" mean?
   c. Keep a list of things you have to do.
   d. Get up earlier.
   e. Watch less television.
   f. Don't try to be perfect. Just get it done.

8. Conclude the activity with a discussion about how it feels not having enough time to finish work or chores or to spend with family or friends. How does it feel to have too much free time or alone time? Ask participants if the way they spend their day impacts their view of themselves. If they changed the way they spend their day, would it change how they see themselves? How do their decisions about time affect their self-esteem? How does feeling frustrated and stressed affect self-esteem? If participants with low self-esteem have difficulty answering some of these questions, try to get them to speculate about how others might feel.

Some ideas for this activity were adapted from Simon, Howe, and Kirschenbaum (1972).

Social Communication

⏰ TIME MANAGEMENT

Directions: The circle or "pie" below represents a regular day in your life. The day is divided into four parts, each of which is six hours. To estimate how you spend your day, answer the following questions:

1. How much time do you spend sleeping? _____
2. How much time do you spend at school? _____
3. How much time do you spend with your family? _____
4. How much time do you spend working at a paying job? _____
5. How much time do you spend watching TV? _____
6. How much time do you spend alone? _____
7. How much time do you spend with friends? _____
8. How much time do you spend doing chores? _____
9. How much time do you spend on personal hygiene? _____
10. How much time do you spend eating? _____

Now draw slices in your "pie" that go with how much time you spend doing the different activities. There is no right or wrong way to divide the "pie."

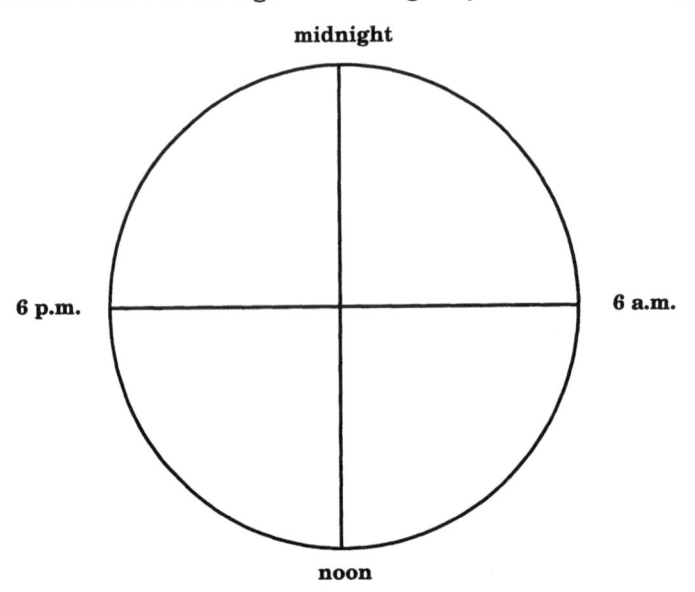

midnight

6 p.m.   **6 a.m.**

noon

© 1992 Thinking Publications
Duplication permitted for educational use only.

Activity 4—Decision Making and Problem Solving
Examining a Problem-Solving Strategy

Language Purpose:

1. To define *a problem*
2. To develop a systematic method of problem solving
3. To formulate a plan to solve a problem

Self-Esteem Focus:

To develop the idea that applying a problem-solving strategy can increase self-confidence in problem situations

Materials:

Problem-Solving Strategy activity pages

Vocabulary:

analysis, avoidance, barrier, consequence, denial, impact, implement, method, monetary, problem, procrastination, realization, solution, strategy

Process:

1. Explain to participants that the purpose of this activity is to define problems and to present a strategy for solving them.
2. Ask participants what *a problem* is. (Answers may include conflict, argument, disagreement, etc.) Ask why learning about solving problems is important. Are there any members of the group who have never had a problem? Explain that this activity is not an exercise in endless problem solving. Instead, this activity will explore a strategy for solving problems when and if they occur.
3. Brainstorm a list of problems, such as disagreeing with parents, losing money, arguing with friends, etc. This list can be limitless. Point out that life can be viewed as being full of problems, from waking in the morning to going to bed at night. Ask participants if they have ever been taught a method for dealing with problems. It seems strange that though problems are an everyday occurrence, few people have been taught to deal effectively with them.
4. Distribute the *Problem-Solving Strategy* activity pages. These will provide participants with a visual aid for the discussion to follow.

Social Communication

    a. Explain that while learning the problem-solving strategy, participants will also be solving a problem situation.

    b. Review the items on the activity pages for vocabulary questions.

5. Explain the items from the activity pages briefly, then use the example below to teach the strategy. Read the Blizzard Problem or Fire Problem from Section 1, Activity 7—"Group Problem Solving," to demonstrate the strategy. (The example used here is based on the Blizzard Problem.) Discuss responses to the following questions:

    a. What is the problem? Explain the problem in detail. Be specific, such as, "You and your sister are stuck in a blizzard."

    b. Whose problem is it? This has to do with accepting responsibility, as well as taking no responsibility for others' problems. Determine the people involved in the problem and decide whose problem it is. If it is not your problem, the strategy could end with this step. (E.g., you and your sister are involved and have a problem.)

    c. Do you choose to solve the problem at this time? At times, you may or may not choose to take action to solve a problem. Procrastination, avoidance, denial, or the realization that the situation will resolve itself can all be reasons for not choosing to take action. If you choose not to solve the problem, the strategy ends with this step. (E.g., if you delay solving the problem, you could freeze to death, so the answer to this question is yes.)

    d. How do you feel about the situation? List or write about your feelings. Getting in touch with emotions can make communication of those feelings easier (e.g., panicked, unsure of yourself).

    e. How can you solve the problem? Use this step for brainstorming various solutions, from the most outrageous to the most practical (e.g., hike to town, carry your sister, stay in the car, start a fire so that airplanes could find you, etc.).

    f. What will happen? Briefly list possible consequences for each solution. (E.g., the town might be farther than you thought or your sister might freeze while you are gone; carrying your sister could tire you; you could freeze in the car; you may not be able to keep the fire going.)

    g. Will anyone be harmed/hurt by the solution? Think about this question before choosing the best solution. While *hurt* can refer to physical harm, it can also refer to emotional, monetary, or other harm. (E.g., your sister could be harmed if left behind; carrying your sister could tire you, but it would be better than freezing to death; staying could harm both of you.)

h. Which is the best solution? Determine which solution is best by looking at the consequences of each alternative and then determining which will best solve the problem while having the least costly consequence. (E.g., you couldn't start a fire because you have nothing to start it with. Carrying your sister and having her walk part of the way might be the best solution.)

i. How can you put the solution into action? Make a plan of action for item *h*. Identify steps, barriers, and deadlines for implementation. This step is similar to goal setting and will make taking action less difficult. (E.g., dress in warm clothing, take snacks, and eat snow for liquid. Start out having your sister walk and when she becomes tired, carry her for a short distance.)

j. What happened? This is the follow-up step. It is as important to evaluate, review, or analyze results as it is to determine what to do to solve the problem. This is the step in which you can determine if your plan was successful or whether it is necessary to implement a different solution. (E.g., when you got out of your car and began walking, the sun began to shine and the snow stopped, making it easy to see the small town just ahead. You were safe. The plan worked.)

8. Present a second problem situation of your choice to allow participants to practice the strategy using the *Problem-Solving Strategy* activity pages.

9. Review the activity pages and participants' strategies as a check for understanding.

10. Conclude the session with a discussion. Is it necessary to have a strategy for solving problems? Why or why not? Why is it important to determine whose problem it is? Is the strategy usable in most problem situations? How can knowing and using a problem-solving strategy improve self-confidence?

Some ideas in this activity were adapted from Schwartz and McKinley (1984).

Social Communication

Problem-Solving STRATEGY

A. What is the problem? (Be specific.)

B. Whose problem is it? (Take responsibility.)

C. Do you choose to solve it at this time? (Take action.)

D. How do you feel about the situation? (Analyze emotions involved.)

E. What are the possible solutions? (Brainstorm solutions.)

   1.   4.

   2.   5.

   3.   6.

Decision Making and Problem Solving: Problem-Solving Strategy

F. What will happen? (Examine consequences.)

1.   4.

2.   5.

3.   6.

G. Will anyone be harmed/hurt by your solution? (Check the impact.)

1.   4.

2.   5.

3.   6.

H. Which is the best solution? (Choose one.)

I. How can you put the solution into action? (Implement the solution.)

J. What happened? (Evaluate the results.)

Social Communication

Activity 5—Decision Making and Problem Solving
Problems for Solving

Language Purpose:

1. To explore problem situations systematically
2. To use a strategy to solve problems
3. To make a systematic plan to solve a problem

Self-Esteem Focus:

To practice a problem-solving technique to build self-confidence

Materials:

Problem Situations activity page

Vocabulary:

input, role play

Process:

(Note: This activity is based on the strategy from the previous activity.)

1. Review the definition of *problem* developed during the last session. Ask participants why it would be beneficial to practice solving problems in the group setting. Answers might include:

    "Practicing something helps people to memorize it."

    "More solutions can be developed in the group."

    "You can learn better by practicing."

2. Review the problem-solving strategy from the previous activity. List the steps where everyone can see them, being sure to allow enough room to fill in answers to the questions presented. The *Problem-Solving Strategy* activity pages can also be redistributed.

3. Distribute a "problem" from the *Problem Situations* activity page to each group member, or have participants suggest situations. (Before the session, copy the situations and cut them apart so each group member receives a different situation.) Choose situations most appropriate for your group members.

4. Ask a participant to read his or her problem situation aloud or role play the problem with another participant without solving it. Using the strategy steps listed, ask the same participant to solve the problem with input from other participants.

5. Select a solution for the problem based on the group discussion. If the situation was role played, have the participants re-enact the situation, this time using the solution selected to complete the role play experience. If participants read the situations, have them develop a plan of action (i.e., step 1 of the strategy). Remind participants that even though they may think their own solutions are best, a better solution might be found when the problem-solving strategy is used.

6. Continue the process with other participants and problems. Problems generated by the participants themselves are frequently more effective to use in teaching the strategy because the personal impact of the situation makes the strategy more relevant.

7. Conclude the session with a discussion about problem solving. Is there a solution to every problem? Does every problem have to be solved immediately? What are the advantages of waiting before solving a problem? Should participants always be able to solve problems without help from others?

Social Communication

Problem Situations

1. Your parents seem to argue all the time. This upsets you.

2. You just got a new haircut. You told the stylist exactly how you wanted it. When she finished, you realized she had ruined your hair.

3. You have been warned by your boss not to visit with the other employees while on the job. A fellow worker has been evicted from his apartment and is telling you about it. You see your boss coming toward you. She looks angry.

4. You're driving down a busy street. Someone cuts in front of you. You swerve to miss him. Honking your horn, you pull up beside him. He looks angrily at you and swerves in front of you again.

5. You have had a terrible morning. You got up late and didn't have time for breakfast. Running to the bus stop, you see the bus coming. You arrive just as the doors begin to close. Reaching into your pocket, you realize you have no money.

6. Your significant other has been in your life for the past three months. Every time you go out, this person argues with others, like the waiter who serves the meal, the ticket taker at the movie, or the cab driver who picked you up. This person's behavior is starting to bother you.

7. For a long time, you have been avoiding a particular person who has expressed an interest in dating you, but whom you don't find attractive. This person has just asked you out Friday night. You're afraid you'll see some of your friends and they will give you a hard time.

8. Your English teacher has just asked for your homework. You didn't do it because you were out with friends last night. Your teacher has told you that if you miss one more assignment, you will fail the course.

9. It is April 14. Tomorrow your income taxes are due. You know you will have to pay $200 and you don't have the money.

10. You borrowed a friend's stereo for a party you were having. You had intended to return it the day after the party. You returned home today and found it missing.

Activity 6—Decision Making and Problem Solving
Writing a Letter to an Advice Column (HS)

Language Purpose:

1. To define *advice*
2. To consider different alternatives to solving problems
3. To use clear and precise language so the listener understands

Self-Esteem Focus:

To provide a variety of contexts for problem solving

Materials:

two or three letters from an advice column

Vocabulary:

alternative, advice, column, legitimate, solution

Process:

1. Explain to participants that today they are going to be discussing advice columns and writing sample letters asking for advice. Ask participants to define *advice* and *advice column*. Ask them if they have ever written a letter asking for advice or thought about writing one. Discuss opinions of advice columns. Who else gives advice?

2. Read two or three short sample advice column letters from a local newspaper. Be sure that the letters are appropriate to the age level, interest level, and/or ability level of participants.

3. Choose one of the letters to discuss. As a group, examine the problem and suggest possible alternative solutions. Discuss whether the advice column gave the "best" solution.

4. Brainstorm problems that participants might encounter in their lives. This list should include 10 to 15 items.

5. Tell the students to think about a problem they have or that someone else has. Instruct them to write a brief, one-paragraph letter describing the problem and requesting a solution. Tell participants not to put their names on the letters. (If this is a small group of three or four members, ask them to write two letters.)

6. Collect the letters. Mix them up and randomly draw them from a hat.

Social Communication

7. Read the first letter and determine a solution as a group. Use the following problem-solving strategy:
   a. What is the problem?
   b. Whose problem is it? (group member's, parent's, friend's, etc.)
   c. Do you choose to solve it at this time?
   d. How do you feel about the situation?
   e. What are the possible solutions?
   f. What will happen?
   g. Will anyone be harmed/hurt by the solution?
   h. Which is the best solution?
   i. How can you put the solution into action?
   j. What happened as a result?

   Repeat the above sequence with the remaining letters.

8. Conclude the activity with a discussion about giving and getting advice. Do people always follow the advice they are given? Why not? Can all problems be solved? What kind of problem has no solution? Point out that advice columns are just one way to get an opinion on how to solve a problem. Discuss if a person such as "Dear Abby" can give legitimate advice. Who is she? Will she know all the facts? Will she know all the details in the situation? How might getting advice from a column differ from getting advice from friends, parents, teachers, etc.? How does it relate to self-esteem?

Additional Activity:

If desirable, participants can actually write letters to an advice column in a local or national newspaper.

Decision Making and Problem Solving: Examining Conflict

Activity 7—Decision Making and Problem Solving
Examining Conflict (C)

Language Purpose:

1. To define *conflict* and compare it to a problem
2. To differentiate between methods of reacting to conflict
3. To describe feelings associated with conflict

Self-Esteem Focus:

To examine reactions to conflicts and feelings during conflicts in order to increase self-confidence in future conflict situations

Materials:

Examining Conflict activity page

Vocabulary:

aggressive, antagonistic, assertive, conflict, denial, hostility, passive, reaction, resolution, resolve

Process:

1. Brainstorm a definition of conflict, such as:

    conflict—what happens when people can't agree on something; a long battle or struggle; a disagreement

    Why is it important to learn about what conflicts are and how to resolve them?

2. Discuss the differences and similarities between problems and conflicts. Answers could include the following:

    - Conflicts and problems are similar in that both involve a question requiring thought.
    - Conflicts involve people and opinions, while problems can involve objects, people, animals, or situations.
    - Unlike problems, conflicts can be antagonistic, involving hostility or fighting.

3. Ask participants to brainstorm a list of conflicts they have been involved in recently. How did they feel when in conflict?

4. Explain to participants that there are three major ways people react to conflict:

Social Communication

   a. Attack the person they are in conflict with (aggressive reaction): One person attacks another physically or verbally. They are not willing to listen to each other.

   b. Deny the conflict exists (passive reaction): One person is angry about a conflict but won't express the problem or anger to the other person.

   c. Solve the conflict (assertive reaction): People talk about the problem and try to think of different ways to solve it. They choose a win-win solution.

5. Distribute the *Examining Conflict* activity page.

6. Select one of the conflicts from the activity page. Have participants role play the situation with three different reactions. One reaction should be to verbally attack, another to deny, and a third to solve the conflict. (This can be continued with other participants and conflicts).

7. Have participants complete the first two columns of the activity page. Explain that after participants complete these columns, they should label each of their reactions (written in the "What Would You Do?" and "How Would You Feel?" columns) as an *attack,* a *denial,* or a *solution* to the conflict. Have them write their labels in the activity page column titled "Type of Reaction."

8. Conclude the activity with a discussion about resolving conflict. What is to be gained by problem solving? Can conflicts be resolved when one person is denying or attacking? What feelings do participants have when a person with whom they are in conflict denies feelings or the existence of the conflict? What feelings do participants have when a person with whom they are in conflict attacks them? Explain that the problem-solving reaction (i.e., assertive reaction) is known as *conflict resolution.* How can knowing about conflict resolution help participants' self-esteem?

Decision Making and Problem Solving: Examining Conflict

Examining Conflict

Directions: For each conflict listed, write how you would react to the conflict and how the conflict would make you feel. There are no right or wrong answers. When you are done, decide what type of reaction you wrote down: an *attack,* a *denial,* or a *solution* to the conflict.

Conflict	What Would You Do?	How Would You Feel?	Type of Reaction
You lost your watch and see someone in your class wearing it.	I accuse the classmate of stealing my watch.	angry	attack
1. You've been waiting in line three hours for concert tickets. Someone cuts in line in front of you.			
2. Your significant other loses an expensive ring you gave him/her.			
3. A teacher accuses you of cheating on a test.			
4. A customer yells at you about the food you served her.			
5. A CD you ordered has come in, but the price has been marked up so that you can no longer afford it.			
6. Your parents don't approve of the person you are dating and tell you so.			

© 1992 Thinking Publications
Duplication permitted for educational use only.

Social Communication

Activity 8—Decision Making and Problem Solving
Conflict Management (C)

Language Purpose:

1. To explore a plan for conflict resolution
2. To employ active listening while resolving a conflict
3. To compare and contrast problem solving and conflict resolution

Self-Esteem Focus:

To explore relationship conflicts and their effect on self-esteem and communication

Materials:

3-by-5-inch note cards

Vocabulary:

complicate, escalate, initiate, mediator, negotiate, perceive, propose, reconcile, resolve, resolution

Process:

1. Remind participants about the difference between problems and conflicts discussed in the previous activity. Ask participants why they need conflict resolution skills. How do participants think conflict resolution is different from problem solving (e.g., in conflict resolution, communication with the conflicting party must take place).

2. Explain that the key to resolving conflicts is communication. Communication involves both listening (active listening) and speaking (*I* messages and feelings). If one person is not aware of the conflict, conflict does not exist. Both parties must be aware of a conflict and want it to be resolved for resolution to take place.

3. Explain that for resolution to take place, one party must initiate or begin the process. Resolution of a problem between two people is not easy. It can be complicated by certain factors such as:

    a. Showing an increase in emotion
    b. Increasing a perceived or suspected threat through physical or verbal actions
    c. Increasing the number of people involved
    d. Lacking knowledge of reconciling skills

Decision Making and Problem Solving: Conflict Management

4. Refer participants back to the *Examining Conflict* activity page from the previous activity. Using those conflicts, role play the situations, complicating them by enacting the factors listed in process step 3:

Conflict	*Complicating Factor*
(1) Person "cuts" into concert ticket line	c. Increase number of people involved
(2) Loss of a ring	a. Increase in emotion
(3) Accused of cheating	b. Increase in verbal threat by student
(4) Unsatisfied customer	b. Increase in physical threat by customer

   The fourth factor, lack of knowledge, is difficult to demonstrate. Did the conflicts resolve themselves or escalate? What skills are needed to resolve conflicts (e.g., negotiating, active listening, etc.)?

5. Explain to participants that to resolve a conflict, both parties should follow these guidelines:

   a. Agree to solve the problem.
   b. Focus attention on the problem, not the person (no blaming).
   c. Engage in no name calling or put-downs.
   d. Use truthful *I* messages.
   e. Express how the conflict makes you feel.
   f. Use active listening (no interrupting).
   g. Propose a solution.
   h. Negotiate a resolution.

   An example of resolution language is:

   Situation: You are working on an assignment at your job. The person with whom you are supposed to work has put off every meeting you've arranged. You are upset with him.

   "I feel really frustrated that this assignment has not been completed. How are you feeling?"

6. Distribute the 3-by-5-inch note cards and instruct participants to write the guidelines on the card as a reminder during role-playing situations.

7. Using the previously mentioned conflicts, focus on the situations using the guidelines in process step 5. Remind participants what happens when guidelines are not followed.

8. Create conflict situations using group input. Practice applying the conflict resolution guidelines to these situations through role plays. The style of

Social Communication

communication in conflict resolution should be assertive, not aggressive or passive. At the successful resolution of a conflict, both parties should feel it is a win-win situation. (Refer to Section 2, Activity 10—"Getting Along with Others.")

9. Conclude the activity with a discussion about conflict resolution. Did participants feel that the methods used would help them resolve conflicts? Why or why not? Did they feel differently during the second role-playing experience than the first? Can all of our conflicts be resolved without help? Is it sometimes helpful to have a third party act as a mediator? How do participants feel about themselves when they are in conflict? Could these feelings have an impact on the participants' self-esteem? Why or why not?

Activity 9—Decision Making and Problem Solving
Relationship Problem Solving

Language Purpose:

1. To describe interpersonal reactions to solving a problem
2. To develop a cooperative plan to reach a goal
3. To consider alternative solutions

Self-Esteem Focus:

To compare the impact of situational and relationship problems on self-confidence

Materials:

a 3-foot length of yarn or string per participant, scissors

Vocabulary:

interpersonal, intrapersonal, situational

Process:

1. Ask participants to summarize past ideas about why it is important to learn about problem solving. Problems come in many forms. Some are interpersonal (such as being unable to get along with a fellow worker), some are intrapersonal (such as whether or not to go out with a person who has a bad reputation), while others are situational (such as when your car breaks down). Ask participants to give examples of each. Not all problems should be solved in the same way using the same strategy.
2. Pair up participants.
3. Tie one end of a piece of yarn around participant #1's right wrist. The other end of that piece should be tied around participant #1's left wrist. Place another piece of yarn over participant #1's yarn, looping it back toward participant #2. Tie each end of the second piece of yarn around participant #2's right and left wrists.
4. Explain that the problem is to separate the two pieces of yarn so that the two participants are no longer hooked together. The rules include no cutting or untying of the yarn.
5. Allow participants 5 to 10 minutes to work out the problem. If at the end of the time period the participants are still tied together, refer to Illustrations A and B at the end of this activity or tell them these instructions to help them separate:

Social Communication

  a. Participant #1, while facing participant #2, should take the overlapping piece of yarn and put it through participant #2's right wrist loop (starting at the inside of the wrist).

  b. Participant #1's overlapping yarn should then be slipped over the palm and fingers of participant #2's hand. This should successfully separate the two participants.

6. Ask participants how this exercise relates to the subject of problem solving and conflict resolution. Answers might include: "The exercise and the resolution process both need an answer. Both try various means to arrive at a solution." Encourage numerous answers.

7. Brainstorm a list of feelings that participants experienced during the exercise. Did the feelings change when a solution was found? If one pair of participants found a solution and another didn't, what were the feelings?

8. Compare the problem-solving strategy from Section 6, Activity 4—"Examining a Problem-Solving Strategy" with the process the participants went through to separate themselves from their partners. Using the *Problem-Solving Strategy* activity pages from Activity 4, ask participants if they went through the various steps. Were there differences in the processes? If so, why?

9. Conclude the activity with a discussion about problem solving. Were there some participants who chose to react by denying, attacking, or problem solving? Were there any similarities between interpersonal relationships and the yarn problem? Who talked? Who made decisions? Who gave directions? What implications, if any, can be made about the participants based on this activity?

Participant #2   *Participant #2*

Participant #1   *Participant #1*

Illustration A   *Illustration B*

Activity 10—Decision Making and Problem Solving
Reaching Consensus: Moon Base Situation (C) (HS)

Language Purpose:

1. To define the concept of *consensus*
2. To use relevant information about a problem and ignore irrelevant information
3. To reach consensus

Self-Esteem Focus:

To develop an understanding that taking others into consideration may foster a sense of positive self-esteem

Materials:

Moon Base activity page

Vocabulary:

asset, collective, consensus, emotional, interact, involved, morale, negotiation, simulation

Process:

(Note: This activity may generate strong emotions. Be sure to include enough time to discuss feelings. If the group consists of fewer than three participants, use a polling or voting method of decision making discussed in the first activity of this section.)

1. Review the different methods of decision making discussed in Section 6, Activity 1—"Learning About Decisions." Define *consensus* by including ideas such as collective agreement, negotiation, and coming to agreement. Explain that *consensus* does not mean voting.

2. Ask participants why learning about consensus is important. What happens when a group tries to act without consensus?

3. Explain that this activity will focus on consensus by discussing a simulation exercise about a NASA team trapped on the moon. Read the Moon Base Situation to the group, being appropriately dramatic whenever possible:

229

Social Communication

Moon Base Situation

The year is 2166. You are the chief scientist on the Tyco Lunar Base on the moon. You and your team of 10 researchers have been on the moon for three years. The original expedition was to have lasted two years; however, six months after arriving, you learned that Earth was struck by a massive meteor shower. All communication with Earth was terminated at that time. It is doubtful that anyone on Earth is still alive. In two weeks, all your food supplies will be exhausted. You have to make a decision now about returning to Earth.

You have an SL-16 re-entry space shuttle that has enough life support to return six people to Earth. You think that the space shuttle can be landed without assistance from Earth. As the chief scientist, it is your job to choose the people who will make the return trip to Earth, knowing there may be no help for those that remain behind. Although you have provided the crew with excellent, expert leadership, you are not sure if you should be included with those who are returning to Earth.

(Note: Ambiguous feelings about the decision of the chief scientist's return to Earth were purposefully included to expand on ideas of values and priorities.)

4. Distribute the *Moon Base* activity page. Read the descriptions of the moon base team aloud as participants follow along.

5. Tell each participant to decide individually who will go and who will stay. Tell them not to discuss ideas at this time. Remind them that the six people who go might be the only six to carry on the human race.

6. Divide participants into small groups (four is an ideal number). Ask group members to explain to their groups why and how they made the choices they did.

7. Tell each small group to come to consensus about who goes and who stays. This process may take 15 to 20 minutes. Remind participants again what *consensus* means.

8. Ask each small group to explain their choices to the other groups. Compare and contrast differences and similarities.

9. Conclude the activity by discussing feelings that surfaced during the activity. Ask participants if they were emotionally involved. Why or why not? How did participants interact in the group? Did people listen to each other? Was reaching consensus easy? Did participants allow themselves to be pressured into changing their minds? What does participating in reaching a consensus have to do with assertiveness? Did anyone feel he or she had the "right" answer? What did people's decisions say about their values? Their self-concepts? How many participants included themselves in those who were returning to Earth? How did they make that decision? How does self-esteem affect trying to reach consensus?

Decision Making and Problem Solving: Reaching Consensus

MOON BASE

Directions: Put a check (✓) by the names of the five people (or six people, if you are not returning) who will return to Earth.

___ 1. Ivan, the base counselor, is in charge of mental health. He is well thought of and always keeps morale high. He is married to Ramona.

___ 2. Ramona is a nutrition expert. She controls the food supply and experimental greenhouse. She is pregnant.

___ 3. Lisa is the computer expert. She first predicted when the food supply would run out. She also knows information vital to making the space shuttle operational.

___ 4. Kelly is the base physician. He is the oldest member of the team; however, he is a vital asset to the team's health.

___ 5. Zara is the telecommunications expert. Since the loss of communication with Earth 2½ years ago, Zara has become bored and moody. Most of the men on the team still find her very attractive.

___ 6. Dennis is the mechanical technician. He has maintained the space shuttle and understands its systems. He is frequently angry and difficult to get along with.

___ 7. Marianne was included on the team in order to study human behavior. She is an expert in interpersonal communication and has helped the team with communication problems.

___ 8. Carlos is a weapons and explosives expert. He was included on the team to provide protection and to clear space for the moon station.

___ 9. Louise is a construction engineer. She supervised building an outpost 20 miles from the moon base.

___ 10. Porter is the very handsome space shuttle pilot. In the last two years, he has frequently been very ill. It is not known if he is strong enough to fly the space shuttle.

© 1992 Thinking Publications
Duplication permitted for educational use only.

Section 7: Analyzing Family Issues

In this section of *Social Communication,* participants begin to examine family history and dynamics. Particular emphasis is placed on understanding how family issues affect self-esteem development. Participants are asked to analyze their family ancestry and to draw conclusions about the impact of significant family relationships and events upon their self-esteem.

As in all activities in *Social Communication: Activities for Improving Peer Interactions and Self-Esteem,* the communication focus is on discourse. The activities are designed to provide the content for discussion.

Activities in this section include:

		Page
1.	Family Tree	234
2.	Writing a Will of Wishes	237
3.	Examining Living Space	239
4.	Birth Order	241
5.	Parents' Character (C) (HS)	244
6.	Family Problems (C)	248
7.	Family Comparison	250
8.	Analyzing Love (HS)	252
9.	Marriage (HS)	255
10.	Examining Divorce (C) (HS)	258

Social Communication

Activity 1—Analyzing Family Issues
Family Tree

Language Purpose:

1. To describe families using family trees
2. To recall family information shared by relatives
3. To discuss the relationship between messages taught by different generations in the same family

Self-Esteem Focus:

To examine family messages and their impact on self-image and self-concept

Materials:

My Family Tree activity page

Vocabulary:

extended, generation, influence, significant

Process:

(Note: Participants who come from nontraditional families may have a difficult time with this activity. [E.g., they may not know one of their parents and thus feel uncomfortable when asked to fill in a family tree. In this case, guide the task so these participants feel at ease describing only one-half of their ancestry.])

1. Explain that today's activity will involve creating a family tree. Define the concept of a *family tree*. Ask participants why they should study their family trees. What does it have to do with self-image and self-concept? Do families influence self-concept?

2. Explain to participants that our families greatly influence the concept we have of ourselves. Our parents are usually the most important people in our lives. Their opinions of us, expressed both verbally and nonverbally, influence the way we see ourselves and our abilities.

3. Distribute *My Family Tree* activity page to each participant. (There are many different types of family trees; if you prefer another format, use that.)

5. Using your own family as a model, fill in the family tree.

6. Instruct participants to fill in their own family trees, including grandparents, parents, brothers, sisters, aunts, and uncles. The important point is not making sure every person in the family is listed, but that

those best known by the participant are listed. The family tree can include extended family members and people who are not related by marriage, such as a parent's significant other or a close family friend who has had a significant role in the participant's upbringing.

7. Allow enough time for participants to complete their family trees. When complete, ask participants to think about their listed family members.

8. Beside each name, or on a separate piece of paper, tell the participants to write a message or lesson that each person taught. (Model this with your tree. Example: father, John, "Get a good education"; mother, Nancy, "Keep your room clean"). If participants cannot think of a message or do not know a relative well, encourage them to ask a parent or family member for the information or leave it blank. This part of the activity may be completed orally, if you prefer.

9. Ask participants to volunteer to tell about their families and messages. While not all messages will be positive, they should not be discounted or made fun of by others.

10. Following participants' explanations of their family trees, encourage them to ask questions of each other. By asking questions, the participants will learn more about each other and their varied backgrounds.

11. Conclude the session with a discussion about families and the messages they give the individual. Did participants learn anything about their view of their families? Were there similarities between the generations in the messages conveyed? Did any of the messages affect the lives of the participants? Did the messages encourage or discourage the participants from attempting certain tasks or interests? Were the participants' self-concepts influenced by the messages they were given by their families? Why or why not?

Social Communication

─────── My Family Tree ───────

| Grandfather | Grandfather |
| Grandmother | Grandmother |

Aunt/Uncle | Aunt/Uncle

Aunt/Uncle | Aunt/Uncle

Aunt/Uncle | Aunt/Uncle

Aunt/Uncle | Aunt/Uncle

Mother | Father

Me

Brother/Sister | Brother/Sister

Brother/Sister | Brother/Sister

My Extended Family

My Stepfamily   Special Friends

_____   _____
_____   _____
_____   _____
_____   _____
_____   _____

© 1992 Thinking Publications
Duplication permitted for educational use only.

Activity 2—Analyzing Family Issues
Writing a Will of Wishes

Language Purpose:

1. To define the concept of *will*
2. To organize information by family member
3. To state a wish assertively for family members

Self-Esteem Focus:

To focus on the needs of participants in family relationships as they pertain to self-esteem

Materials:

My Family Tree activity page from the previous activity

Vocabulary:

affirmation, constructive, declaration, dispose, heirs, influential, possession, will

Process:

1. Ask participants to define the word *will*, such as:

    will—a declaration of how a person wishes his or her possessions to be disposed of upon death

    What do participants think a "Will of Wishes" would involve? Because few young people own many material possessions, wishes are easier to come by. In this activity, participants will imagine what wishes they would like to leave for their heirs. How is this process like leaving a will that tells who gets which possessions?

2. Use the list of relatives and influential others generated during Activity 1—"Family Tree," or have participants make a list of their relatives and influential others.

3. Brainstorm some wish statements (i.e., what you want another person to have or do). The wish statements should be constructive or affirmative (see Section 2, Activity 2—"Constructive Criticism" or Section 4, Activity 7— "Affirmations"):

    Examples:

    Mom— I wish you could always be as happy as you are now.

Social Communication

> *Dad—* You're a wonderful provider for the family. I wish that you could relax more and be more understanding when people don't live up to your expectations.
>
> *Grandma—* You're a great story teller. I wish you would take more time to tell me about your dreams.

4. Tell participants to choose one or two family members from their family tree for whom they would like to write a wish. Tell them to write the wish beside the name(s).

5. Ask participants if they would like to share some of their wishes with the group. Group members should be reminded that this group is a safe environment. Participants should reveal only what they feel comfortable revealing.

6. After sharing wish statements, ask participants to make a list of wish statements for their future offspring. In other words, if participants had children, what would be the most important messages they could pass on to them? Participants should list at least three messages, and more if they want to. (E.g., I wish for you to get a good education. I wish for you to be happy in your chosen work.)

7. Conclude the activity by sharing some of these important messages. Did anyone share their wishes with their relatives? Why or why not? Who would benefit from the "Will of Wishes"? The participant? The relatives or influential others? Which is more valuable, a possession or a life message? Why? Why don't relatives speak honestly with each other at times? Why is it sometimes easier to talk with friends than relatives? Why are we sometimes afraid of telling relatives how we feel and what our needs are? How does that fear affect self-concept? How does being honest with others affect self-esteem?

Activity 3—Analyzing Family Issues
Examining Living Space

Language Purpose:

1. To describe and define *living space*
2. To discuss the need for privacy
3. To examine personal living space and answer questions concerning it

Self-Esteem Focus:

To examine participants' living space and discuss related issues of self-worth and self-concept

Materials:

11" x 14" paper, pencils (no pens), rulers

Vocabulary:

dimension, domain, privacy, private, public

Process:

1. Explain to participants that the purpose of this activity is to examine living space in a different way. Living space is the place where a person lives. It can be a house, a townhouse, an apartment, a trailer, etc.
2. Ask participants why it is important to examine their living space. Can one's living space affect self-worth or self-concept? How?
3. Distribute a large sheet of paper to each participant. Instruct them to draw the floor plan of their homes and to include labels for each room. The dimensions do not have to be precise, but doorways should be included to explain traffic flow and privacy concerns.
4. Ask for volunteers to tell about their completed floor plans. Gather information, such as:
   a. Do you share a room?
   b. Is your house quiet or noisy? Busy or laid back?
   c. If you have a room, do people knock before entering?
   d. Where do you study or read?
   e. Where do you entertain friends?
   f. Is privacy respected in your home?
   g. Where can you be alone?

- h. Can you play your music without disturbing others? Where?
- i. Are you expected to help with household chores?
- j. Do you spend more time at home or away?
- k. If you could change anything about your home, what would it be (e.g., having a private entrance, a soundproof room for a stereo, a separate living room for you and your friends)?
- l. Is your room public or private domain?
- m. Are there two sets of rules in your house, one for parents and another for children? Why?
- n. How would you feel if the person or people you live with looked through your things while you weren't home?

5. Conclude the activity with a discussion about living space. Remind participants that Americans generally require more living space than people of other cultures. Did the participants learn anything new about other group members? Why is it important to have space of your own? Is privacy an issue with participants? Why or why not? If privacy is not allowed, how do participants feel? Is there a connection in our society between a person's home and his or her self-concept? Why? Were the participants supportive in the sharing portion of the activity? How did the support make the sharing participant feel?

Activity 4—Analyzing Family Issues
Birth Order

Language Purpose:

1. To discuss the concept of *birth order*
2. To categorize group members by birth order descriptions
3. To examine the effects of birth order

Self-Esteem Focus:

To develop an understanding that birth order may have an impact on self-concept and self-esteem

Materials:

Birth Order Quiz

Vocabulary:

order, sibling, theory

Process:

1. Tell participants that this activity is about birth order. Ask them what they think that means. Explain that birth order is based on the theory that *when* one was born, in relation to siblings (e.g., first, middle, last), may affect one's personality. It could also affect job choices, who people marry, and how well they get along with others.
2. Distribute the *Birth Order Quiz*. Define any terms that may need explaining.
3. Ask participants to tell their actual birth order and to choose the description on the quiz that describes them best. Explain that the descriptions correspond to birth order as follows:

    Description A—the first child or the only child

    Description B—the second or middle child

    Description C—the youngest or last-born child

    Are there any participants whose actual birth order and description do not match? What could that mean? Are the descriptions correct?

4. Ask each participant to describe problems and advantages that were unique to his or her childhood. Include ideas such as:

    a. Were you treated differently? How?

    b. Did you have to take care of anyone?

241

    c. Were you the only child at any time?

    d. Did you get things your siblings didn't?

5. Write the names of all participants where everyone can see them under the appropriate birth-order categories (i.e., first/only; middle/second, third, etc.; youngest/last).

6. Review the descriptions on the *Birth Order Quiz*. Beginning with the first/only category, discuss the descriptions in relation to each person. As an example, ask if the group perceives firstborn Stephanie as being reliable, goal-oriented, serious, etc. How do the group's perceptions of the person relate to the *Birth Order Quiz* descriptions? Are they similar? Does Stephanie act like a firstborn child? Repeat this process for each participant.

7. Conclude the activity by discussing participants' opinions of the theory of birth order. Is it an acceptable theory? Why? Why not? How might knowing about birth order help a person analyze his or her self-esteem? Can birth order affect self-esteem? How? Birth order may affect personal qualities, but does it control them? Have participants explain their answers to that question. Remind participants of other ways personal qualities are formed (e.g., type of family, values, personal dreams, etc.). Should birth order be used as an excuse for failure or lack of personal accomplishments? Why not?

Some ideas in this activity were adapted from Leman (1985).

Birth Order Quiz

Directions: Check (✔) which category you are most like or that describes you best.

_____ A. You like things to be perfect. You are neat and tidy, well-organized, serious, helpful, dependable, fault-finding, patient, and goal-oriented. You get good grades, follow the rules, and like to please people.

_____ B. You do not like conflict and you are a peacekeeper. You are loyal, very independent, secretive, friendly, and balanced. You tend to stay in relationships for a long time.

_____ C. You are charming, outgoing, messy, independent, carefree, and influential. You are sometimes seen as a clown or a showoff.

Social Communication

Activity 5—Analyzing Family Issues
Parents' Character (C) (HS)

Language Purpose:

1. To identify character traits of parents
2. To create interview questions for parents
3. To analyze how a parent's character can affect children

Self-Esteem Focus:

To develop an understanding that a parent's personality can have an impact on a child's self-esteem

Materials:

Parents' Character activity pages

Vocabulary:

caregiver, character, personality, trait

Process:

(Note: Given the sensitivity of this activity, you should know participants' backgrounds before beginning. Delete questions on the activity pages that are inappropriate for your participants.)

1. Tell participants that in this activity they will be focusing on their parents or caregivers (i.e., the people who are raising them). Ask how knowing more about parents or caregivers leads to a better understanding of one's own past and present.

2. Explain that often one can find interesting clues to parents' personalities by thinking about one's parents' lives before they had children. We may forget that they had individual lives, dreams, fears, and goals that perhaps had nothing to do with the thought of having children.

3. Remind participants of the interviews that they conducted in Section 1, Activity 2—"Group Interviews: Getting to Know Each Other." Brainstorm questions participants may want to ask their parents or caregivers about their lives before they had children. Participants are to imagine questions that might be interesting to ask; they will not be required to actually ask their parents these questions. Ideas might include:

   a. How would you describe yourself?
   b. How did you feel about getting married?

c. If you're married, how did you feel about your spouse before you had children?
   d. Did you want to have children?
   e. What have been the happiest days of your life? The most difficult?
   f. What were your main worries before you had children?
   g. What was your best quality before you had children?

4. Distribute the *Parents' Character* activity pages. Tell participants to keep the list of questions in mind as they complete the sentences. Ask for volunteers to read their responses. Ask participants to be active listeners by giving each other feedback about responses. (E.g., "It sounds like your parents were happy." "You must have had a difficult time with your father." "I know what you mean.")

5. Conclude the activity with a discussion about how parents' characters can affect children. What happens when a parent or caregiver has a negative character? Do children take on negative as well as positive character traits? Why? How can parents' characters affect their children's self-esteem? What can parents do if they know they have negative personality traits? Do people always know which negative traits they have? Why not?

Social Communication

Parents' Character

Directions: Complete the following sentences about your parents or caregivers. You will need to imagine that you know the information. Think about their personality, self-concept, and self-esteem.

1. Before my mother had children, she was a woman who _____
   _____
   _____

2. One of the most important experiences of her young life was _____
   _____
   _____

3. One of her goals as a young woman was to _____
   _____
   _____

4. When I think about what kind of mother she is now, I think that _____
   _____
   _____

5. When my mother was younger, I would describe her personality and character as _____
   _____
   _____

6. Before my father had children, he was a man who _____
   _____
   _____

246

© 1992 Thinking Publications
Duplication permitted for educational use only.

Analyzing Family Issues: Parents' Character

7. One of the most important experiences of his young life was _____

   _____

   _____

8. One of his goals as a young man was to _____

   _____

   _____

9. When I think about what kind of father he is now, I think that _____

   _____

   _____

10. When my father was younger, I would describe his personality and character as _____

    _____

    _____

11. When they were younger, my parents were similar in that they _____

    _____

    _____

12. When I think of how my parents were different when they were younger, I see _____

    _____

    _____

Social Communication

Activity 6—Analyzing Family Issues
Family Problems (C)

Language Purpose:

1. To define qualities of *an ideal family*
2. To name common family problems
3. To formulate solutions to family problems

Self-Esteem Focus:

To develop an understanding that families influence self-esteem

Materials:

none

Vocabulary:

asset, con, foster, ideal, identity, liability, pro, traditional

Process:

1. Explain that people usually agree that the most important factor in the development of one's self-esteem is the family in which one was raised. Remind participants that much of what the group has discussed previously was related to the idea that people achieve their identity through relationships with other people. Ask how learning about family interaction can help to achieve higher self-esteem.

2. Ask participants to define *an ideal family*. Write a definition where everyone can see it that combines participants' responses. Ask how many grew up in an ideal family. Stress the idea that most people do not grow up in an ideal family.

3. Brainstorm the types of families that exist in today's society (e.g., traditional families, single-parent families, stepfamilies, adopted families, extended families, two single people living together, dual-career families, etc.). Define all unfamiliar terms. Discuss pros and cons of each, if appropriate for your group.

4. Brainstorm "ideal" family qualities. In an ideal situation, what should families provide for children? Include ideas such as:

    a. security
    b. privacy
    c. honesty
    d. positive role model
    e. kindness
    f. trust

Analyzing Family Issues: Family Problems

g. respect

h. guidance

i. pleasant atmosphere

j. prompt attention to illness

k. a feeling of being an asset, not a liability

l. demonstration of love and affection

5. Explain that families are very complicated. Family members are not always able to give each other what is needed, and every family has problems. Brainstorm common family problems. Ideas may include:

a. overly stern parent

b. sibling jealousy

c. abuse

d. divorce

e. not enough money

f. not enough space

g. parents who don't set limits

h. alcoholism

6. Ask participants to choose three of the problems mentioned to discuss in depth. For each of the three problems, help participants to create a scenario that includes type of family, family members' names, specific details of the problem, an analysis of the problem, and possible solutions. (See Section 6, Activity 4—"Examining a Problem-Solving Strategy.")

7. Conclude the activity with a discussion about the kind of family each participant would like to have in the future (if they are not already in adult-like situations). How will they foster self-esteem in their future families? How will they continue to maintain high self-esteem for themselves in their current families?

Social Communication

Activity 7—Analyzing Family Issues
Family Comparison

Language Purpose:

1. To compare and contrast different types of families
2. To use practical guides as opposed to impractical ideals when thinking about family issues

Self-Esteem Focus:

To explore families as they really are without imposing unrealistic expectations

Materials:

none

Vocabulary:

characteristic, compare, comparison, contrast, expectation, ideal, normal, nuclear, portray, unrealistic

Process:

1. Remind participants of the discussion in the previous activity about ideal families. Ask participants why it would be important to compare ideal and normal families. For example, why might we want to compare our families with some of the ideal families presented on TV? What can be gained from such a comparison? What can we learn?
2. Ask participants to brainstorm a list of current TV programs based on family situations. Be ready to offer your own examples.
3. As a group, select one TV family as the "Ideal American Family."
4. List characteristics, where everyone can see them, that describe the family under the "Ideal American Family" heading. Some characteristics might include *nuclear family, married, rich, large house, and great relationships* (i.e., everyone likes each other).
5. Under a "Normal American Family" heading, list characteristics that might describe the typical family, such as *divorced parents, both parents work, finances are tight,* etc.
6. Compare and contrast the lists.
7. Answer the following questions:
    a. Are there any similarities in the two lists? What are they?

    b. Why are families on TV usually portrayed so unrealistically?

    c. What happens when we try to achieve the ideal family model? Can we?

    d. Is a family normal if it doesn't live up to the ideal?

8. Reassure participants that many different family models are acceptable, though not all families are healthy. There are no two families exactly alike. Comparing a real family with a fantasy family can cause conflicts. Real families have real problems and real personalities. On major holidays or at family gatherings, for example, wishing one's family could live up to an ideal may cause sadness. Discuss this idea.

9. Conclude the activity with a discussion about families and comparisons to an ideal. Should participants try to change, or *can* they change, their families? Why or why not? Who can they change? (Answer: themselves.) Why do human beings compare themselves to others? What was gained by comparing participants' real families with the TV fantasy families? What can unrealistic expectations do to self-concept?

Social Communication

Activity 8—Analyzing Family Issues
Analyzing Love (HS)

Language Purpose:

1. To define the concept of *love*
2. To differentiate between types and levels of love
3. To categorize quotations about love

Self-Esteem Focus:

To associate love with self-esteem

Materials:

Analyzing Love activity page

Vocabulary:

categorize, familial, fascination, infatuation, jealousy, ownership, permanent, quotation, relationship, romantic

Process:

(Note: The activity page includes high-level figurative language and requires abstract thinking to interpret some of the quotations.)

1. Tell participants that this activity is about love. Ask them how knowing more about love could affect their self-concept and self-esteem.
2. Ask each participant to write a definition of *love* on a board or where everyone can see it. (If writing is a problem, they can tell their definitions.) When everyone has finished, discuss each definition. Responses may include:

    "It's a stronger feeling than friendship."

    "Love is caring how someone else feels."

3. As a group, try to combine as many definitions as possible to come up with a composite definition.
4. Brainstorm different types of loving relationships, such as:
    a. parent-child
    b. boyfriend-girlfriend
    c. lover-lover
    d. husband-wife
    e. friend-friend

    Ask participants to categorize the types of love that they listed, i.e., familial, romantic, or friendship.

252

5. Brainstorm different terms for *love,* such as:

   a. romance
   b. puppy love
   c. a crush
   d. marriage-based
   e. sex
   f. fascination
   g. true love
   h. infatuation

   Ask participants to which types of loving relationships these terms apply.

6. Discuss the meaning and importance of the types of loving relationships listed. Why does one person love another? Do people fall in love because of how someone looks? Is there a difference between "loving" someone and "being in love"?

7. Distribute the *Analyzing Love* activity page. Discuss the quotations and help participants to understand the meaning of each. Point out that the author's name appears at the end of each quotation. When completed, ask participants to read their answers and explain why they categorized the quotations as they did. If participants' answers vary, encourage discussion of their differences of opinion. For example, quotation #1 could be referring to love between friends, or it could be referring to romantic relationships, which are also based on friendship. There will be variances in responses and differences of opinion that will encourage group interaction. Listed below are potential responses, although participants should be allowed to defend other answers as well:

   ### *Analyzing Love* Activity Page Answers

   1. 1 or 3
   2. 1, 2, or 3
   3. 1, 2, or 3
   4. 2
   5. 3
   6. 1, 2, or 3
   7. 1, 2, or 3
   8. 1, 2, or 3
   9. 1, 2, or 3
   10. 1 or 3
   11. 2
   12. 2 or 3

8. Conclude the activity with a discussion about how participants view love at this time. Does love mean the same now as it did 100 years ago? Why or why not? Do people love each other for the same reasons? Does love bring rights and responsibilities? Does love mean ownership? What is jealousy? Is it healthy for a relationship? Can there be jealousy between parents and children? Is love the joy of giving or receiving? Is there a *double standard* in love? (Discuss what that term means, if necessary.) Do males love differently than females? Is love a permanent emotion? Is marriage the best step to take after romantic love? What does love have to do with self-esteem? Can you be unloved and still have high self-esteem? Why or why not?

Social Communication

Analyzing LOVE

Directions: These quotations describe one or more of the following types of love: familial, romantic, friendship. Decide which type(s) of love the quote is describing and write 1, 2, or 3 beside it.

   1 = Familial
   2 = Romantic
   3 = Friendship

____ 1. Friendship is love without his wings. (L. Byron)

____ 2. All for love, and nothing for reward. (E. Spenser)

____ 3. How do I love thee? Let me count the ways. (E. Browning)

____ 4. Live with me and be my love, and we will all the pleasures prove. (W. Shakespeare)

____ 5. Greater love hath no man than this, that a man lay down his life for his friends. (St. John)

____ 6. Time was when love and I were well acquainted. (W. Gilbert)

____ 7. Love built on beauty, soon as beauty, dies. (J. Donne)

____ 8. Love conquers all things. (Virgil)

____ 9. Love is like the measles; we all have to go through it. (J. Jerome)

____ 10. Thou shalt love thy neighbor as thyself. (Leviticus)

____ 11. Men love in haste, but they detest in leisure. (L. Byron)

____ 12. Tis better to have loved and lost, than never to have loved at all. (S. Butler)

© 1992 Thinking Publications
Duplication permitted for educational use only.

Activity 9—Analyzing Family Issues
Marriage (HS)

Language Purpose:

1. To express ideas about marriage
2. To analyze marriage and alternatives to marriage

Self-Esteem Focus:

To develop an understanding that self-concept can affect marriage choices and results

Materials:

Marriage activity page

Vocabulary:

alternative, faithful, guarantee, ideal, legal, mate, monogamous, security, trial

Process:

1. Ask participants to define *marriage*. Is everyone in total agreement? Why or why not? Ask how many people plan to get married (or are married). Ask why it is important to discuss marriage even if a person has no plans to marry.
2. Explain that people often talk about an ideal marriage. However, what is ideal for one couple might not be ideal for another. Brainstorm ideas about why people get married (e.g., security, love, sex, companionship).
3. Brainstorm qualities that participants think are "ideal" or necessary in a marriage partner. Are the qualities the same for males and females? Why or why not? Include ideas such as love, understanding, sense of humor, faithfulness, patience, and honesty. How are personal qualities reflected in mate selection? How is self-concept reflected?
4. Distribute the *Marriage* activity page. Explain any unfamiliar terms. When participants have completed it, discuss differences and similarities in responses. Help participants with the last two questions, if necessary.
5. Explain that many people consider alternatives to marriage. Ask for examples and list them where everyone can see them. Ideas might include:
   a. Living together—partners feel that their relationship does not have to be legal to be significant. They may not know if they want to marry.

Social Communication

    b. Trial marriage—partners want to get married, but they decide to first live together; this arrangement usually does not involve having children.

    c. Not marrying or not living together at all—partners keep individual living places. Partners may or may not be monogamous.

6. Conclude the activity with a discussion about how important love is to marriage. Does love conquer all? Do people live *happily ever after*? Can a marriage exist without love? Why or why not? Why are there no guarantees in marriage? How does trust affect a marriage? What happens when there isn't enough trust? Ask participants how having high self-esteem could make them better marriage partners (e.g., how would assertiveness, active listening, and using constructive criticism make them better partners)?

Additional Activity:

Have participants investigate requirements for marriage such as age, blood test, disease test, physical exam, prohibitions, cost, and license.

Analyzing Family Issues: Marriage

MARRIAGE

Directions: Check (✓) if you agree or disagree with the following statements.

Agree Disagree

_____ _____ 1. People should discuss their feelings about having children before they get married.

_____ _____ 2. People who live together before getting married will probably never get married.

_____ _____ 3. Children are a necessary part of marriage.

_____ _____ 4. The husband should earn more money than the wife.

_____ _____ 5. Marriage based on true love can solve people's personal problems.

_____ _____ 6. Couples should not marry if one partner is going to school.

_____ _____ 7. It is not a problem if people marry before they are financially secure.

_____ _____ 8. People who never marry are never really happy.

_____ _____ 9. Most men never want to get married.

_____ _____ 10. Most women want to get married.

11. What messages about marriage did you get from your parents or from a couple you know?

12. Write your suggestion for a happy marriage.

Social Communication

Activity 10—Analyzing Family Issues
Examining Divorce (C) (HS)

Language Purpose:

1. To discuss the effect of divorce on self-concept
2. To recognize cause-and-effect relationships in divorce

Self-Esteem Focus:

To develop an understanding that divorce can affect self-concept and self-esteem

Materials:

Divorce activity page

Vocabulary:

alternative, arrangement, depression, society, stable, statistic

Process:

1. Ask participants why learning about divorce may give information about self-concept and self-esteem. Why might someone who has not experienced divorce in his or her family want to learn about divorce?

2. Explain that almost all societies provide some arrangement for divorce. In some societies, divorce is rare, while in others a permanent marriage is unusual. Ask participants if *society* views divorce as good or bad. Why? Explain that generally the public view of divorce is that it is unfortunate, but often necessary. Ask participants to offer ideas about why it is unfortunate.

3. Explain that the divorce rate in the United States is approximately 55 percent (National Center for Health Statistics, 1991). Ask participants why they think the rate is so high. What did they learn about marriage in the previous activity that might account for such a high divorce rate? Ask if statistics are helpful in understanding divorce. Will high divorce statistics slow the marriage rate? Why or why not?

4. Brainstorm possible reasons for divorce. Include ideas such as:

    a. money problems

    b. immaturity

    c. emotional differences

    d. frequent moving to a new location

Analyzing Family Issues: Examining Divorce

   e. sexual freedom

   f. dishonesty

   g. loneliness

   Discuss the list and why such reasons could lead to a divorce.

5. Brainstorm effects of divorce on children and parents. Include ideas such as:

   a. sense of loss

   b. depression

   c. dwelling on the past

   d. taking sides

   e. legal effects (child support money, legal custody)

   f. feelings of personal failure

   g. learning from past mistakes

   Discuss situations in which each effect may occur.

6. Continue discussing the effects of divorce by asking questions such as:

   a. Why do parents worry so much about the effect of divorce on children?

   b. What is lost when couples break up?

   c. Should some marriages end? Is there such a thing as a "good divorce"?

   d. Is a bad marriage better than a good divorce?

   e. Should parents stay together for the sake of the children?

   f. Why do some children feel responsible for their parents' divorce?

   g. Why are children sometimes forced to take sides in a divorce? How does this affect children?

   h. Why is society concerned about marriages staying stable?

7. Distribute the *Divorce* activity page. Explain any unfamiliar terms. When participants have completed it, discuss differences and similarities in responses.

8. Conclude the activity with a discussion about participants' personal experiences with divorce. Have most participants experienced some aspect of divorce? If so, did the divorce influence their self-concept in some way? How can divorce be avoided? Is one person in the marriage usually the cause of divorce? Can marriage partners remain friends after they divorce? Are there danger signals that can alert couples and children that a divorce is coming? Are children helpless when their parents are breaking up? Why are some people afraid to live alone after a divorce? Are there or should there be required alternatives to divorce (e.g., counseling, trial separation)?

Social Communication

DIVORCE

Directions: Write **T** (True) or **F** (False) for each statement. Your answers may be different from other people's. Be ready to explain your responses.

_____ 1. Divorce runs in families. If your parents divorced, you probably will also.

_____ 2. Divorce always affects children in a negative way.

_____ 3. Divorce laws make it too easy to get a divorce.

_____ 4. A divorced person will probably marry another divorced person.

_____ 5. Mothers should always have custody of children.

_____ 6. If people really love each other, they won't divorce.

_____ 7. Happily married people are happy all the time.

_____ 8. Fathers are always the cause of divorce.

9. In your opinion, what is the main cause of divorce?

10. How would you advise people who are thinking about divorce?

Section 8: Social Values and Myths

In this section, participants examine the effects of society and culture on self-concept and self-esteem. Particular social values and pressures are analyzed to develop an understanding of the important effects that group norms, conformity, and mass media have on individual development.

As in all activities in *Social Communication: Activities for Improving Peer Interactions and Self-Esteem,* the communication focus is on discourse. The activities are designed to provide the content for discussion.

Activities in this section include:

		Page
1.	Examining Social Myths (HS)	262
2.	Image and Conformity	265
3.	Examining Body Image and Personal Style	268
4.	Friendship	271
5.	Negative Peer Pressure	274
6.	Sexual Beliefs and Attitudes (C) (HS)	278
7.	Analyzing Advertising	280
8.	Sports and Society	282
9.	Music and Society	285
10.	An Ideal Education	287

Social Communication

Activity 1—Social Values and Myths
Examining Social Myths (HS)

Language Purpose:

1. To define the concept of *myth*
2. To discuss myths that illustrate values
3. To create examples of myths

Self-Esteem Focus:

To develop an understanding that myths and values may not be the same

Materials:

Social Statement Test

Vocabulary:

expectation, fictional, myth, social, society, value

Process:

1. Define *society*, for example:

    society—all people as a group; a group of people with beliefs and interests in common

    Integrate the idea of being social: living together in an organized group or similar closeness. Ask participants what happens when people don't know about social expectations of the group.

2. Explain to participants that societies have common values. Ask them to define *values*, keeping in mind ideas from other activities. Remind them of concepts from Section 4, Activity 8—"Personal Values." Ask for a few examples of social values (working hard, staying married, raising a family, saving money, etc.).

3. Explain that social values are frequently found in myths. Discuss the definition of a myth, such as:

    myth—a story or idea (usually fictional) that reflects society's values

    Ask if anyone knows of a myth.

4. Explain that one of our society's values is that if children behave themselves and are good, they will be rewarded. Ask if anyone knows of a myth or social story that illustrates this idea (e.g., Santa Claus will bring more or better gifts to children who are "good"). Explain that some

Social Values and Myths: Examining Social Myths

myths can be dangerous if people don't know whether they are based on fact or fantasy. Children often do not know the difference.

5. Brainstorm ideas in society that may be related to myths. Ideas may include:

   a. Tooth fairy—Good children will be rewarded.

   b. Weddings—Husband and wife will live happily ever after.

   c. Thanksgiving—People are all thankful for what they have.

   d. Love—There is a perfect mate for everyone.

   Discuss the values on which these myths are based. Are these myths helpful? Why or why not?

6. Distribute the *Social Statement Test*. Explain that the statements are based on myths. After participants have completed the test, discuss and compare answers. Ideally, all statements would be labeled false. Depending on the value system of the group, explain why false is the preferred answer, or accept both true and false answers. What were the similarities and differences among participants' responses? How do these myths affect people's lives?

7. Brainstorm social values that participants think are important. Examples may include:

   a. Be a person of integrity.

   b. Understand and affirm your values.

   c. Take care of your physical health.

   d. Take responsibility for your actions.

   e. Protect the environment.

   f. Help others.

8. Break participants into small groups. Ask each group to choose one of the values in process step 7 and jointly write or act out a myth (story or idea) about it. Give participants help if necessary to complete this task. When participants have completed their myths, ask them to read the myths to the large group or act them out.

9. Conclude the activity with a discussion about how myths can be helpful and/or harmful. What happens when myths become "shoulds"? How do people learn myths? How can myths be changed, or can they? How can a myth affect self-esteem? What happens when society turns a myth into a value that you don't support? How will a person with low self-esteem look at a myth differently than a person with high self-esteem? What are the advantages of supporting a myth? What are the disadvantages?

Social Communication

SOCIAL STATEMENT test

Directions: Write "true" or "false" beside the following statements. Be prepared to defend your answers.

_____ 1. Money brings happiness.

_____ 2. If you work hard, you can get rich.

_____ 3. Anybody can grow up to be president.

_____ 4. People probably never learn anything when they are asleep.

_____ 5. Famous people tend to be born of poor but hardworking parents.

_____ 6. If a child must be punished, it is best to let the father do it.

_____ 7. Attractive people are usually happier than unattractive people.

_____ 8. You can be anything you want to be.

_____ 9. Bad things don't happen to good people.

_____ 10. People should put others' happiness before their own.

© 1992 Thinking Publications
Duplication permitted for educational use only.

Activity 2—Social Values and Myths
Image and Conformity

Language Purpose:

1. To define the concepts of *image* and *conformity*
2. To explore one's personal image and compare it to conformity
3. To discuss the link between image and the need to conform

Self-Esteem Focus:

To examine the issues of image and conformity and their effect on self-concept

Materials:

Image and Conformity activity page

Vocabulary:

concept, conform, consensus, convey, image, myth, project, style

Process:

1. Brainstorm a definition for *image,* such as the following:

    image—an exact likeness of another; an idea or concept projected by a person

2. An old saying claims, "The clothes make the man." What does that mean? Brainstorm possible answers:

    "You are what you wear."

    "People can tell a lot about you by your clothes."

    "Clothes can make you feel different in different situations."

    Is the saying a myth? How does image pertain to self-concept?

3. Brainstorm descriptions or images of different types of people, such as:

    a. Business executive (e.g., three-piece suit, short hair, etc.)

    b. Rock star (e.g., fancy costumes, tight clothes, heavy makeup, etc.)

    c. Teacher (e.g., comfortable pants or dress, flat shoes, etc.)

    d. Mechanic (e.g., khaki pants, steel-toed boots, etc.)

    e. Athlete (e.g., sweat pants, sweat band, etc.)

Social Communication

4. Ask participants if it was easy or difficult to form a description of the persons in process step 4. Using consensus, label each as easy or difficult to describe. Why were some difficult and some easy? Why do people dress similarly (e.g., money, acceptance)?

5. Instruct participants to think about their peers as they write a descriptive image of a teenager.

6. Share the descriptions. Are any of them similar? Write similar descriptions where everyone can see them. They may include such items as blue jeans, T-shirt, high tops, etc. Just as body language can convey a message, clothing, accessories, makeup, and hair style can also convey messages. What are the messages?

7. Do adolescents with similar interests also have a similar style of dress and behavior? What are some common styles? How are the different groups labeled (e.g., rockers, jocks)?

8. Remind participants that to *conform* means to become similar or identical—to act in acceptance of current rules or customs. Are any of the descriptive images or common styles based on conformity? List the pros and cons of conformity.

9. Distribute the *Image and Conformity* activity page. Remind participants that since some of the questions might be considered personal, they should only share what they would like to. When participants have completed the task, encourage them to talk about what they wrote.

10. Conclude the activity with a discussion about why people dress in the ways they do. Can clothes change your mood? How? Can different clothes change your self-image? How? How does your personal style or image pertain to your self-concept? What is the connection between social myths and conformity?

Social Values and Myths: Image and Conformity

Image and Conformity

Directions: Answer the following questions for yourself. You will be asked to share only those answers you would like to.

1. What hair style do you wear? _____

    What does it say about your personality?

2. What do your clothes say about you?

3. What kind of jewelry do you wear? _____

    How does it convey your personality?

4. Do you dress differently when you are away from your friends? _____

    Why or why not?

5. Does your behavior conform to a certain group style? _____

    If so, which one? _____

    If not, how did you arrive at your personal style?

6. What does your personal style say about you as a person?

7. Do you conform to society's customs or rules? _____

    Is conforming important to you? _____

    Why or why not?

© 1992 Thinking Publications
Duplication permitted for educational use only.

267

Social Communication

Activity 3—Social Values and Myths
Examining Body Image and Personal Style

Language Purpose:

1. To examine the concept of *body image*
2. To compare participants' body images to their ideal selves
3. To use active listening techniques

Self-Esteem Focus:

To reinforce the idea that body image and self-concept are closely linked

Materials:

Body Image and Personal Style activity page

Vocabulary:

accessory, feature, ideal, image, insecure, physique, prominent, self-conscious, standard, stereotype, style

Process:

1. Ask participants why it is important to learn about the connection between their bodies and self-concept. Can the way we think about our bodies influence our self-concept? Review information discussed in Section 5, Activity 5—"Body Image and Self-Esteem."
2. Explain that body image begins to form in childhood and adolescence. This is a significant time for body image development. Explain that a number of ideas are related to body image. List, so all can see, and discuss these ideas adapted from Palmer and Froehner (1989):

    a. *Rate of change*—Rapid growth and changes in the adolescent's body can make acceptance of the new physique difficult (e.g., feet growing more rapidly than other body parts can give the adolescent the feeling of being "all feet").

    b. *Lack of knowledge*—Sometimes the adolescent has not been adequately prepared for body changes and this can cause feelings of self-doubt and a loss of control.

Social Values and Myths: Examining Body Image and Personal Style

   c. *Comparison to an ideal*—If a body part varies greatly from an ideal self the adolescent has developed in childhood, the adolescent may have difficulty accepting himself or herself.

   d. *Social acceptance*—Adolescents compare their body type or parts to those of significant others in their lives. What the adolescent believes others think can influence acceptance of the body.

   e. *Stereotypes*—If the body build or facial features of a person begin to resemble those of an unfavorable group, the adolescent may have a lowered self-concept.

   f. *Insecurity*—Physical appearance can affect social acceptance. An unattractive feature can cause social insecurity.

3. Discuss the concept of body image with participants. Can one of the above factors influence how they view themselves? Who determines what is or is not attractive for the individual? Do friends seem more accepting than the individual? Why?

4. Ask participants what role clothing, makeup, hair style, and accessories play in developing body image and self-image. What is involved in developing style? How does a person determine a personal style?

5. Distribute the *Body Image and Personal Style* activity page. When participants have completed it, instruct individuals to pair up with the person they know the least. Instruct them to share their answers with one another, remembering to be active listeners. Allow 5 to 10 minutes for the sharing of answers. For participants who have a difficult time writing, allow the entire activity to be completed orally.

6. Conclude the activity with a discussion about body image and personal style. How do body image and style affect self-concept? Does everyone experience self-doubt and self-consciousness about their appearance at times? How can these doubts be dealt with effectively? How do society's standards for good looks affect self-esteem? Is there a connection between body image and myths? Why do we compare ourselves to others? How does this affect self-concept?

Social Communication

Body Image and Personal Style

Directions: Write answers to the following questions. Use the back side of this paper if you need more space. You will be sharing your answers with another group member.

1. How would you describe yourself? (Include your body type, prominent features, hair color, eye color, and your feelings about them.)

2. What would you like to change about the description above?

3. How would you describe the person you admire most? (Use the ideas from #1 and also include a description of style of clothing and hair, use of accessories, and/or makeup.)

4. How would you describe your personal style? (Include a description of your style of clothing and hair, use of accessories, and/or makeup.)

5. What would you like to change about your personal style described above?

© 1992 Thinking Publications
Duplication permitted for educational use only.

Activity 4—Social Values and Myths
Friendship

Language Purpose:

1. To define *friendship*
2. To identify important characteristics of friendship

Self-Esteem Focus:

To explore how friendships can affect self-esteem

Materials:

Characteristics of Friends activity page, large piece of paper

Vocabulary:

acquaintance, attitude, attract, characteristic, friend, friendship, gender

Process:

1. Ask participants why they think most people consider friendship to be an important social and personal value. How does the fact that people have groups of friends affect society? Why is friendship important on a personal level?
2. Engage participants in a discussion of how friendships develop by asking questions such as:
   a. How do people choose their friends?
   b. How do people choose their best friends?
   c. Why do people feel closer to some friends than to others?
   d. Why do some friendships start but never really develop?
   e. How do people attract new friends?

   Summarize and write responses for all to see.
3. Explain that there are general ideas about choosing friends, such as:
   a. Friendships often happen between neighbors.
   b. Friendships often happen between people who share similar experiences, such as being in the same class or having the same interests.
   c. Friendships often happen between people who share similar attitudes.
   d. Friendships often happen between people who meet each other's needs.

   Discuss these ideas as you proceed.

Social Communication

4. Relate the information in process step 3 to the information from process step 2. Ask participants to identify the similarities.

5. On a large piece of paper (that later can be removed from view), brainstorm and list characteristics of people that would make them good friends. Include characteristics such as:

   a. kind
   b. sharing
   c. trusting
   d. fun
   e. loyal
   f. honest
   g. understanding
   h. generous

   Make sure participants understand all terms.

6. Break participants into small groups. Remove the list of characteristics from view. Distribute the *Characteristics of Friends* activity page to each participant. Read the directions to all participants. When participants have completed the task, ask each small group to share its list and how it ranked each characteristic. Compare information from all groups. Discuss differences and similarities.

7. Conclude the activity with a discussion of participants' personal experiences developing friendships. How do acquaintances become good friends, and how do good friends become best friends? What's the difference between having friends of the same gender and friends of the opposite gender? What happens when parents don't like their children's friends? Why do friendships end? How can friends increase or lower one's self-esteem? What happens if a person doesn't have a friend?

Social Values and Myths: Friendship

Characteristics of FRIENDS

Directions:
1. Think about the characteristics of a good friend that the group just listed and discussed.
2. As a team, list as many characteristics of a friend as possible on your paper. You may list characteristics discussed as a group or list new characteristics. Everyone on the same team should have the same list.
3. As a team, place the number 1 beside the characteristic the team feels is the most important. Place a number 2 by the next most important, etc. Remember to discuss your opinions with your team.

Characteristics of Friends   **Team Ranking**

1. _____   _____

2. _____   _____

3. _____   _____

4. _____   _____

5. _____   _____

6. _____   _____

7. _____   _____

8. _____   _____

9. _____   _____

10. _____   _____

Social Communication

Activity 5—Social Values and Myths
Negative Peer Pressure

Language Purpose:

1. To define and recognize *peer pressure*
2. To develop a strategy to deal with negative peer pressure
3. To use assertive communication to counteract negative peer pressure

Self-Esteem Focus:

To explore peer pressure and its effect on identity and acceptance

Materials:

Negative Peer Pressure activity pages

Vocabulary:

assertive, negative, peer, positive, pressure, reply, statement

Process:

1. Ask participants to define *peer pressure*. Have they ever been the recipients of peer pressure? Ask participants why it is important to learn about peer pressure. What advantage is there in being able to recognize and respond to peer pressure?

2. Explain that while peer pressure can be negative (which is the subject of this activity), it can also be positive, such as when it encourages people to join extracurricular activities or clubs. Pressure can come in many forms, but the topic of this activity is pressure messages. Sometimes when we know what we want to do, pressure messages can make us rethink our decisions. When this happens, there are assertive messages we can give to others to let them know about our decisions without putting others down or being untrue to our feelings.

3. Distribute the *Negative Peer Pressure* activity pages. If participants have difficulty formulating assertive responses, they might find one of the following techniques helpful:

    a. Say no. You don't need to give reasons or excuses.

    b. Tell the person how pressure makes you feel.

    c. Don't continue to discuss the matter. Walk away.

4. Ask participants to share their answers with the rest of the group. Participants should check for assertiveness and ensure there are no put-downs.

5. Conclude the session with a discussion about pressure messages and negative peer pressure. What effect could giving in to negative peer pressure have on self-concept? Discuss advantages of recognizing messages as negative or positive peer pressure. Why is it important to be assertive in pressure situations? How does a person with high self-esteem respond differently to peer pressure than a person with low self-esteem?

Some ideas for this activity were adapted from Gregg, Hunter, Renner, Peterson, Casey, and Kastor (1984).

Social Communication

NEGATIVE PEER PRESSURE

Directions: Next to each pressure message, write an assertive reply. Remember, use no put-downs.

STATEMENT   **REPLY**

Example:

1. It's either now or never.   I guess it will have to be never. I have thought about it a lot and it's not for me.

2. Everybody's going to be there.

3. Come on, try it. You know you want to.

4. I know you want to go; you're just afraid of what people will say.

© 1992 Thinking Publications
Duplication permitted for educational use only.

Social Values and Myths: Negative Peer Pressure

STATEMENT   **REPLY**

5. If you were my friend, you would do it.   _____
                                                 _____
                                                 _____

6. You don't want people to think you're a chicken.   _____
                                                      _____
                                                      _____

7. If you don't, someone else will.   _____
                                                 _____
                                                 _____

8. If you'll do it, I'll be your friend.   _____
                                                 _____
                                                 _____

9. I dare you to do it.   _____
                                                 _____
                                                 _____

10. If you want to be popular, you'll have to get it.   _____
                                                        _____
                                                        _____

Social Communication

Activity 6—Social Values and Myths
Sexual Beliefs and Attitudes (C) (HS)

Language Purpose:

1. To compose a broad definition of *sexuality*
2. To identify social beliefs about sexuality

Self-Esteem Focus:

To develop an awareness that sexuality is a reflection of the entire person, and as such is a reflection of self-concept

Materials:

magazines, scissors, tape, large sheet of paper

Vocabulary:

aspect, assertive, attitude, conflict, intimacy, representation, sex, sexuality, significant, value

Process:

(Note: This activity may not be appropriate for all groups. Use discretion.)

1. Tell participants that the topic of this activity is how beliefs and attitudes affect the way people think about sexuality. Explain that some people find it difficult to discuss sex. Many people feel uncomfortable or embarrassed, and those feelings are acceptable. Sexuality is a significant part of human development that is important to discuss. Ask participants what may happen if people don't know why they think what they do about sex and sexuality.
2. Explain that sexuality is made up of many things other than genitals and sexual intercourse. It affects how a person thinks, feels, acts, and sees the world. It also affects how the world sees males and females. Ask participants to describe where people learn about sexual-social attitudes or beliefs (parents, friends, church, etc.).
3. Brainstorm common attitudes about sex held by society. (Emphasize that these are attitudes and not facts.) Ideas may include:
   a. People should be virgins when they marry.
   b. Women should be virgins when they marry.
   c. Sex outside of marriage is bad.
   d. Men should know more about sex than women.
   e. Women should have less sexual experience than men.

Social Values and Myths: Sexual Beliefs and Attitudes

    f. Children are not sexual.

    g. Elderly people are not sexual.

    h. Sex is dirty.

    i. Sex is wonderful.

    j. Sex is dangerous.

    Discuss conflicting ideas and messages. Why/how do conflicting ideas develop? What effect do conflicting ideas have on people (e.g., confusion)? Why does society have so many conflicting ideas?

4. Ask participants to think about something they have seen on TV or in a movie recently that was related to sexuality. List responses for everyone to see. If responses represent a narrow definition of sexuality (sexual encounters, sexy bodies or clothes, having a baby), point out that a broader definition of sexuality exists (sex roles, intimacy, body image, affection, conversation, nonverbal communication). Define terms if necessary.

5. As a group, compose a definition of *sexuality* based on thoughts generated so far. Include ideas such as male/female roles, social roles, feelings about oneself and others, relationships, self-esteem, etc. An example of a definition is:

   > *Sexuality* includes the whole person and personality. Sexuality begins at birth and ends in death. It includes feelings about self-concept and self-esteem, how you feel about being male or female, and how well you get along with others. Sexuality also includes intercourse and having children.

6. Break the group into pairs. Give each pair several magazines. Ask them to cut out examples of other aspects of sexuality not found in their TV/movie list. For example, they should be able to find ads and articles that deal with body image, affection, intimacy, sensory pleasures (fragrance, textures, visual images), and relationships. The goal is to find visual representations of what sexuality means to them. Allow 15 minutes.

7. Bring the group back together and tell participants to tape their visual representations on a large sheet of paper labeled "Aspects of Sexuality." When completed, ask participants to define *sexuality* again according to what participants have chosen as their representations.

8. Conclude the activity with a discussion of the confusion that exists about sexuality. Why can sexuality be so difficult to talk about? Why is it included in so many TV programs and movies? Do people feel pressured by TV, movies, and friends to become sexually active? Why or why not? How does negative peer pressure affect sexuality? Does having sex make a girl into a woman or a boy into a man? What does self-esteem have to do with sexuality? What does assertive behavior have to do with sexuality? How does understanding personal values relate to sexuality?

Social Communication

Activity 7—Social Values and Myths
Analyzing Advertising

Language Purpose:

1. To identify advertising techniques
2. To evaluate advertising appeal
3. To relate the effect of advertising on self-concept

Self-Esteem Focus:

To develop an understanding that advertising can influence self-concept and self-esteem

Materials:

ads from magazines and/or taped commercials from TV

Vocabulary:

advertise, appeal, approval, attraction, endorsement, intelligence, technique

Process:

1. Explain that the goal of this activity is to discover how advertising affects us. Ask participants why it is important to learn more about advertising. Explain that advertising can help people discover new products or show where to buy products on sale. Advertising can also mislead customers by making false claims through ad appeal. It is important to be skilled at telling the difference. Ask participants if they believe all the advertising that they see or hear.
2. Brainstorm different sources of advertising (e.g., radio, TV, movies, magazines, billboards, books, etc.), and have participants name examples of each.
3. Ask participants how they think advertisers create particular ads. What are some common types of ads? Explain that one way to examine an ad is to look at advertising techniques. Ask what *technique* means. Then ask participants to guess what the following techniques mean before giving them the information:

    a. *Peer approval*—appeals to feelings of acceptance by others; "join the gang"

    b. *Sexual attraction*—appeals to desires to be sexually attractive

Social Values and Myths: Analyzing Advertising

   c. *Hero endorsement*—appeals to desires to be like a hero or heroine

   d. *Good looks*—appeals to feelings about personal appearance or attractive physical appearance

   e. *Intelligence*—appeals to your intelligence; thinking people buy "_____."

4. Show participants several ads from a magazine or commercials taped from TV. Ask them to tell which technique was used in each ad or commercial.

5. Explain that once participants can identify the technique used in an ad, it is also helpful to examine why an ad appeals to them and how it involves their feelings, wishes, and dreams. Explain that ads attempt to make products look luxurious, modern, fun, patriotic, or any one of dozens of other desirable qualities. Ad appeal can be categorized in different ways, including the following:

   a. *Type of person*—child, cowboy, young woman

   b. *Setting*—outdoors, mansion, small house, bathroom

   c. *Family situation*—family members participating in various activities (positive or negative)

   d. *Animals*—having fun, suffering pain

   e. *Flowers*—delicacy, softness

6. Distribute a variety of magazine ads and/or show a variety of TV commercials. For each ad, ask participants to identify what technique was used and what type of ad appeal was stressed. Within ad appeal, be certain to have participants identify the group (e.g., age, gender, income level) the advertiser was trying to reach.

7. Conclude the activity with a discussion about how advertising can affect our values. What happens when people believe that they need to be sexy, strong, young, hardworking, rich, etc.? How does advertising affect self-concept? Does a person with high self-esteem relate differently to advertising than a person with low self-esteem? Can understanding advertising techniques increase self-esteem? How? (E.g., We can look at ads in terms of techniques and ad appeal instead of as realistic situations that reflect what we should do or be.)

Additional Activity:

Ask participants to write or draw an ad for some service or quality like peace, the end of poverty, care of the environment, better education, love, etc.

Social Communication

Activity 8—Social Values and Myths
Sports and Society

Language Purpose:

1. To name characteristics associated with sports
2. To analyze particular characteristics associated with sports figures
3. To debate the pros and cons of different aspects of sports

Self-Esteem Focus:

To develop an understanding that sports can affect self-concept and self-esteem

Materials:

sports pages from newspapers

Vocabulary:

affiliation, aggressive, athlete, attribute, characteristic, competition, model, role, society, value, violence

Process:

1. Remind participants of the definition of *society* (see Section 8, Activity 1—"Examining Social Myths"). This activity focuses on how sports affect our society (e.g., bring people together, influence our values, provide role models, etc.). Ask how learning more about sports can be beneficial to self-concept.
2. Explain to participants that sports activities can be divided into two categories: team sports (e.g., basketball, football) and individual sports (e.g., gymnastics, tennis). Brainstorm examples of each.
3. Tell participants that particular characteristics can be associated with team sports and with individual sports. Brainstorm examples of each, such as:

Team	*Individual*
cooperation	independence
unity	individual achievement
role within team	individual role
specific skill ability	general skill ability
team communication	self-motivation
team recognition	individual recognition

Social Values and Myths: Sports and Society

4. Engage participants in a discussion of how characteristics associated with sports figures can affect society's values. Include ideas such as:

endurance	consistency
ability/skill	winning
competition	sportsmanship
aggression	ethics
cooperation	health
sacrifice	high salaries
goals	heroes/heroines
time management	identity/role models
work ethic	entertainment

   Explain any unfamiliar terms.

5. Ask participants to tell what *affiliation* means. Elaborate on the definition by discussing the concepts of feeling a part of a group, choosing a team or individual to cheer for, or lending support to and encouraging athletes. Ask how being affiliated with a team or individual makes fans feel. What benefit do fans get from affiliation?

6. Ask participants what a *role model* is. What kinds of role models are associated with sports? Brainstorm the attributes of sports figures who are role models. Are there positive and negative role models in sports? Why? Ask participants to discuss the importance of sports figures who are role models to them. How do sports figures become heroes or heroines? Is having a hero or heroine important? Why?

7. Ask participants to tell you what *competition* means. What ideas do sports reflect about competition? How is that value reflected in society? What forms of competition does our society encourage? What forms does society discourage?

8. Explain that many sports are associated with aggressiveness. Ask what part aggressiveness plays in sports. Is aggression in sports a social value? Why? Is aggression necessary in sports? Which sports are the most aggressive? Why? Is aggression in sports approved of by society? Is aggression okay? If appropriate to your group, repeat this discussion using the term *violence* instead of *aggression*.

9. Give each participant the sports page from a newspaper. Ideally, everyone should have a different sports page. The date of the sports page is not particularly important. Tell participants to find articles that discuss sports as a social issue. If reading is a problem, help participants to choose an article and assist them in reading it. After articles have been read, ask participants to give the group a brief summary of the main idea and tell how the article relates to society.

10. Conclude the activity with a discussion about the pros and cons of society's emphasis on sports. Are there any cons? What do sports teach about aggression? Are most sports played by men or women? What does that say about social values? How could society's emphasis on sports affect self-concept? What happens when a person is not good at athletics? Is self-esteem affected? How?

Activity 9—Social Values and Myths
Music and Society

Language Purpose:

1. To recognize emotions that music can generate
2. To analyze the cultural importance of music
3. To judge lyrics by a set of criteria

Self-Esteem Focus:

To develop an awareness that music can affect self-concept

Materials:

lyrics contributed by participants (see note below), equipment necessary to play contributions brought in by participants (e.g., cassette player, turntable, CD player)

Vocabulary:

associate, culture, impact, influence, inspire, lyric, quality, value

Process:

(Note: Before doing this activity, ask participants to bring examples of music they like or find interesting and that are appropriate for the group setting. If they bring vocal music, ask them also to write down a few lines of the lyrics so that everyone is sure to understand them. If you think that some participants may bring extremely explicit music, screen it before using it in the group.)

1. Tell participants that the focus of this activity is to become aware of the impact music has on society and on self-concept. Ask how learning more about music may be important to understanding society and culture.

2. Brainstorm as many different types of music as possible (e.g., rock, heavy metal, gospel, classical, jazz, blues, salsa, rap). You could also play examples of different types of music. Ask participants to associate emotions, feelings, or moods with the different types of music (e.g., blues—sad). Accept a wide range of answers and remind participants that they may have differing points of view. Ask them why they might disagree on the emotions associated with different types of music.

3. Discuss differences and similarities in music. Is rock always upbeat and happy? Is classical always serious and thought provoking? How is Cajun music similar to jazz, etc.?

285

4. Ask participants how they think music might have been invented or discovered. Why did music develop? What purpose did/does it serve in society? Do different cultures have different music? Why is that? Has your culture adopted music from other cultures? Why? How? What does that have to do with values?

5. Ask participants how music is used to inspire loyalty, patriotism, or courage. What songs might relate to those qualities? What do those qualities have to do with values?

6. Ask participants who brought vocal music to play brief sections of their songs, read two or three lines of the lyrics, and explain why they like the songs they picked.

7. As a group, analyze the lyrics, discussing ideas such as:

    a. the meaning of the words

    b. appropriateness of the lyrics—Do participants agree with what the lyrics are saying?

    c. quality of the lyrics—Are the words pleasant or interesting to listen to? Are they poetic?

    d. related emotions

8. On a scale from 1 to 5 (5 being a great song), have participants rate each song for overall quality, then justify the ratings.

9. Conclude the activity with a discussion of the impact of music in today's society. Why are parents afraid of some of the music their children listen to? Should parents decide what children can't listen to? Can music influence people to do things that they normally would not do (i.e., affect them in positive or negative ways)? Does music have anything to do with self-concept or self-esteem? What? Ask participants to speculate about whether a person with low self-esteem would listen to different types of music than a person with high self-esteem. How can music raise or lower self-concept, or can it? (The last two questions were included to stimulate discussion about the possibility that some music may encourage people to act in particular ways. Conversational focus at this point could revolve around whether or not music has the power to change how people think.)

Activity 10—Social Values and Myths
An Ideal Education

Language Purpose:

1. To discuss the present educational system
2. To define *an ideal educational system*

Self-Esteem Focus:

To explore the educational system and create alternatives that would enhance self-esteem

Materials:

none

Vocabulary:

ideal, influence, negative, positive, system

Process:

1. Tell participants that this activity is about defining *an ideal education*. Discuss the concept of *ideal* in some detail.
2. Tell participants that in order to think of an ideal educational system, it will be helpful to briefly describe their experiences with education. Brainstorm educational experiences and expectations such as:
    - three years of middle school
    - four years of high school
    - four to five required courses a year
    - one or two elective courses
    - 45-minute class periods
    - overcrowded classes
    - boring classes
    - assemblies
    - interesting class discussions
    - homework
3. Explain to participants that the remainder of the activity requires use of their imaginations. They are to imagine themselves as the Earth's educational representatives. They are being sent to Mars to help Martians set up an educational system. The Martians want to know the

best kind of educational plan they can use. They also want to know what not to do.

4. Break participants into small groups. Tell them to discuss ideas about an ideal education for children on Mars. They also should discuss things to avoid when planning Martian schools. Each group is to choose a recorder who will write down positive and negative ideas. They should try to list at least ten positive ideas and five things to be avoided. Plan on at least 10 to 15 minutes for this part of the activity.

5. Ask groups to share their information. Discuss differences and similarities among responses. Compile all information agreed upon by the small groups into a document to be presented to the Martians.

6. Conclude the activity with a discussion about how participants could influence their current educational system if they chose to (e.g., writing letters, giving suggestions to the principal, talking to teachers). How can self-esteem be increased or decreased by an educational system?

Section 9: Differences and Similarities Among People

After examining the impact that family members have on each other, participants are better able to explore how self-concept and self-esteem are affected by their gender and race. After exploring basic concepts of gender identification and stereotyping, activities in this section focus on prejudice and discrimination. The underlying theme of all activities in this section is how cultural pressures can limit feelings of self-worth and self-confidence.

As in all activities in *Social Communication: Activities for Improving Peer Interactions and Self-Esteem,* the communication focus is on discourse. The activities are designed to provide the content for discussion.

Activities included in this section include:

		Page
1.	Gender Identification	290
2.	Female/Male Values (C) (HS)	293
3.	Social Expectations of Males and Females (HS)	296
4.	Defining Stereotyping	299
5.	Sexual Stereotyping (HS)	301
6.	Stereotypical Roles and Occupations	306
7.	Differing Communication Styles Between Males and Females (HS)	310
8.	Sexual Stereotyping on TV	313
9.	Defining Prejudice (HS)	316
10.	Defining Discrimination	319

Social Communication

Activity 1—Differences and Similarities Among People
Gender Identification

Language Purpose:

1. To define the concept of *gender identification*
2. To differentiate between physiological and learned factors associated with gender identification
3. To complete sentences that express ideas about gender

Self-Esteem Focus:

To foster nonstereotypical definitions of gender identification and self-concept

Materials:

large paper

Vocabulary:

biology, feminine, gender, identity, implication, masculine, physiological, traditional

Process:

1. Explain that this activity focuses on gender identity. Ask participants to recall how the term *identity* was used in previous activities (sense of self, personal characteristics). Elaborate on the concept of *gender* by explaining that it pertains to how people acquire an awareness that they are either male or female. By age three to four years, girls learn what it means to be female and boys learn what it is to be male (i.e., they learn what it means to be members of the opposite sex). Ask participants why it is important to learn about how gender identity develops. What does gender identity have to do with self-concept?

2. Explain that as people grow, they start to behave in ways that society says are appropriate for men and women. Traditionally, people believed that gender identity was based on physiological differences. Ask participants to brainstorm general physiological differences between the sexes. For example:

Males	*Females*
taller	shorter
heavier	lighter
stronger	weaker
shorter life expectancies	longer life expectancies

Differences and Similarities Among People: Gender Identification

Ask participants to think about the implications of the differences (e.g., men might be viewed as better fighters/hunters; women might be viewed as safer at home).

3. Explain that current ideas suggest that people acquire gender identity based on their physiology as well as what they learn from their families (i.e., social learning) and from social pressures. Both biology and social learning affect what it means to be male and female. Explain what those terms mean. Brainstorm ways that one's family or society teaches about gender identification. For example:

Males	*Females*
Boys are made of snakes and snails and puppy dog tails.	Girls are made of sugar and spice and everything nice.
Boys wear blue.	Girls wear pink.
Boys are rough, tough, and strong.	Girls are soft, gentle, and sweet.
Boys shouldn't cry.	Girls shouldn't be loud.
Boys play with cars and trucks.	Girls play with dolls.

Ask participants to discuss their responses. Do they agree with what society teaches?

4. Read the phrase, "You've come a long way, baby." Explain to participants that this phrase is commonly used to explain changes women have made in society and in their lives. Ask participants for examples of how women's roles have changed in the last 100 years.

5. Ask participants to give examples of how men's roles have changed in the last 100 years. If they can't come up with as many changes for men as for women, ask them to speculate about why men may have made fewer changes than women.

6. Divide the group into several small, same-gender groups. Ask each group to write as many endings as they can to the following sentences:

    Male group—"I'm glad I'm a male because…"

    Female group—"I'm glad I'm a female because…"

    Give an example to help them get started. Allow about 10 minutes.

7. Have the same groups write endings to a second sentence in the same way:

    Male group—"If I were a woman, I would…"

    Female group—"If I were a man, I would…"

8. Ask groups to tape their responses to the wall, chalkboard, or large piece of paper. Read their responses to the whole group. Discuss the responses.

Social Communication

> Were any of the responses the same for both genders? What does that mean? Can both genders have similar characteristics? Why? How?

9. Conclude the activity with a discussion about how gender identification might limit what it means to be masculine and feminine. Are there certain ways that men and women are supposed to behave? Is a man any less of a man because he cries? Is a woman any less of a woman because she is strong? What are admirable masculine and feminine qualities? Is there overlap? How could gender identity influence people to have negative feelings about themselves? How can gender identity affect self-concept positively?

Activity 2—Differences and Similarities Among People
Female/Male Values (C) (HS)

Language Purpose:

1. To differentiate between traditional female/male values
2. To categorize values as being associated with males or females
3. To compare female/male values

Self-Esteem Focus:

To show how female/male values can affect self-concept

Materials:

Female/Male Values Assessment activity page

Vocabulary:

gender, identification, speculate, traditional, value

Process:

1. Remind participants of previous discussions about values (see Section 4, Activity 8—"Personal Values"). Ask them to recall several values that were important to them. Ask them also to speculate about the possible content of a discussion on female and male values. Why is it important to learn what men and women value in this society?

2. Remind participants of the previous activity about male-female gender identification. With those gender differences in mind, brainstorm traditional values that many men and women have in this society. Remind participants that there are no right or wrong answers. For example:

Men's Values	*Women's Values*
work	family
single life	marriage
being rich	getting a man with money
competition	cooperation

   Ask participants why men and women might traditionally have different values (e.g., gender identity).

3. Distribute the *Female/Male Values Assessment* activity page. Define terms as necessary. If it is helpful to your group, ask participants to look

Social Communication

up unfamiliar terms in the dictionary. After participants have completed the assessment, discuss each item, asking participants to explain why they responded as they did. Compare and contrast differences between males and females.

4. Conclude the activity with a discussion about how female/male values are changing. Why do so many women work outside the home? Why do so many men have heart attacks? Do men still have a difficult time crying and expressing emotions? Why or why not? Do women express emotions too easily? How did the gender values of your parents affect you? What will you teach your child to value as a man/woman? How do female/male values affect self-concept?

Differences and Similarities Among People: Female/Male Values

FEMALE/MALE VALUES ASSESSMENT

Directions: Below is a list of values. Some ideas may be more valued by men. Some may be more valued by women. Some may be valued by both. Write M (Male), F (Female), or B (Both) in front of each item, depending on who you think values the idea more. There are no right or wrong answers. Count the number of M values and total them. Do the same for the F values and B values.

____ 1. honesty

____ 2. education

____ 3. assertiveness

____ 4. risk taking

____ 5. mystery

____ 6. independence

____ 7. freedom

____ 8. equality

____ 9. alone time

____ 10. privacy

____ 11. protection

____ 12. trust

____ 13. approval

____ 14. control

____ 15. safety

____ 16. comfort

____ 17. security

____ 18. sexual relationships

____ 19. conversation

____ 20. love

____ 21. children

____ 22. intimacy

____ 23. physical closeness

____ 24. commitment

____ 25. money

____ 26. leadership

____ 27. responsibility

____ 28. work

____ 29. emotional expression

____ 30. goals

TOTAL Male Values _____
TOTAL Female Values _____
TOTAL Both Values _____

Social Communication

Activity 3—Differences and Similarities Among People
Social Expectations of Males and Females (HS)

Language Purpose:

1. To elaborate on the concept of *expectation*
2. To list traditional social expectations for men and women
3. To formulate ideas about how men and women behave similarly

Self-Esteem Focus:

To develop an awareness that social expectations can negatively affect self-esteem

Materials:

Social Expectations activity page

Vocabulary:

conformity, expectation, habit, vulnerable

Process:

1. Ask participants for a definition of *expectation,* such as:

    expectation—something considered likely or certain; something you are supposed to do; a certain way you are supposed to act

    Ask participants what expectations they have of a teacher or the group facilitator (e.g., show up on a regular basis, be knowledgeable, be educated). People expect teachers to act in certain ways. Explain that sometimes expectations can turn into "shoulds" when they are related to conformity or habits. If people think all teachers should act in one certain way, then problems can develop. Discuss what some problems might be.

2. Explain that society places certain expectations on males and females. Society expects people to act in certain ways depending on their gender. Ask participants to recall any expectations put on them because of gender. Ask why it is important to learn about expectations.

3. Distribute the *Social Expectations* activity page. Read the first item in the "A Real Man..." column. Point out the equivalent example in the "A Real Woman..." column. Read the second item. As a group, finish the statement "A Real Woman..." for item 2 and write it on the activity

Differences and Similarities Among People: Social Expectations

page. Proceed through the activity as a group. Discuss the negative aspects of each item. Possible answers include these:

"A Real Woman..."

1. should not earn more money than a man.
2. should never act too strong.
3. should act helpless.
4. should act like she doesn't know more than a man.
5. should express emotions easily.
6. should always be a lady.
7. should express painful feelings.
8. should rely on a man to keep her safe.
9. should not become muscular.
10. should be emotionally weaker than a man.

4. Brainstorm current positive expectations or characteristics that could apply to both males and females. Ideas could include these:

   a. being honest
   b. communicating openly
   c. expressing anger assertively
   d. accepting mistakes
   e. doing your best
   f. working hard
   g. asking for help
   h. expressing feelings
   i. acting confidently
   j. being vulnerable
   k. being patient
   l. getting a good education

5. Conclude the activity with a discussion about how negative expectations and "shoulds" can limit experiences. If females or males only do what is expected of them, what are they missing? Why might trying new behaviors be difficult? How might it feel to try new behaviors while friends are still behaving in old patterns? How could participants find new role models? How do negative expectations affect self-esteem?

Social Communication

SOCIAL EXPECTATIONS

Directions: Fill in the traditional expectations in the "A Real Woman" column that go with those in the "A Real Man" column.

"A Real Man…"	"A Real Woman…"
1. should be the primary money earner in a relationship.	*Example:* should not earn more money than a man.
2. should never show his weaknesses.	
3. should be able to handle everything by himself.	
4. should act like he knows everything.	
5. should never lose control.	
6. should prove his manhood continually.	
7. should not give in to pain.	
8. should always be fearless.	
9. should always be physically strong.	
10. should always be emotionally strong.	

© 1992 Thinking Publications
Duplication permitted for educational use only.

Activity 4—Differences and Similarities Among People
Defining Stereotyping

Language Purpose:

1. To define *stereotyping*
2. To examine commonly held beliefs about groups of people
3. To explore reasons behind stereotyping

Self-Esteem Focus:

To recognize the ease with which stereotyping occurs and the complexity it creates for people or groups being stereotyped

Materials:

paper

Vocabulary:

extreme, inferior, label, stereotype, superior

Process:

(Note: The focus of this activity is on exploring how some people stereotype others. If ideas arise from discussion about being the recipient of stereotyping, incorporate it into the activity in a way that is appropriate for your group.)

1. Define the word *stereotype*:

    stereotype—a way of thinking about people that pays no attention to individual differences; a description of how some persons judge others; previously formed opinions about a race or group of people

    Remind participants of the discussion about labeling people in Section 3, Activity 1—"Who Am I?" Explain that unaware people often use stereotyping labels. They feel they know all about people by looking at them. They decide about a person's character, social standing, or ability at a moment's glance.

2. Explain that stereotypes are usually extreme (all-or-none) statements, such as "Everyone from that part of town is a snob." Brainstorm a list of stereotyping statements. The statements are not to be judged, just listed.

3. Ask participants why people of certain groups, religions, races, or backgrounds seem to act in certain ways. When people have had similar experiences, are from the same area, and are taught similar values, they

Social Communication

may seem the same. Similarities are not inherited and not all people in a group are the same. Getting to know a person as an individual and not as part of a stereotyped group is important in changing a stereotypical thinking process.

4. Look at the list of stereotyping statements generated in process step 2. Put a check mark beside those that are "all-or-none" statements. Do any of the statements include the words *some, a few,* or other words indicating only part of a group?

5. Explain that some people would say stereotyping is for lazy people—people who don't want to think or become familiar with a person as an individual. Why might getting to know a person as an individual change stereotypical thinking?

6. Write the following sentence starters (or your own) in a place where all participants can see them:

    a. All teachers...

    b. People in jail...

    c. Left-handed people...

    d. All athletes...

    e. Homeless people...

    f. All jocks...

7. Ask participants to complete the sentences on a sheet of paper.

8. List the answers where everyone can see them. Are there any answers that are similar? Why are there differences in answers? Did the participants feel comfortable doing the exercise? Why or why not?

9. Conclude the activity with a discussion about stereotyping others. What effect does a stereotype have on a group? An individual? Does stereotyping occur every day? Why or why not? When others are stereotyped, how do participants feel in relation to them (superior/inferior)? Why? Who does more stereotyping, people with high or low self-esteem? Ask group members to explain their answers. What effect does stereotyping others have on the self-concept and self-esteem of those being stereotyped? Of those doing the stereotyping?

Activity 5—Differences and Similarities Among People
Sexual Stereotyping (HS)

Language Purpose:

1. To define *sexism*
2. To recognize sexist ideas sometimes accepted by society
3. To compare beliefs about males and females

Self-Esteem Focus:

To determine the effects of sexism and sexist beliefs on the individual's self-esteem

Materials:

Sexual Stereotyping Questionnaire activity pages

Vocabulary:

attitude, enlightened, gender, narrow-minded, role, sexism, stereotype

Process:

1. Define *sexism* for the participants:

    sexism—an attitude, action, or social practice that places a person in a lower position on the basis of gender

    Sexual stereotyping means to group all people of one gender and assume that the roles they play are the same for all people of that gender (e.g., all men are macho). Why is it important to learn about sexual stereotyping? Can or should people be stereotyped? What are the advantages/disadvantages? Answers may include: "It is easier to group people than to get to know them as individuals." "You can feel superior to certain groups of people." "Not everyone fits a stereotype."

2. Distribute the *Sexual Stereotyping Questionnaire* activity pages and have participants complete them.

3. After participants have finished the questionnaire, write the following scale where everyone can see it:

Total	*Interpretation*
26–50	Narrow-minded. You might want to reexamine your view of gender roles.

301

Social Communication

> 10–25 Workable. You are aware of some differences in men's and women's roles in life.
>
> 0–9 Enlightened. You look at individuals in terms of personal roles and do very little stereotyping.

4. Read each statement from the questionnaire and have participants vote on each item, answering the way they did on the questionnaire. On more controversial statements (one-third to one-half of the group voting "true"), ask for a representative to explain each side's answer. Remind participants not to interrupt, as they will also have a chance to voice an opinion.

5. Remind participants that some stereotypical views can be linked with cultural differences, religious values, or familial traditions. This exercise does not take away from the value of those sources, but rather opens the door for different experiences and opinions. All people are different, whether they are men or women. Share the expression, "There are strengths in differences." What does that statement mean? When a person is limited by previously formed ideas about a group, then stereotyping becomes a source of frustration for both the stereotyper and the person being stereotyped. Discuss this concept.

6. Conclude the activity with a discussion about sexual stereotyping. Ask participants how it felt to have their opinions challenged. Does stereotyping help or hurt male/female relationships? How? Have group members ever found a previously formed idea to be in error? Can participants change others' stereotypical views to meet their own? Why or why not?

Differences and Similarities Among People: Sexual Stereotyping

SEXUAL STEREOTYPING QUESTIONNAIRE

Stereotype—a way of thinking about people that pays no attention to individual differences; a description of how some persons judge others; previously formed opinions about a race or group of people

Directions: Circle **T** for True or **F** for False for each statement listed. When you're finished responding to all of the statements, total all true answers and put the sum in the space indicated at the end of the questionnaire.

True **False**

T F 1. Men shouldn't change diapers.

T F 2. Women need men to protect them.

T F 3. It's more important for a man to continue his education than for a woman.

T F 4. Men are better athletes.

T F 5. Women are better at caring for children.

T F 6. Women should not work. They should stay home.

T F 7. Women should wait on men.

T F 8. Men are better drivers than women.

T F 9. Only women gossip.

T F 10. Men don't watch soap operas.

T F 11. Men need to tell women what to do.

T F 12. Women should do what they're told.

T F 13. Men shouldn't shop for groceries.

T F 14. Women follow their feelings.

Social Communication

T	F	15.	Men act after thinking. Emotions are not involved.
T	F	16.	Only men ask for dates.
T	F	17.	Men should make more money than women.
T	F	18.	Only boys should play with guns.
T	F	19.	Only girls should play with dolls.
T	F	20.	All men are aggressive.
T	F	21.	All women are weak.
T	F	22.	Only men should propose marriage.
T	F	23.	Women are more careless about driving than men.
T	F	24.	Men are better at fixing things. (They are more mechanical than women.)
T	F	25.	A man's job is more important than a woman's.
T	F	26.	Women don't like sports.
T	F	27.	Women spend more money than men.
T	F	28.	Women should be more polite than men.
T	F	29.	Women are smarter than men.
T	F	30.	Men are smarter than women.
T	F	31.	All men are stronger than women.
T	F	32.	Women should be attractive.
T	F	33.	Women should be more concerned about their appearance than men.
T	F	34.	Men are sloppy.
T	F	35.	Women are neat.
T	F	36.	Men shouldn't cry.
T	F	37.	Men are independent.
T	F	38.	Women are dependent.
T	F	39.	All women are smaller than men.

© 1992 Thinking Publications
Duplication permitted for educational use only.

Differences and Similarities Among People: Sexual Stereotyping

    T   F   40. Men are better leaders/supervisors/bosses.

    T   F   41. Women don't know how to lead.

    T   F   42. Women aren't good at math or science.

    T   F   43. Women think too much about situations. They analyze everything.

    T   F   44. Men like to watch more TV than women.

    T   F   45. Men should barbecue, women should cook.

    T   F   46. Men are better at outdoor things.

    T   F   47. Women are better at indoor things.

    T   F   48. It's OK for men to get angry, but not for women.

    T   F   49. Women should not say what is on their minds.

    T   F   50. Women like to spend more time in the bathroom than men.

_____ **Total number of true answers**

Social Communication

Activity 6—Differences and Similarities Among People
Stereotypical Roles and Occupations

Language Purpose:

1. To explore stereotypical roles
2. To examine *traditional* and *nontraditional* roles
3. To determine the effects of stereotyping on occupational choices

Self-Esteem Focus:

To explore the relationship between traditional and nontraditional roles and their effect on self-determination and self-concept

Materials:

Stereotypical Roles and Occupations activity pages

Vocabulary:

analytical, expectation, mechanical, nontraditional, occupation, profession, role, signature, traditional

Process:

1. Review the definition of *stereotype* (see Section 8, Activity 4—"Defining Stereotyping"). Ask why learning about stereotyping in role expectations and professions is important.
2. Explain that men's traditional role expectations include mechanical and analytical occupations such as medicine or engineering. Women's traditional role expectations include helping professions such as teaching or nursing. Some people feel trapped by traditional roles concerning occupations or jobs. This activity is designed to open possibilities for participants' occupational futures.
3. Explain that traditionally men have made more money than women. Men who have gone into "traditionally" female jobs make less money than their counterparts in "traditionally" male occupations. Brainstorm a short list of jobs that are traditionally male or female.
4. Distribute the *Stereotypical Roles and Occupations* activity pages. Explain that participants are to complete the fill-in-the-blank portion on the first page of the activity. Responses will be used for discussion.
5. Discuss with participants the answers listed in the male professions/occupations category. Are all the jobs listed by participants still totally male occupations?

Differences and Similarities Among People: Stereotypical Roles and Occupations

6. Have participants share answers listed in the female professions/occupations category. Should there be occupations which are only female jobs? Why or why not?

7. Brainstorm a list of household chores that traditionally belong to men and another list for women. Are there families in which both genders share chores and responsibilities? Does sharing confuse roles or strengthen the partnership?

8. Ask participants to complete the signature portion of the activity pages. This portion of the activity may require homework to collect the signatures. Did this exercise change the participants' views of traditionally male and female occupations and roles?

9. Conclude the activity with a discussion about expected male/female roles. If a person goes into a nontraditional occupation, does that make him or her less of a person? Why are there traditional roles and occupations based on gender? Do participants feel role expectations are changing or will change in the future? Why or why not? Ask participants why it is important to continue to learn about traditional or stereotypical roles and occupations. Could knowing a person who has a nontraditional role or occupation change the participants' views of that role/occupation? Why or why not?

Social Communication

STEREOTYPICAL ROLES AND OCCUPATIONS

List six traditionally male professions/occupations.

1. _____ 4. _____

2. _____ 5. _____

3. _____ 6. _____

List six traditionally female professions/occupations.

1. _____ 4. _____

2. _____ 5. _____

3. _____ 6. _____

List five jobs around the house that traditionally have been:

Men's Jobs   **Women's Jobs**

1. _____ 1. _____

2. _____ 2. _____

3. _____ 3. _____

4. _____ 4. _____

5. _____ 5. _____

Differences and Similarities Among People: Stereotypical Roles and Occupations

Directions: Collect signatures from participants or others outside the group who fit each of the statements.

Signature   **Find someone who:**

_____   1. has a female doctor.

_____   2. is male and has been a baby sitter.

_____   3. is a female athlete.

_____   4. has been cared for by a male nurse.

_____   5. is male and has taken family and consumer education (home economics).

_____   6. has taken auto mechanics with a female student.

_____   7. knows a female company executive.

_____   8. is a female who has asked a male for a date.

_____   9. is a male who has taken typing.

_____   10. has had a male hairdresser.

Social Communication

Activity 7—Differences and Similarities Among People
Differing Communication Styles Between Males and Females (HS)

Language Purpose:

1. To create a model of sender-receiver communication
2. To recognize that differences frequently exist between male and female communication styles
3. To analyze why differences exist

Self-Esteem Focus:

To develop the awareness that communication difficulties between the genders may be based on differing communication styles rather than differences in skill

Materials:

Differing Communication Styles activity page

Vocabulary:

aspect, gender, identity, model, process, rapport, receiver, sender, skill, style

Process:

(Note: Remind participants that *style* is a generic term used to describe various aspects of communication. For example, the term was used in Section 1, Activity 8 in reference to "introvert-extrovert" style and in Section 2, Activity 8 in reference to "aggressive-passive-assertive" style.)

1. Ask participants to review various aspects of communication using examples that they have discussed previously (e.g., assertiveness, trust, active listening, exchanging ideas and feelings). Explain that researchers believe males and females frequently use different communication styles. Ask participants why it is important to know about the differences that frequently exist between the communication styles of men and women. Make sure that participants understand the discussion is about communication *style,* not communication *skill*.

2. Explain that before examining the communication differences between men and women, you would like to create a model of communication focusing on the sender and receiver. Explain that when people (senders) talk, what they say is influenced by their backgrounds and histories.

Differences and Similarities Among People: Differing Communication Styles

Brainstorm other factors that influence how people talk and what they say, such as:

a. culture	g. gender
b. feelings	h. race
c. attitudes	i. age
d. opinions	j. values
e. education	k. health
f. perceptions (hearing, sight, etc.)	

Give examples of each factor and discuss how each factor affects the sender's message.

3. Ask participants which factors influence what the receiver hears or perceives. These factors should be the same as the sender's.

4. Point out that communication is a very complicated process. Explain that because of social pressures, males and females frequently communicate in different ways. Ask participants to think of examples of differences between how males and females communicate.

5. Distribute the *Differing Communication Styles* activity page. Explain that ideas from the activity were suggested by Tannen (1990) in a book titled *You Just Don't Understand*. Ask participants to speculate what the book is about. Define terms on the activity page as necessary. Go over each item on the activity page, comparing and contrasting ideas. Discuss participants' agreement or disagreement with the two lists (i.e., "Males" and "Females").

6. Conclude the activity with a discussion about why males and females communicate differently. What do gender identity and sexual stereotyping have to do with the differences? Why is understanding that the differences exist important? What happens when men and women have their own rules for communication? What can be done about the differences? How can men and women communicate more comfortably? How can the activity page be used to establish rapport between males and females in this group? How can differences in communication styles and rules between the genders affect self-esteem?

Social Communication

Differing Communication Styles

Directions: The ideas below represent how males and females sometimes communicate differently. Discuss your agreement or disagreement with each idea.

Males	Females
1. May find it difficult to identify and discuss feelings	Talk openly about feelings
2. Talk more easily in public	Talk more easily at home
3. Talk to give information	Talk to establish closeness
4. Jump from one topic to another	Talk at length about one topic
5. Feel a need to come up with solutions to problems	Want understanding when talking about problems
6. See conversation as a debate	Use conversation to establish rapport
7. Don't like to talk about personal things	Like to talk about personal things
8. Portray that independence is very important	Portray that interdependence is very important
9. Tend to give orders	Tend to make decisions based on discussions
10. Feel uncomfortable about asking personal questions	Feel that asking probing questions is important

Ideas for this activity were taken from Tannen (1990).

Activity 8—Differences and Similarities Among People
Sexual Stereotyping on TV

Language Purpose:

1. To identify attributes of TV commercials and programs
2. To analyze TV commercials and programs for sexual stereotypes
3. To assess the impact of TV on gender identification

Self-Esteem Focus:

To develop an awareness that watching TV can affect self-concept and self-esteem

Materials:

Sexual Stereotyping on TV activity page

Vocabulary:

attribute, character, gender, identification, impact, quality, role

Process:

(Note: This activity requires homework.)

1. Explain that in this activity participants will examine gender roles that appear on TV. Ask participants why TV might be an important source of investigation of male/female expectations.
2. Assign one hour of TV viewing to the group to be completed before the group meets again. If TVs are not available at home to some participants, discuss possible alternatives:
   a. Watch the TV in a school library.
   b. Watch TV with a friend or neighbor.
   c. Have a TV available for the group.

   Tell participants that the one hour of viewing must include five commercials that involve people and a weekly situational program (i.e., comedy or drama).
3. Distribute the *Sexual Stereotyping on TV* activity page and instruct participants to complete it as they watch television. Go over the example and discuss any questions. Tell the group to bring the completed activity to the next group interaction.
4. When participants have completed their assignment, ask them to draw some conclusions about what they watched. Discussion might focus on these questions:

Commercials

a. What kind of activities were the females engaged in?
b. What kind of activities were the males engaged in?
c. What kind of products were the women selling?
d. What kind of products were the men selling?
e. Was there a reason that a male or female was selling a particular product?
f. Was the commercial realistic?
g. Was there sexual stereotyping involved? Explain.

TV Program

a. What roles did males and females play?
b. Who was the most important character in the program?
c. Was anyone playing a nontraditional role?
d. Did the situation seem real?
e. Was there sexual stereotyping involved? Explain.

5. Conclude the activity with a discussion of the impact that TV has on gender identification. How traditional is TV with respect to gender roles? Have there been changes in how gender roles are portrayed on TV? If not, are changes needed? Why? Does TV affect how you see yourself as a male/female? Does TV limit people's possibilities? In what way? Does it matter if men and women do the same activities (e.g., cook, wash dishes, fix a faucet)? Should children be able to watch all the TV they want? What are they learning about gender identification and sexual stereotyping? What effect does stereotyping have on self-esteem?

Differences and Similarities Among People: Sexual Stereotyping on TV

Sexual Stereotyping on TV

Directions: Watch five TV commercials that involve people and fill in the blanks below.

Name of Product	Gender of Main Character	Role of Main Character	Location
Example: Nutro Cooking Oil	Female	Mother	Kitchen
1.			
2.			
3.			
4.			
5.			

Directions: Watch a TV program and describe the main characters.

Name of Program: _____

Characters	Gender of Characters	Qualities, Attributes of Characters	Characters' Activities
1.			
2.			
3.			
4.			
5.			

© 1992 Thinking Publications
Duplication permitted for educational use only.

Social Communication

Activity 9—Differences and Similarities Among People
Defining Prejudice (HS)

Language Purpose:

1. To define *prejudice*
2. To examine beliefs about prejudice

Self-Esteem Focus:

To examine prejudice and its impact on society and the self-concept of those involved

Materials:

Defining Prejudice Quiz activity page

Vocabulary:

attitude, minority, prejudice, prior, racial, victim

Process:

1. Write a definition for *prejudice* where everyone can see it, such as:

    prejudice—an attitude, opinion, or feeling formed without prior knowledge, thought, or reason; judging in favor of or against a person, group, gender, etc. without prior knowledge or facts

2. Ask participants why it is important to learn about prejudice. Has anyone in the group experienced prejudice? Is everyone prejudiced to some extent? Why or why not? If participants have done the previous activities on stereotyping, ask them how prejudice and stereotyping are the same.

3. Distribute the *Defining Prejudice Quiz* activity page. Remind participants that they do not have to share any answer they're not comfortable with.

4. After participants have completed the quiz, read the statements and discuss the answers with participants.

    1) *False*—Prejudice is learned, though it can be taught within families.

    2) *False*—Both those who reject others and the victims of prejudice suffer some personality damage.

    3) *False*—Most people are very aware they are prejudiced. Some prejudiced people's lives are complicated by their desire to avoid those whom they are prejudiced against.

316

Differences and Similarities Among People: Defining Prejudice

    4) *True*—Being prejudiced toward all people of a group is much easier than being prejudiced toward an individual you know personally who is a member of that group.

    5) *True*—Some people feel it is smart or popular to voice feelings of prejudice.

    6) *False*—People can be prejudiced about any minority group, including those with a disability, people of a different gender, religious groups, etc.

    7) *True*—Prejudice is learned, but not always from parents. Peer groups, significant others, or almost anyone who exerts influence over another can steer a person toward prejudice.

    8) *False*—Most people who are prejudiced against a particular group do not live near, work with, or socialize with members of that group.

    9) *False*—By virtue of the fact that a group is in a minority, its members get less attention until they bring their group to the attention of the majority.

    10) *False*—If a person is prejudiced against or in favor of a particular group, that person has already acted on that prejudice by the way he or she thinks about that group.

6. Conclude the activity with a discussion about prejudice. Does everyone have prejudices about some group? What part does prejudice play in society? Can a prejudiced person change? What would it take? How does prejudice affect the self-concept of the person holding it? Of the victim?

Some ideas in this activity were adapted from Riker and Riker (1977) and from Smuin (1978).

Social Communication

DEFINING PREJUDICE QUIZ

Directions: Read the statements. Circle **T** for True and **F** for False.

True   False

T   F   1. Some people are born with prejudices.

T   F   2. Being prejudiced doesn't really hurt anybody.

T   F   3. People don't consciously think about prejudice.

T   F   4. Prejudice is easier against groups than individuals.

T   F   5. People may like being prejudiced.

T   F   6. Prejudice only applies to racial groups.

T   F   7. Prejudice is learned.

T   F   8. Prejudice is learned by being around those you are prejudiced against.

T   F   9. People don't mind having minority status. They get more attention that way.

T   F   10. Prejudice is all right if you don't act on it.

Differences and Similarities Among People: Defining Discrimination

Activity 10—Differences and Similarities Among People
Defining Discrimination

Language Purpose:

1. To define *discrimination*
2. To examine discrimination from various perspectives
3. To consider alternatives to discriminatory situations

Self-Esteem Focus:

To examine discrimination's role in society and its effect on self-esteem

Materials:

Discrimination Scripts

Vocabulary:

character, discrimination, forum, injustice, minority, prejudice, quota, reverse, script

Process:

1. Explain to participants that the purpose of this activity is to define *discrimination* and examine its effects on our lives. Ask participants to review the definition of *prejudice* from the previous activity. How are *discrimination* and *prejudice* similar?

2. Agree on the definition of *discrimination*, such as:

    discrimination—a prejudiced outlook or treatment of people on the basis of race, religion, age, gender, or handicapping condition; to act on a prejudice

3. Ask participants why learning about discrimination is important. How does discrimination affect a person's self-esteem? Is discrimination still an issue in our society?

4. Discuss and brainstorm a list of instances when people within or outside the group have been discriminated against, such as when applying for jobs, seeking acceptance in schools, moving into particular neighborhoods, etc.

5. Ask participants which groups are affected by discrimination. Answers may include minority races, women, old people, people with disabilities, etc. Is there a group not affected by discrimination? If participants name white males as such a group, then define and discuss the concept of

Social Communication

    reverse discrimination, where a white male may be turned down for employment because the employer must hire minority applicants to fulfill guidelines set by the government.

6. Remind participants that this activity is not designed as a forum to discuss past injustices or to raise tensions, but as a strategy for reexamining or looking at discrimination in a different way.
7. Ask for two volunteers to participate in a role-playing exercise. Explain that they will be reading from a script and that no memorization will be necessary.
8. Distribute a *Discrimination Script* to each of the volunteers. Ask them to read over the scripts for any questions they might have.
9. Identify the characters and the situation for the other participants. Help the volunteers to perform the role-playing exercise. Debrief using the following questions:

    a. What is the situation?
    b. Who is being discriminated against? Why?
    c. What effect can this situation have on self-esteem?
    d. What will be the outcome of the situation?
    e. What do you think has caused this discrimination?
    f. Can discrimination of this sort be changed? Why or why not?
    g. How did the volunteers feel about the role-playing situation?

    Proceed in the same manner with the remaining scripts.
10. Conclude the activity with a discussion about discrimination. Why does discrimination exist? Does discrimination affect self-esteem? How can or should discriminatory practices be challenged? Who in the participants' group has not been discriminated against? How does it feel to be discriminated against?

Differences and Similarities Among People: Defining Discrimination

Racial Discrimination Script

Situation: John, a member of a minority race, is applying for a job as a bank teller. Ms. Smith is the personnel director for the bank.

Ms. Smith: Good morning, John. I see you're applying for a job as a teller.

John: Yes, I am.

Ms. Smith: What is your work experience?

John: I am currently working in a restaurant as a cashier, and I'm going to college at night to become an accountant.

Ms. Smith: Why do you want to leave your present job?

John: I want to learn more about banking, and I feel that I can offer a lot as far as experience and knowledge in this job.

Ms. Smith: I'm sure we'd be happy to have you here, but we don't have any openings at this time.

John: I was under the impression there was an opening. I read your "Help Wanted" ad in the paper.

Ms. Smith: That may have been run in error. You're not the kind of person we're looking for at this time. You don't project the image our bank is known for.

John: Ms. Smith, I am highly qualified for this position. I am a good employee. Please check my references.

Ms. Smith: You don't understand. We are looking for someone who is more in line with our image. Our customers would not feel comfortable with you. We would lose business. I'm sorry.

Social Communication

Sexual Discrimination Script

Situation: Marge has always wanted to be a firefighter. Captain Jones is interviewing her for the training program.

Capt. Jones: Come in, Marge. It's nice to meet you. So you're interested in becoming a firefighter.

Marge: Yes, I am. I've wanted to be a firefighter since I was eight years old.

Capt. Jones: That's very nice. As you probably realize, there is more to being a firefighter than passing a test.

Marge: I'm aware of that. I'm prepared to do whatever it takes to become a firefighter.

Capt. Jones: I see you're wearing a wedding ring.

Marge: Yes, why?

Capt. Jones: We don't have a separate restroom or sleeping facilities for men and women. As you know, we have no female firefighters. Their husbands and boyfriends wouldn't like them sleeping in the same room with men.

Marge: But other cities are hiring women.

Capt. Jones: Well, we need to train people who will be with us for a long time. If you're married, you're likely to have children. We can't have a pregnant firefighter endangering her crew mates because she can't do her part.

Marge: What are you trying to say?

Capt. Jones: Because we don't have the facilities for you, and knowing that women aren't as strong as men, maybe it would best if you looked into some other line of work.

Differences and Similarities Among People: Defining Discrimination

Reverse Discrimination Script

Situation: Frank Green is a first-year teacher at Washington Elementary. Maria Gomez is the principal of the school.

Maria: Frank, I'm glad you could take time out to meet with me.

Frank: No problem. What did you need?

Maria: The board of education has just sent out racial quotas for our staff next year. According to the figures, we will need two more minority staff members for next year.

Frank: How does that affect me?

Maria: Since you were the last staff member hired, you'll probably not be asked to come back next year.

Frank: Is it my performance? When we had the evaluation meeting last month, you seemed happy with my performance.

Maria: I am very happy with your work with the children. I must do what the board says. That means you will have to go. I wish it could be different. I need you on my staff. You're a great teacher.

Frank: Is there anything I can do? Isn't there anything that can be done?

Maria: (Shakes her head no.) Maybe one of the other schools can use you.

Section 10: Examining Our Role in the World

In this section, activities move participants from a social/cultural focus to a global focus. Discussion emphasizes seeing oneself as a member of the world community. As such, participants explore how local community issues affect and are similar to global issues. Topics such as environmental protection and social problems stress the idea that individuals can make a difference in bettering significant situations. Participants also learn how being socially responsible can improve self-esteem.

As in all activities in *Social Communication: Activities for Improving Peer Interactions and Self-Esteem,* the communication focus is on discourse. The activities are designed to provide the content for discussion.

Activities in this section include:

		Page
1.	Acting Responsibly Toward Others (HS)	326
2.	Adolescent Rights (C)	329
3.	Why Is This a Rule?	332
4.	Solving Social Problems	335
5.	Taking a Stand (HS)	338
6.	Creating a Support Network	342
7.	Community Services	346
8.	Bettering the Community	349
9.	Exploring Environmental Concerns	352
10.	Ways to Help the Earth	355

Social Communication

Activity 1—Examining Our Role in the World
Acting Responsibly Toward Others (HS)

Language Purpose:

1. To recognize principles of acting responsibly toward others
2. To make a plan with needed steps to reach a goal

Self-Esteem Focus:

To show how acting responsibly toward others can improve self-esteem

Materials:

Acting Responsibly Toward Others activity page, paper, variety of magazines, glue or tape

Vocabulary:

anxious, appreciate, dignity, neglect, principle, respect, responsible, unique, worth

Process:

1. Remind participants of the knowledge they have about self-esteem. Briefly review the self-esteem principles discussed in Section 5, Activity 1—"Analyzing the Concept of Self-Esteem." Ask participants how acting responsibly toward others relates to appreciating the worth of others. Also ask them why it is important to appreciate those around us.

2. Explain that the more we appreciate our own worth, the more we can appreciate the worth of others. Part of self-esteem is recognizing our own uniqueness and recognizing the uniqueness of others. Briefly brainstorm ideas about how people are unique (e.g., gender identification, race, culture, age, history, family background).

3. Explain that being aware of differences and accepting them is not enough. Appreciating others leads to treating them with dignity and respect, and acting responsibly toward them. Read the following quote:

   The primary way in which we show respect to others is to step out of the state of anxious self-concern long enough to give others our attention—to listen, to understand, to care. (California Task Force to Promote Self-Esteem and Personal and Social Responsibility [1990], p. 21)

Ask participants to explain what they think the quote means. Tell them what you think it means. Discuss how your explanations are the same and how they are different.

4. Distribute the *Acting Responsibly Toward Others* activity page. Explain that appreciating the worth of others and acting responsibly toward them can be approached by examining the principles listed on the activity page. Read each item on the activity page, defining vocabulary, concepts, and phrases (e.g., *sense of belonging*) when necessary. Engage participants in discussions about each principle, encouraging them to share examples from their lives. Also discuss what happens when these principles are neglected. (Ideas for this process step were taken from *Toward a State of Self-Esteem* by the California Task Force to Promote Self-Esteem and Personal and Social Responsibility [1990].)

5. Divide the group into pairs. Distribute magazines. Tell the pairs to find a picture or pictures that represent one of the principles listed on the activity page and to glue, tape, or staple it to a piece of paper. Tell pairs to write the corresponding principle at the bottom of the paper. Encourage participants to discuss the task and come to joint decisions.

6. Ask a member of each pair to share the chosen picture and explain how it relates to acting responsibly toward others.

7. Ask each participant to choose one of the principles as a personal self-esteem goal. Use the goal format presented in Section 4, Activity 8—"Personal Values."

8. Conclude the activity with a discussion about how participants are acting responsibly toward others at this time. Do participants feel that most people act responsibly toward them? What principles are generally the most neglected? Why? How difficult is it to act responsibly toward others? What do participants do if people won't cooperate with their feelings of good will? What kind of life changes do participants need to make in order to act responsibly toward others? How does acting responsibly toward others improve self-esteem?

Social Communication

Acting Responsibly Toward Others

Directions: Read the following principles. Choose one that you would like to work on as a personal goal.

1. *Respect the dignity of being human.* Recognize that our most valuable assets are within us. Every person has an inborn worth.

2. *Encourage independence, autonomy, and competence.* An old Chinese proverb says, "To give a man a fish is to feed him for a day. To teach him how to fish is to feed him for a lifetime."

3. *Create a sense of belonging.* People need to be accepted for themselves, including their weaknesses and mistakes.

4. *Develop basic skills.* Being able to read, write, speak, and listen effectively are crucial to being able to participate in society. Developing basic skills leads to a sense of competence and self-esteem.

5. *Provide physical support and safety.* Self-esteem expresses itself in the tenderness and courage to stand up for others who cannot stand up for themselves.

6. *Foster a democratic environment.* Organizations, families, employers, and schools need to adopt joint decision-making processes in order for members to gain self-esteem and strengthen their sense of belonging.

7. *Recognize the balance between freedom and responsibility.* Freedom without responsibility leads to confusion and lawlessness. Responsibility without freedom leads to imprisonment of the human spirit.

8. *Cooperate instead of compete.* Competition divides people into winners and losers. Cooperation leads to win-win situations.

9. *Serve humanity.* Realize we live in a "global village." Serving others improves self-esteem and helps develop a sense of personal fullness.

Activity 2—Examining Our Role in the World
Adolescent Rights (C)

Language Purpose:

1. To define *adolescent rights*
2. To develop a list of adolescent rights
3. To examine the responsibilities that go along with rights

Self-Esteem Focus:

To examine self-efficacy as it relates to basic adolescent rights

Materials:

Adolescent Rights activity page

Vocabulary:

assure, authority, curfew, democracy, entitle, figure, privilege, respect, responsible, restriction, right

Process:

1. Ask participants why it is important to know your rights. Tell participants to define *a right*. Answers may include: a power or privilege that a person is entitled to.
2. Explain that part of becoming personally responsible and growing to adulthood includes separating or growing away from parents or other authority figures and becoming a responsible person. Ask participants to define *authority figure*.
3. Remind participants that most democracies have laws that protect people's rights in some way. For example, in the United States, the Declaration of Independence states that people have certain rights such as life, freedom, and the search for happiness. It also states that all people should be treated equally. Ask participants how such laws affect their lives today.
4. Establish that even though some laws assure citizens of their rights, many times adolescents feel they don't have rights or that their rights are not respected. Ask why that is so.
5. Brainstorm a list of restrictions adolescents usually have to accept, such as curfew, limited use of the car, parental control of stereo volume, etc.
6. Explain that while there are restrictions at every age, adolescents are stuck between childhood and adulthood. Rules that applied to them as

Social Communication

children, such as going to bed at 8 p.m. or eating everything a parent puts on the plate, no longer apply. At the same time, adolescents do not have adult rights, such as coming and going as they please or the ability to purchase alcoholic beverages. Ask about other rights that adolescents don't have. Ask participants why it is appropriate to limit the rights of adolescents sometimes. What problems might arise if some adolescents' rights were not limited?

7. Distribute the *Adolescent Rights* activity page. Explain that participants are to compose their own list of rights pertaining to the subjects listed on the activity page.

8. Remind participants that with rights come responsibilities. The rights they list should not interfere with the rights of others. For example, say a participant makes this response to item 2: "I deserve the right to express my feelings whenever and wherever I please." This right could interfere with others' rights unless the response to item 10, "My responsibility," covers the protection of others' rights when feelings are expressed.

9. Divide into small groups (three to four persons is ideal). Have participants compare and discuss their individual lists of rights. Then have them combine their individual lists of rights into small-group lists of rights.

10. Combine small-group lists of rights to formulate one large-group list of rights for adolescents.

11. Conclude the activity with a discussion about rights. Was it easy or difficult to develop a list of adolescent rights? Why? Was there a right on an individual list that was left off a small-group list? What was it? Ask participants how having their rights respected makes them feel. Should all people have rights? If so, why? If not, under what circumstances should they lose their rights? How does having rights affect self-esteem? How does a person who has few rights feel?

Some ideas in this activity were adapted from Palmer and Alberti-Froehner (1990).

Examining Our Role in the World: Adolescent Rights

Adolescent Rights

Directions: Create your own list of rights using the subjects listed below:

I deserve the right...

1. **Example:** Respect—to be treated with respect and to respect others.

2. Expression of feelings—

3. Expression of opinions—

4. Listening—

5. Making decisions—

6. Needs—

7. Making mistakes—

8. My body—

9. Privacy—

10. My responsibility—

Social Communication

Activity 3—Examining Our Role in the World
Why Is This a Rule?

Language Purpose:

1. To examine current social rules
2. To discuss why rules are needed in a society
3. To explore the link between the need for a rule and the consequences of breaking the rule

Self-Esteem Focus:

To examine rules and their purpose in society in order to enhance self-determination

Materials:

paper clips, *Why Is This a Rule?* activity page

Vocabulary:

consequence, consistency, global, rule, stability, tenant

Process:

1. Ask participants for their definitions of *rule*. Ask participants why it is important to follow rules. Should people question rules? Are rules correct or fair just because they are accepted?
2. Brainstorm a list of rules, such as:
   a. Do not park in a handicapped zone without a permit.
   b. Do what authority figures tell you.
   c. Do not shoplift.
   d. Do not carry a gun on an airplane.
3. Examine the consequences of breaking these rules:
   a. Your car will be towed away.
   b. You will get into trouble.
   c. You will be arrested.
   d. You will be arrested.
4. Remind participants that almost all aspects of life contain rules. Groups of people such as club members, tenants, drivers, adolescents, citizens, etc., all have rules to follow. When a new group forms, it adopts rules, either written or unwritten, to help the group meet its objectives. Rules

Examining Our Role in the World: Why Is This a Rule?

provide groups with consistency, stability, and a certain amount of comfort. To make the need for rules more apparent, ask participants to get into small groups (three to four persons works best).

5. Explain that they are going to play a new game. Instruct each group to form a line. Give the first person in each line a paper clip.

6. Say "Ready, set, go." Participants will probably either make up a game, look confused, or demand to know how to play the game.

7. Ask participants why they couldn't play the game. What was missing? How did they feel during the exercise? Is there a connection between trying to play a game with no rules and being in a group which has no rules? If so, what?

8. Distribute the *Why Is This a Rule?* activity page. Using the brainstormed list of rules from process step 2, participants should fill in the blanks on the activity page and share answers when completed.

9. Conclude the activity with a discussion about rules and summarize why they are necessary. How do we feel when there are no rules in a situation? Are rules needed in relationships? Why? What are some relationship rules? Do adolescents have more rules to follow than others? Why or why not? How can unfair rules be changed? What are some rules that apply on a national or global level? Are they as easy to enforce or follow? Why or why not? How might a person with high self-esteem view rules differently than a person with low self-esteem?

Social Communication

Why Is This a Rule?

Directions: Fill in the "Rule" column from the list that your group brainstormed. Fill in the blanks beside each rule listed.

Rule	Group Being Ruled	Group Making Rules	What Would Happen If There Was No Rule:
Example: Drive on the correct side of the road.	Drivers	Police	Cars would run into each other.
1.			
2.			
3.			
4.			
5.			

© 1992 Thinking Publications
Duplication permitted for educational use only.

Activity 4—Examining Our Role in the World
Solving Social Problems

Language Purpose:

1. To examine social problems
2. To develop solutions or alternatives to resolve social problems
3. To compare and contrast solutions

Self-Esteem Focus:

To develop an awareness of personal responsibility for social problems and its effects on individual self-esteem

Materials:

Solving Social Problems activity page

Vocabulary:

bureaucracy, compatible, feasible, perspective

Process:

(Note: If writing is too taxing for some participants, instruct them to select a group secretary to take notes, or to complete the activity page orally.)

1. Explain that the purpose of this activity is to examine and develop solutions to social problems.
2. Ask participants to brainstorm a list of social problems such as:

automobile pollution	nuclear power and waste
poverty	acid rain
hunger	lack of funding for education
illiteracy	waste disposal

   Beside each problem, write the levels (local, state, national, international) that go with each problem. For instance, education funding may be a local, state, or national problem. Acid rain, however, may not be categorized as a local problem in some communities.

3. Select one problem to work on as a total group (e.g., illiteracy).
4. Divide participants into small groups. Distribute the *Solving Social Problems* activity page to each participant. Explain that each group has unlimited funds with which to solve the problem. Their assignment is first to define the specifics within the selected problem, such as

determining the illiteracy rate in their area. They are then to figure out ways to solve the problem (e.g., teach more reading in school, build more libraries, start reading classes for adults). Tell participants to complete the activity page in their small groups. Encourage joint decision making.

5. Allow 15 to 20 minutes for the groups to discuss the problem and create solutions. Upon completion of the assignment, each small group is to report its solutions to the larger group.

6. Compare solutions. If the same aspects of the problem were discussed by two different groups, were the solutions compatible? Did every small group take the same perspective when seeking a solution? Why or why not? (An added dimension would involve a joint small group meeting to decide on one solution to a problem that all groups could accept. One to two members would act as representatives from each small group).

7. Conclude the activity with a discussion about social problems and our role in solving them. Can one individual make a difference? Is it helpful to place blame for the problem? Why or why not? How can taking responsibility for social problems affect the individual's self-esteem? Did participants learn anything about bureaucracy from this exercise? If so, what? Are social problems easy to solve? Why or why not?

Examining Our Role in the World: Solving Social Problems

SOLVING SOCIAL PROBLEMS

Directions: Fill in the blanks for your group.

1. Define the problem:

2. Level(s) of problem: local, state, national, international

3. Brainstorm solutions (remember, all answers are acceptable):

    a.   f.

    b.   g.

    c.   h.

    d.   i.

    e.   j.

4. Best solution:

5. Resources needed (funding, time, laws, etc.):

6. Is this solution feasible? What steps can this group take to make the solution a reality?

Social Communication

Activity 5—Examining Our Role in the World
Taking a Stand (HS)

Language Purpose:

1. To express opinions on various social problems
2. To consider different viewpoints
3. To use clear and concise language to express opinions

Self-Esteem Focus:

To examine the effect that expressing opinions and listening to others' opinions have on self-esteem

Materials:

Taking a Stand activity pages

Vocabulary:

hypothetical, neutral, opinion, position, pressure, stand

Process:

1. Ask participants what *taking a stand* means. Answers might include "expressing your opinion" or "telling others about your opinion on a particular subject." Why is it important to express your opinion? How does taking a stand relate to personal responsibility and social responsibility?
2. Explain to participants that they are going to be asked to make decisions on a variety of hypothetical situations. They are to take a stand concerning that situation. Ask them to explain what *hypothetical* means.
3. Remind participants that there are no right or wrong answers. They are expressing opinions. If they choose to, they can change their positions at any time. This is not a popularity contest. The activity is designed to help them learn where they stand on particular social issues. Do they feel pressured to be with certain members of the group whose opinions they feel are more accepted or acceptable than their own? That is also valuable information about how they feel about themselves and their opinions.
4. Ask participants to stand in the center of the room. Read a situation from the *Taking a Stand* activity pages. Instruct the participants to move to the left side of the room if they agree with the statement/question or to the right side of the room if they disagree. (Participants are to literally move to the left or right side of the room to indicate their

Examining Our Role in the World: Taking a Stand

opinions. The figurative interpretation of "left" or "right" positions or viewpoints could be further explored with participants but is not the overall intent of this activity.) Participants may stay in the center of the room if they have no opinion or are neutral on the topic. Select the situations which are most appropriate to your group's age and interests. Be sure participants understand vocabulary terms in the situations selected.

5. Ask participants to explain their positions for each situation. This changes the exercise into a learning and sharing experience.

6. Conclude the activity with a discussion about taking a stand. Was it easy for participants to stand up for their opinions? Why or why not? Were participants swayed to change their beliefs? How? Did they feel any pressure to rethink their opinions? If so, where did the pressure come from—from within themselves or from others in the group? Were they surprised by some of their own or others' responses? Why do they think that was? Is taking a stand easier if you have high self-esteem? Why? Why might it be difficult for a person with low self-esteem to take a stand?

Social Communication

Taking a STAND

Directions: Read a situation below. Participants should move to the left side of the room to indicate agreement (yes), go to the right side of the room to indicate disagreement (no), or remain in the center of the room to indicate that they are neutral or have no opinion.

1. Your friend is in a car accident and is in a coma. She is on life-support equipment. Before the accident, she had told you she would not want to be kept alive by machines. Should the doctor pull the plug on the equipment?

2. Your friend is pregnant. Her parents have made it clear that if she ever got pregnant, she would be thrown out of the house. The father, a 17-year-old football player, has said he will not support her. Would you advise her to keep the baby?

3. You're concerned about the environment. When you take your car into a mechanic, he tells you your cooling system is leaking Freon (a potential hazard to the ozone layer). It will cost $250 (which you don't have) to repair the leak or about $10 every two months to replace the Freon. Do you repair the leak?

4. There are many homeless people in the town where you live. You feel sorry for them, especially for their children. You are asked by a teacher to help prepare and serve a meal to the homeless twice a month. It would cost you nothing but time. Do you help out?

5. A student in your school is always being picked on by others because she is handicapped. Would you confront the students who are picking on her?

Examining Our Role in the World: Taking a Stand

6. Your sister's boyfriend wants to move in with her. He's out of work and treats your sister rudely. Should she let him move in?

7. You go to a controversial movie with an older, more sophisticated friend. When you arrive at the theater, there are picketers outside. Their desire is to have the movie banned. You go past them into the theater. Ten minutes into the movie, you realize it is extremely offensive to you and people of your race. Do you leave and join the protesters?

8. You are walking along the street and find a wallet containing an I.D., credit cards, and $100 in cash. Would you return it to the owner without taking anything out?

9. A teacher misgrades your test. Instead of receiving a D, you receive an A. Would you tell your teacher?

10. You're at a party where alcohol is being served. Your friend Tom has had several drinks. He insists that he is not drunk and can drive himself home. Do you let him?

Social Communication

Activity 6—Examining Our Role in the World
Creating a Support Network

Language Purpose:

1. To define *support network*
2. To explore the need for and advantages of support networks
3. To develop alternatives to dealing with problems alone

Self-Esteem Focus:

To examine the possible effects of a support network on the individual's self-esteem

Materials:

newspaper classified section, *Creating a Support Network* activity pages

Vocabulary:

confidant, confidentiality, network, support

Process:

1. Define *support network*:

    support network—a person or group of persons who help others in their time of need

    Support networks can include close friends, parents, counselors, teachers, organizations, clubs, significant others, or a formal support group. The academic or school setting can provide participants with support, but knowledge of support networks and how to meet personal needs is a life skill. Not all support networks are designed to improve self-esteem or self-concept. Some involve shared interests which, if begun early in adolescence, can provide support outside the academic setting.

2. Ask participants why it is important to have a support network when we are stressed, depressed, or emotionally upset. What purposes does a support network serve?

3. Inform participants that, at times, individuals come together as a group to support and care for each other. These groups usually have a common interest, problem, or reason for being formed. Many times, these groups and their meeting times and places are listed in the classified section of the newspaper. Some of the more familiar groups include Alcoholics Anonymous, Al-Anon, etc.

Examining Our Role in the World: Creating a Support Network

4. Tell participants to look through the newspaper and then list the support groups they find or ones they know about. Also list support groups that exist within the school.

5. Brainstorm a list of common problems people may have, such as:

   a. friendship problems
   b. family problems
   c. arguments with a significant other
   d. rumors being spread
   e. anorexia
   f. problems in a class or on the job
   g. pregnancy
   h. substance abuse

   As a group, link these problems with the support groups in process step 4.

6. Research and discuss the groups appropriate for adolescents, such as Al-Anon, which is for families of alcoholics. Professional counselors, psychologists, and other mental health professionals are available for support. Professionals take an oath to preserve the confidentiality of their clients. If your newspaper does not list any support groups, discuss other groups that have a common purpose and support their members, such as clubs, scouting organizations, athletic or academic teams, etc. While the emphasis of these groups is not in dealing with personal problems, they can be a source of friendship and support in a time of need.

7. Distribute the *Creating a Support Network* activity pages. Explain that the answers given on the activity pages will be seen only by yourself and the participant completing the activity.

8. Collect the completed activity pages. Look at each to determine if the participants are aware of the support network resources available. Arrange time to discuss one-on-one with the participants the alternative resources that are available. This conversation and the activity page responses are confidential.

9. Conclude the activity with a discussion about why it is important to feel support. What advantages are there to feeling that others care? How does having a support network affect self-esteem? What are important qualities to look for in a confidant? How does not having anyone to rely on to listen to your problems feel? Remind participants that although they may feel alone at times, they are never really without confidants. Explain how professional counselors can be located and utilized. Are friends always the best support network? Why or why not?

343

Social Communication

CREATING A SUPPORT NETWORK

Directions: Under the heading "Problem Situation," write a problem you might encounter. Under the heading "Support Network," write the name of the *Confidant* you might go to with the problem and the *Reason* you would choose to go to that person or group. (In this case, *Confidant* can mean an individual or a group you could look to for support.)

Problem Situation **Support Network**

Example: Family problems

Confidant: school counselor

Reason: She listens to me and doesn't judge.

1.

Confidant:

Reason:

2.

Confidant:

Reason:

3.

Confidant:

Reason:

4.

Confidant:

Reason:

Examining Our Role in the World: Creating a Support Network

5. *Confidant:*

    Reason:

6. *Confidant:*

    Reason:

7. *Confidant:*

    Reason:

8. *Confidant:*

    Reason:

9. *Confidant:*

    Reason:

10. *Confidant:*

    Reason:

Social Communication

Activity 7—Examining Our Role in the World
Community Services

Language Purpose:

1. To examine the concept of *community services*
2. To identify community problems
3. To assemble information about community services

Self-Esteem Focus:

To relate personal responsibility to social responsibility

Materials:

Community Services Needs List activity page

Vocabulary:

community, locale, neighborhood, service

Process:

(Note: This activity requires homework.)

1. Present the concept of *community* by discussing ideas such as:

    community—people living in the same area; people living closely together and having similar interests; people with ideas in common

    Explain that a community can be an entire town or smaller grouping of people within a town or city. Ask participants why it is important to understand one's community.

2. Ask participants to describe their communities. If they live in large cities, ask them to focus on a smaller locale within the city, such as their neighborhood.

3. Explain that healthy communities make healthy people and healthy people make healthy communities. Ask participants to explain what that means. Incorporate ideas previously discussed about acting responsibly toward others (see Section 10, Activity 1—"Acting Responsibly Toward Others").

4. Brainstorm ingredients of a healthy community. Include ideas such as:

    a. healthy environment (e.g., clean air and water, free of drugs)
    b. safe environment (e.g., free of crime, violence, homelessness)

Examining Our Role in the World: Community Services

   c. community services (e.g., assistance provided to those in need; enrichment resources available like libraries, parks, swimming pools)

   Briefly discuss each category.

5. Explain that some community services are designed to help people in need. These services are meant to help people get through difficult times. Brainstorm a list of problems that may lead people to seek community service for help. Include problems such as:

   a. unemployment
   b. single parenting
   c. natural disasters
   d. illness
   e. child abuse
   f. lack of food
   g. homelessness

6. Distribute the *Community Services Needs List* activity page. Explain that it is sometimes difficult to know where to find help. This list represents possible areas of help that people need to know about. Review the list, add your own items, and ask participants to add any they can think of. From this list, ask each participant to choose an area to research, investigate, and report on to the group. (If the group is small, ask that each participant investigate two or three areas.) Depending on the abilities of group participants and the group structure, information can be obtained in the following ways:

   a. Looking in the telephone directory to find services that are available.
   b. Making telephone calls.
   c. Writing letters asking for information.
   d. Interviewing people who are knowledgeable.
   e. Visiting an agency or community service office.

7. When information has been compiled and reported to the group, create a resource guide to have available. (This process can vary in complexity, depending on the abilities of participants.)

8. Conclude the activity with a discussion about how easy/difficult it was to get the necessary information. Were people at community service locations helpful? Knowledgeable? Friendly? Also talk about who uses community services. Might everyone have a need at some time? Is there anything wrong with asking for help? What are the alternatives to not asking for help? Can high or low self-esteem affect whether or not people ask for help? How? Why? What does asking for help have to do with assertiveness?

Social Communication

COMMUNITY SERVICES NEEDS LIST

Directions: Below is a list of commonly needed community services. Read the list and add to it, if possible.

1. How to find a child-care center
2. How to get a job through an employment service
3. How to find an apartment
4. How to apply for food stamps
5. How to apply for welfare assistance
6. How to receive legal services
7. How to apply for college financial aid
8. How to find psychological or counseling services
9. How to get temporary shelter
10. What to do if you are worried about suicide
11. What to do if you have an alcohol or drug problem
12. What to do if you think a child is being abused
13. What to do if you think you have a sexually transmitted disease
14. What to do if you have been discriminated against
15. What to do if you have been raped
16. What to do if you think you are pregnant
17.
18.
19.
20.

© 1992 Thinking Publications
Duplication permitted for educational use only.

Activity 8—Examining Our Role in the World
Bettering the Community

Language Purpose:

1. To identify areas of need in the community
2. To define community problems and determine what needs to be done
3. To make a plan with needed steps to reach a goal

Self-Esteem Focus:

To relate personal responsibility to social responsibility

Materials:

Bettering Your Community activity page

Vocabulary:

cause, commitment, community, environment, feasible, recycle, registration

Process:

1. Explain that this activity is about how to improve a community. Ask participants to review their definition of *community* from ideas discussed in the previous activity. Ask why it is important to learn about bettering one's community. How can it help participants personally?

2. Brainstorm problems that need attention in the community. These could include:

    a. violence
    b. environment (pollution, water quality, recycling)
    c. homelessness
    d. education
    e. family relations
    f. youth employment
    g. traffic/public transportation
    h. lack of parks and recreation sites
    i. racism

    Define and discuss each problem.

Social Communication

3. Point out that there may not be a direct benefit to all participants from working on some of the problems listed. Read the following quote by the California Task Force to Promote Self-Esteem and Personal and Social Responsibility (1990):

   Persons with healthy self-esteem choose to serve others out of the sense of personal fullness and their joy of being alive. In this process of serving, they deepen and reinforce their own self-esteem. (p. 38)

   Help participants to analyze the meaning of the quote. How does bettering one's community relate to serving others? How does that improve self-esteem? Why may some people not be concerned about helping others or bettering the community? (Some reasons may be poverty, hopelessness, hunger.)

4. Distribute the *Bettering Your Community* activity page. Read each item with participants, briefly explaining the social significance of each and defining vocabulary terms if necessary.

5. Ask each participant to choose a project that interests him or her. When each participant has focused on a project, instruct them to:

   a. Plan an outline of the steps to take to become involved in the project.

   b. Investigate sources of information about the process of becoming involved in the project. Make contact with organizations.

   c. Report the information to the group, in writing or orally.

6. Conclude the activity with a discussion about the feasibility of actually following through with a project. How much commitment would be involved? Would projects require money? How much time would projects require? What is a *cause*? Do participants have any particular causes they believe in? Could a project be accomplished if people worked together as a group? How might a group decide on a project? Some of the projects on the list have to do with bettering the world. How does that help the community? What is a *world community*?

Examining Our Role in the World: Bettering the Community

Bettering Your COMMUNITY

Directions: Read the list of suggestions for bettering your community. Add to the list, if possible. Choose the one that is of most interest to you.

1. Join an environmental organization such as the Sierra Club, Cousteau Society, Greenpeace, or Audubon Society and become involved in an activity suggested by the club.

2. Ride on a public transportation system and evaluate it. Is it efficient? Write a letter to a public official about your impressions.

3. Get involved in a voter registration drive. Start with all the people that you know who can legally vote.

4. Organize a committee to give the school board ideas about bettering schools or education.

5. Write a letter protesting the cruel treatment of animals such as elephants, tigers, seals, wolves, whales, etc.

6. Organize a committee that will advise your local government about problems facing today's youth.

7. Establish a recycling center or volunteer time at an existing center.

8. Volunteer your time at a suicide prevention center, health clinic, hospital, or home for the elderly.

9. Write letters to editors of newspapers about causes that concern you.

10. Get the local media to donate air time for a public service announcement.

Social Communication

Activity 9—Examining Our Role in the World
Exploring Environmental Concerns

Language Purpose:

1. To identify environmental concerns
2. To define environmental problems and effects of such problems

Self-Esteem Focus:

To relate personal responsibility to social responsibility

Materials:

Environmental Concerns activity page

Vocabulary:

environment, extinct, greenhouse, pollution, resource, responsibility

Process:

(Note: This activity is to be done in conjunction with Activity 10—"Ways to Help the Earth," which explores ways to improve and protect the environment.)

1. Review the areas included in the definition of *self-esteem* in Section 5, Activity 1—"Analyzing the Concept of Self-Esteem." Point out that one aspect of self-esteem relates to social responsibility. Explain to participants that part of social responsibility involves protecting the environment. Ask participants to fully define *environment* (air, water, soil, etc.). Ask how acting socially responsible by protecting the environment might improve one's self-esteem.

2. Distribute the *Environmental Concerns* activity page. Engage participants in a discussion about what they know to be environmental problems. Include ideas and details that cover local as well as world issues. Be sure to discuss the idea that the earth's natural resources are not in endless supply.

   Instruct participants to fill in the blocks on the activity page using information from the discussion. An "Environmental Concerns Facilitator Guide" has been provided for you after process step 3; however, allow participants to generate as much information as possible before you contribute ideas. If it is appropriate to the group, or if participants are interested in more details, assign topics to be researched and reported back to the group.

3. Conclude the activity with a discussion about what or who has caused the existing environmental problems. Whose fault is it? Why is it so

Examining Our Role in the World: Exploring Environmental Concerns

difficult for people to stop harming the earth? What is the future of the earth if people don't change their thinking and take action? What does this mean for today's children? Whose responsibility is it to make changes for the better? How might a person with low self-esteem act differently toward the environment than a person with high self-esteem?

Environmental Concerns Facilitator Guide

Problem	Definition	Effect on the Environment
Air pollution	Pumping pollutants into the air	Smog is generated. Air is so polluted in some areas that it is harmful to breathe.
Acid rain	Generating harmful gases that mix with water in the form of rain, producing an acid mixture	Acid rain is extremely harmful to plants, rivers, and lakes. In some places, it is killing forests.
Disappearing animals	Displacing animals which sometimes have no other place to live; also, some animals are being killed for profit	Animals can become endangered or extinct. Animals on the endangered list include elephants, tigers, zebras, mountain lions.
Water pollution	Poisoning rivers, lakes, oceans by dumping waste and chemicals into them	Most rivers and streams are no longer safe to drink from. Some rivers, lakes, and oceans are not safe to swim in, and the fish are not safe to eat.
Ozone hole	Destroying the ozone layer that protects the earth from the harmful rays of the sun	Harmful sun rays do damage to humans.
Greenhouse effect	Generating gases which trap more heat and warm up the planet	Heat could affect the weather patterns. Places that are warm could become too hot to live in or grow food.
Garbage	Making so much garbage that in some places there is not enough room to bury it	Piles of garbage, most of which is not biodegradable, are ever-increasing.

Social Communication

ENVIRONMENTAL CONCERNS

Directions: Fill in the blocks as you discuss environmental problems.

Problem	Definition	Effect on the Environment

Activity 10—Examining Our Role in the World
Ways to Help the Earth

Language Purpose:

1. To recognize personal power
2. To define environmental problems and determine what needs to be done

Self-Esteem Focus:

To develop the awareness that protecting the environment can improve self-esteem

Materials:

None

Vocabulary:

commit, con, empower, involve, power, pro, reaction, toxic

Process:

1. Ask participants to summarize ideas from the previous activity. Ask if anyone had other thoughts that related to that discussion.

2. Remind participants that the environmental problems identified are enormous. Ask participants for ideas about what people might commonly do or feel when faced with enormous problems:

   a. seek help
   b. feel frightened
   c. feel hopeless
   d. feel powerless
   e. do nothing

   Discuss the pros and cons of each reaction.

3. Discuss the concept of *power*. Explain that having power relates to feeling that one can influence others. Power also relates to feeling that one can effect changes, be respected, and be effective. Ask participants how a feeling of personal power relates to environmental issues. What do people who feel powerless do about environmental problems?

Social Communication

4. Read the following paragraph:

   Now, more than ever, people are aware that the planet's natural resources are not only in short supply, but what's left may already be in danger of being permanently destroyed. There are oil spills on our coastlines, chemical waste in the drinking water, and a possible hole in the ozone layer. Can one person really make a difference?

   Ask participants how one person can make a difference concerning the problems that were identified previously (e.g., acid rain, endangered animals, polluted air and water). Can an individual be powerful? Ask them if they have ever written a letter to anyone in government who is in a position to effect changes. If appropriate to the group's structure, encourage each person to write a letter expressing concern. Ask participants why more people do not call or write government officials.

5. Explain that the discussion is now going to focus on how individuals can more directly protect the environment and make a difference. Read each problem situation below to participants. Discuss the vocabulary terms if necessary and the implications of each statement. Then brainstorm what people can do to help solve the problem, discussing as many details as possible:

   a. As a nation, we consume 450 billion gallons of water a day.
   b. The more electricity we use, the more toxic fumes we create.
   c. We throw away 28 billion glass bottles and jars a year.
   d. Americans use 2.5 million plastic bottles every hour.
   e. Styrofoam, a form of plastic, is not biodegradable and is a great danger to sea animals.
   f. One gallon of paint or a quart of motor oil can seep into the earth and pollute 250,000 gallons of drinking water.
   g. Water in most streams is unfit to drink.
   h. Half of the African elephants have been killed in the last 10 years.
   i. Six-pack rings are frequently deadly to sea animals and fish.
   j. The average American uses seven trees a year in paper, wood, and other products made from wood.
   k. There are millions of cars and factories pumping carbon dioxide into the air every day.
   l. Rain forests are being cut down at a rate of 100 acres per minute.

Examining Our Role in the World: Ways to Help the Earth

    m. A 100-watt light bulb left on half a day for a year uses enough electricity to burn 400 pounds of coal.

    n. If all Americans turned their heat down six degrees in the winter, they would save 500,000 barrels of oil each day.

Add to the list if possible. The above statistics were taken from the Earth Works Group (1990).

6. Conclude the activity with a discussion of how empowered people feel. What are participants doing at this time to protect the environment? Would they like to make any changes in what they are doing? Would self-esteem be improved if they were more involved and committed? How? How do people get involved and become more committed?

Appendix A
Communication Summation Form I: How Did We Do?

	Yes	Somewhat	No
1. We listened to each other.	___	___	___
2. We made positive comments to one another.	___	___	___
3. We helped each other.	___	___	___
4. Everyone talked about the same amount of time.	___	___	___
5. We stayed on topic.	___	___	___
6. We used active listening skills. Explain:	___	___	___
7. We used assertive interaction skills. Explain:	___	___	___
8. We encouraged each other. Explain:	___	___	___

9. Next time we will be better at _____

_____

_____

Social Communication

Communication Summation Form II: Rules of Conversation

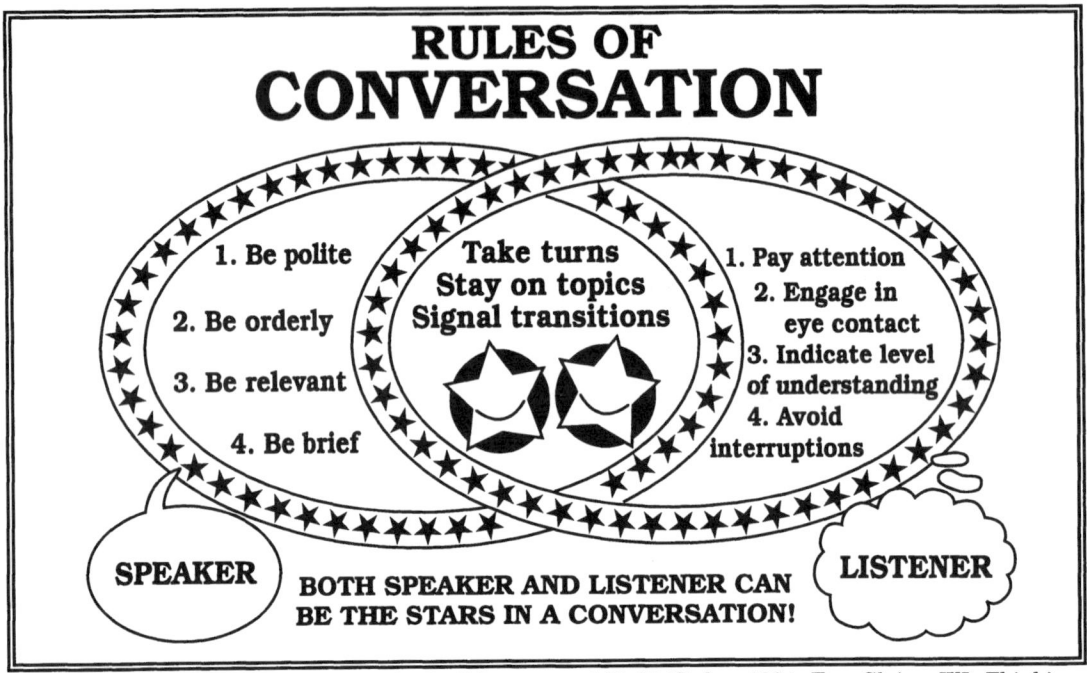

RULES OF CONVERSATION

1. Be polite
2. Be orderly
3. Be relevant
4. Be brief

Take turns
Stay on topics
Signal transitions

1. Pay attention
2. Engage in eye contact
3. Indicate level of understanding
4. Avoid interruptions

SPEAKER   LISTENER

BOTH SPEAKER AND LISTENER CAN BE THE STARS IN A CONVERSATION!

From *Daily Communication* (p. 123) by L. Schwartz and N. McKinley, 1984, Eau Claire, WI: Thinking Publications. Reprinted with permission.

	Yes	No
1. Did we follow all the rules for speakers? Explain your answer:	___	___
2. Did we follow all the rules for listeners? Explain your answer:	___	___
3. Did we follow all the mutual speaker-listener rules? Explain your answer:	___	___

Appendix B
Social Communication Goals and Objectives

Use a check mark (✓) to indicate teaching goals and objective(s) to be targeted while using *Social Communication: Activities for Improving Peer Interactions and Self-Esteem.*

Individualized Education Program (IEP) Goal: Improve discourse skills

Teaching Objectives: During group discussion, the participant will:

_____ respond to initiations of others

_____ ask questions requesting information

_____ ask questions requesting clarification about what others have said

_____ initiate and close conversations appropriately

_____ maintain a topic

_____ make informative contributions to the conversation

_____ make truthful contributions to the conversation

_____ make relevant contributions to the conversation

_____ make clear and orderly contributions to the conversation

_____ incorporate narrations within conversations in a relevant manner

IEP Goal: Improve thought-processing skills

Teaching Objectives: The participant will:

_____ increase knowledge (define, list, recall, relate, remember, repeat)

_____ improve comprehension (associate, consider, describe, discuss, express, identify, locate, recognize, report, restate)

Social Communication

     _____ apply concepts
     (apply, employ, illustrate, interpret, practice, show, use)

     _____ improve analytical skills
     (analyze, categorize, classify, compare, contrast, debate, diagram, determine, differentiate, examine, explore, question)

     _____ synthesize information (arrange, assemble, collect, compose, create, design, develop, formulate, generate, organize, plan, propose)

     _____ improve evaluation skills (assess, evaluate, judge, predict, rate)

Adapted from Bloom (1956) and Larson and McKinley (1987).

IEP Goal: Improve interpersonal communication

Teaching Objectives: The participant will:

     _____ participate comfortably in conversations

     _____ modify or clarify messages upon request

     _____ recognize different social situations and adapt speech style accordingly (e.g., formal/informal, peer/adult)

     _____ demonstrate comprehension of the body language of others

     _____ use appropriate body language

     _____ demonstrate competency with mixed cues or messages

     _____ acknowledge the right of others to have different points of view

IEP Goal: Improve affective skills

Teaching Objectives: The participant will:

     _____ identify own feelings

     _____ recognize feelings of others

     _____ talk about self appropriately

     _____ share ideas appropriately

Appendix B: Social Communication *Goals and Objectives*

_____ express negative feelings appropriately

_____ express positive feelings appropriately

IEP Goal: Improve self-esteem

Teaching Objectives: The participant will:

_____ demonstrate self-awareness

_____ use affirmations as one form of improving self-esteem

_____ increase knowledge about self-esteem

_____ decrease low self-esteem symptoms
(see Appendix C: Low Self-Esteem Symptom Checklist)

_____ state that he or she feels better about himself or herself

Social Communication

Appendix C
Low Self-Esteem Symptom Checklist

Participant's Name _____ Preintervention Date _____
_{mo/date/yr}

Facilitator _____ Post-intervention Date _____
_{mo/date/yr}

(Note: Although some listed traits and characteristics are also related to problems other than self-esteem, they are generally indicative of low self-esteem.)

Use a check mark (✓) to indicate problem behavior present during group activities. Preintervention measure should take place during or before the first activity, and post-intervention measure should take place during or after the final activity.

	Frequently		Seldom		Never	
	Pre	Post	Pre	Post	Pre	Post

A. Physical Characteristics:

	Pre	Post	Pre	Post	Pre	Post
1. Inappropriate eye gaze						
2. Sloppy and dirty appearance						
3. Sagging posture						
4. Weak and uncertain voice						
5. Habitually unhappy face						
6. Seriously over- or underweight						

B. Personality Traits:

	Pre	Post	Pre	Post	Pre	Post
1. Timid						
2. Withdrawn						
3. Arrogant						

© 1992 Thinking Publications
Duplication permitted for educational use only.

Appendix C: Low Self-Esteem Symptom Checklist

	Frequently		Seldom		Never	
	Pre	Post	Pre	Post	Pre	Post
4. Boastful						
5. People pleaser						
6. Perfectionistic						
7. Name dropper						
8. Critical of self or others						
9. Harsh						
10. Condemning						
11. Demanding						
12. Resentful						
13. Complaining						
14. Rebellious						
15. Domineering						
16. Aggressive						
17. Passive						
18. Loner						
19. Helpless						
20. Stubborn						
21. Indecisive						
22. Distrustful						
23. Uncooperative						

© 1992 Thinking Publications
Duplication permitted for educational use only.

Social Communication

	Frequently		Seldom		Never	
	Pre	Post	Pre	Post	Pre	Post
24. Controlling						
25. Hostile						

C. Psychological Characteristics:

	Pre	Post	Pre	Post	Pre	Post
1. Depressed						
2. Anxious						
3. Suspicious						
4. Envious						
5. Jealous						
6. Insecure						
7. Guilty						
8. Worried						
9. Sad						
10. Bored						

D. Behavior Traits:

	Pre	Post	Pre	Post	Pre	Post
1. Overly sensitive to criticism						
2. Lacking in motivation						
3. Preoccupied with what others think						
4. Difficulty taking risks						

© 1992 **Thinking Publications**
Duplication permitted for educational use only.

Appendix C: Low Self-Esteem Symptom Checklist

	Frequently		Seldom		Never	
	Pre	Post	Pre	Post	Pre	Post
5. Difficulty expressing feelings						
6. Lacking a sense of humor						
7. Difficulty being responsible for self						
8. Negative self-talk						
9. Overly stressed						
10. Lacking in empathy						

Items in this checklist reflect a compilation of ideas from activities in *Social Communication: Activities for Improving Peer Interactions and Self-Esteem* and suggestions from McGreevy (1990).

Appendix D
Closure Activity—Suggestions for Ending the Group

Individuals who have spent a substantial period of time in a group situation generally come to experience a closeness and a bond. For this reason, most groups will benefit from a discussion about bringing the group to a close. This will be especially true if group members have interacted over several months.

If the group met in a school setting, the general anxiety of ending a school year will probably be experienced within group dynamics. By discussing how it feels to end the group, students can also incorporate feelings about ending the school year. In addition to a structured conversation about the group's ending, group members should be prepared for the idea two or three sessions before the last session. Reminding group members that the last group meeting will be coming up soon should be enough to start them to think about the implications of the group's termination.

Most group members will probably feel that the end of the group is a loss. Group members come to realize that the group will never reconvene as it is even if some of the same members remain friends or participate in a similar group in the future. *If appropriate to the group,* discuss ideas such as:

1. *Loss*—Define it and talk about it in terms of the group.
2. *Separation*—Help participants understand how separation can be a loss.
3. *Growth*—Help participants to think about how growth can come from loss.

Lead a discussion about ending the group. Include some of these ideas:

1. What did you learn about yourself? About being a group member?
2. What did you learn about communication?
3. What were some of your favorite activities? Why?
4. Which activities were the most difficult? Why?
5. What did you contribute to the group?
6. What is the most important lesson or idea that you learned?
7. How did this group help your self-esteem?
8. How have you changed since this group first began?
9. What suggestions do you have about making this kind of group better?

The group facilitator needs to find a balance between preparing members for closure and helping them to keep working until the last minute. Failure to find the balance could lead to ineffective "lame duck" sessions.

References

Audet, L.R., and Hummel, L.J. (1990). A framework for assessment and treatment of language-learning disabled children with psychiatric disorders. *Topics in Language Disorders, 10,* 57–74.

Bailey, L. (1984). *How to get going when you can barely get out of bed.* New York: Prentice Hall.

Baker, L., and Cantwell, D. (1985). Interrelationship of communication, learning, and psychiatric disorders in children. In C. Simon (Ed.), *Communication skills and classroom success: Assessment of language-learning disabled students* (pp. 43–64). San Diego, CA: College-Hill Press.

Baltaxe, C., and Simmons, J.Q. (1988). Pragmatic deficits in emotionally disturbed children and adolescents. In R. Schiefelbusch and L. Lloyd (Eds.), *Language perspectives* (pp. 223–253). Austin, TX: Pro-Ed.

Baltaxe, C.A., and Simmons, J.Q. (1990). The differential diagnosis of communication disorders in child and adolescent psychopathology. *Topics in Language Disorders, 10,* 17–31.

Battle, J., and Blowers, T. (1982). A longitudinal comparative study of the self-esteem of students in regular and special education classes. *Journal of Learning Disabilities, 15,* 100–102.

Baum, D., Duffelmeyer, F., and Geelan, M. (1988). Resource teacher perceptions of the prevalence of social dysfunction among students with learning disabilities. *Journal of Learning Disabilities, 21,* 380–381.

Beane, J., and Lipka, R. (1986). *Self-concept, self-esteem, and the curriculum.* New York: Teachers College Press.

Berg, R., and Wages, L. (1982). Group counseling with the adolescent learning disabled. *Journal of Learning Disabilities, 15,* 276–278.

Blank, M., and Marquis, A. (1987). *Directing discourse.* Tucson, AZ: Communication Skill Builders.

Bloom, B. (Ed.). (1956). *Taxonomy of educational objectives: The classification of education goals.* In *Handbook I: Cognitive domain.* New York: Longman.

Bolton, R. (1979). *People skills.* New York: Simon and Schuster.

Borba, M. (1989). *Esteem builders: A K-8 self-esteem curriculum for improving student achievement, behavior, and school effectiveness.* Rolling Hills Estates, CA: B.L. Winch and Associates.

Bormaster, J., and Treat, C. (1982). *Talking, listening, communicating.* Austin, TX: Pro-Ed.

Bourgault, R. (1991). Mass media and pragmatics: An approach for developing listening, speaking, and writing skills in secondary school students. In

C. Simon (Ed.), *Communication skills and classroom success: Assessment and therapy methodologies for language and learning disabled students* (pp. 358–383). Eau Claire, WI: Thinking Publications.

Branden, N. (1987). *How to raise your self-esteem.* New York: Bantam Books.

Brewner, M., McMahon, W., Paris, K., and Roche, M. (1987). *Life skills attitudes in everyday living.* New York: Educational Design.

Brinton, B., and Fujiki, M. (1989). *Conversational management with language-impaired children.* Rockville, MD: Aspen Publishers.

Bryan, T. (1974). An observation study of classroom behaviors of children with learning disabilities. *Journal of Learning Disabilities, 7,* 25–34.

Burke, G.M. (1990). Unconventional behavior: A communicative interpretation in individuals with severe disabilities. *Topics in Language Disorders, 10,* 75–85.

Butler, K. (1985). Discourse and language-impaired children: Clinical issues. *Topics in Language Disorders, 5,* iv–v.

Butler, K. (1990). World knowledge and language: Development and disorders. *Topics in Language Disorders, 10,* iv–vi.

Calhoun, M., and Beattie, J. (1987). School competence needs of mildly handicapped adolescents. *Adolescence, 22,* 555–563.

California Task Force to Promote Self-Esteem and Personal and Social Responsibility. (1990). *Toward a state of self-esteem.* Sacramento, CA: California Department of Education.

Camarata, S., Hughes, C., and Ruhl, K. (1988). Mild/moderate behaviorally disordered students: A population at risk for language disorders. *Language, Speech, and Hearing Services in Schools, 19,* 191–200.

Canfield, J., and Wells, H. (1976). *100 ways to enhance self-concept in the classroom.* Englewood Cliffs, NJ: Prentice-Hall.

Canino, F. (1981). Learned-helplessness theory: Implications for research in learning disabilities. *The Journal of Special Education, 15,* 471–484.

Center, D., and Wascom, A. (1986). Teacher perceptions of social behavior in learning disabled and socially normal children and youth. *Journal of Learning Disabilities, 19,* 420–425.

Coleman, J. (1983). Self-concept and the mildly handicapped: The role of social comparisons. *The Journal of Special Education, 17,* 37–44.

Coleman, L. (1980). *Encyclopedia of serendipity.* Littleton, CO: Serendipity House.

Cooley, E., and Ayres, R. (1988). Self-concept and success-failure attributions of nonhandicapped students and students with learning disabilities. *Journal of Learning Disabilities, 21,* 174–78.

Cormier, L., and Hackney, H. (1987). *The professional counselor: A process guide to helping.* Englewood Cliffs, NJ: Prentice-Hall.

Craig, H. (1983). Applications of pragmatic language models for intervention. In T. Gallagher and C. Prutting (Eds.), *Pragmatic assessment and intervention in language* (pp. 101–128). San Diego, CA: College-Hill Press.

Damico, J.S. (1991). Clinical discourse analysis: A functional approach to language assessment. In C. Simon (Ed.), *Communication skills and classroom success: Assessment and therapy methodologies for language and learning disabled students* (pp. 125–148). Eau Claire, WI: Thinking Publications.

Dembrowsky, C. (1988). *Affective skill development for adolescents.* Lincoln, NE: Selection Research.

Donahue, M., and Bryan, T. (1984). Communicative skills and peer relations of learning disabled adolescents. *Topics in Language Disorders, 4,* 10–21.

Duco, J. (1986). *Self-image is the key.* Nashville, TN: Joyce Duco.

Earth Works Group. (1990). *50 simple things kids can do to save the earth.* Kansas City, MO: Andrews and McMeel.

Ellis, D., and Davis, L. (1982). The development of self-concept boundaries across the adolescent years. *Adolescence, 17,* 695–708.

Farmer, S., and Farmer, J. (1989). *Supervision in communication disorders.* Columbus, OH: Charles E. Merrill.

Fey, M., and Leonard, L. (1983). Pragmatic skills of children with specific language impairment. In T. Gallagher and C. Prutting (Eds.), *Pragmatic assessment and intervention in language* (pp. 65–82). San Diego, CA: College-Hill Press.

Gajewski, N., and Mayo, P. (1989). *SSS: Social skill strategies (Book A* and *Book B).* Eau Claire, WI: Thinking Publications.

Galbo, J. (1984). Adolescents' perceptions of significant adults: A review of the literature. *Adolescence, 19,* 951–970.

Goldstein, A., Sprafkin, R., Gershaw, M., and Klein, P. (1980). *Skillstreaming the adolescent: A structured approach to teaching prosocial skills.* Champaign, IL: Research Press.

Gregg, C., Renner, S., Peterson, L., Casey, S., and Kastor, A. (1984). *Life planning educator.* Washington, DC: Center for Population Options.

Gresham, F., and Elliott, S. (1987). The relationship between adaptive behavior and social skills: Issues in definition and assessment. *The Journal of Special Education, 21,* 167–181.

Gresham, F., Evans, S., and Elliott, S. (1988). Self-efficacy differences among mildly handicapped, gifted, and nonhandicapped students. *The Journal of Special Education, 22,* 231–239.

Grice, H. (1975). Logic and conversation. In P. Cole and J. Morgan (Eds.), *Syntax and semantics: Vol. 3, Speech acts.* New York: Academic Press.

Gualtieri, C., Koriath, U., Van Bourgondien, M., and Saleeby, N. (1983). Language disorders in children referred for psychiatric services. *Journal of American Academy of Child Psychiatry, 22,* 165–171.

Hartzell, H. (1984). The challenge of adolescence. *Topics in Language Disorders, 4,* 1–9.

Haynes, N. (1990). A comparison of learning and motivation among high school students. *Psychology in the Schools, 27,* 163–171.

Heath, S. (1986) Taking a cross-cultural look at narratives. *Topics in Language Disorders, 7,* 84–94.

Helmstetter, S. (1987). *The self-talk solution.* New York: Pocket Books.

Holmes, T., and Rahe, R. (1979). The social readjustment rating scale. *Journal of Psychosomatic Research, 11,* 213–218.

Hoskins, B. (1987). *Conversations: Language intervention for adolescents.* Allen, TX: DLM/Teaching Resources.

Hoskins, B. (1990). Language and literacy: Participating in the conversation. *Topics in Language Disorders, 10,* 46–62.

Jacobs, M., Turk, B., and Horn, E. (1988). *Positive self-concept.* Portland, ME: J. Weston Walch.

Jaffee, D., and Scott, C. (1984). *Self-renewal.* New York: Simon and Schuster.

Juhasz, A. (1985). Measuring self-esteem in early adolescents. *Adolescence, 20,* 877–887.

Kershner, J. (1990). Self-concept and IQ as predictors of remedial success in children with learning disabilities. *Journal of Learning Disabilities, 23,* 368–374.

Klecan-Aker, J. (1985). Syntactic abilities in normal and language disordered school children. *Topics in Language Disorders, 5,* 46–54.

Klein, H., Moses, N., and Altman, E. (1988). Communication of adults with learning disabilities: Self and other's perceptions. *Journal of Communication Disorders, 21,* 423–436.

Knepflar, K., and Laguaite, J. (1991). Relaxation therapy for improving classroom skills. In C. Simon (Ed.), *Communication skills and classroom success: Assessment and therapy methodologies for language and learning disabled students* (pp. 256–265). Eau Claire, WI: Thinking Publications.

Knoff, H. (1983). Learning disabilities in the junior high school: Creating the six-hour emotionally disturbed adolescent? *Adolescence, 18,* 541–550.

Larson, V., and McKinley, N. (1985). General intervention principles with language impaired adolescents. *Topics in Language Disorders, 5,* 70–77.

Larson, V., and McKinley, N. (1987). *Communication assessment and intervention strategies for adolescents.* Eau Claire, WI: Thinking Publications.

Leman, K. (1985). *The birth order book.* New York: Dell Publishing Co.

Madden, N., and Slavin, R. (1983). Effects of cooperative learning on the social acceptance of mainstreamed academically handicapped students. *The Journal of Special Education, 17,* 171–182.

Margalit, M. (1985). Role perception of therapeutic teaching. *The Journal of Special Education, 19,* 205–213.

Markoski, B. (1983). Conversational interactions of the learning disabled and nondisabled child. *Journal of Learning Disabilities, 16,* 606–609.

Mathinos, D. (1988). Communicative competence of children with learning disabilities. *Journal of Learning Disabilities, 21,* 437–443.

Mayo, P., and Waldo, P. (1986). *Scripting: Social communication for adolescents.* Eau Claire, WI: Thinking Publications.

Mboya, M. (1989). The relative importance of global self-concept and self-concept of academic ability in predicting academic achievement. *Adolescence, 24,* 39–46.

McElmurry, M., and Bisignano, J. (1985). *My relationship with others.* Carthage, IL: Good Apple.

McGreevy, P. (February, 1990). *Facilitating group interaction.* Paper presented to Albuquerque Public Schools, Albuquerque, NM.

McKinley, N., and Lord Larson, V. (1985). Neglected language-disordered adolescent: A delivery model. *Language, Speech, and Hearing Services in Schools, 16,* 2–15.

Miller, L. (1990). The roles of language and learning in the development of literacy. *Topics in Language Disorders, 10,* 1–24.

Milosky, L. (1990). The role of world knowledge in language comprehension and language intervention. *Topics in Language Disorders, 10,* 1–13.

Minskoff, E. (1980). Teaching approach for developing nonverbal communication skills in students with social perception deficits. *Journal of Learning Disabilities, 13,* 118–124.

National Center for Health Statistics. (1991). Monthly vital statistics report. *Department of Health and Human Services Bulletin, 19,* 3–4.

Nelson, N. (1989). Curriculum-based language assessment and intervention. *Language, Speech, and Hearing Services in Schools, 20,* 170–184.

Palmer, D., Drummond, F., Tollison, P., and Zinkgraff, S. (1982). An attributional investigation of performance outcomes for learning-disabled and normal-achieving pupils. *The Journal of Special Education, 16,* 207–219.

Palmer, P., and Alberti-Froehner, M. (1990). *Teen esteem: A self-direction manual for young adults.* San Luis Obispo, CA: Impact Publishers.

Patten, M. (1983). Relationships between self-esteem, anxiety, and achievement in young learning disabled students. *Journal of Learning Disabilities, 16,* 43–45.

Peck, D. (1981). Adolescent self-esteem, emotional learning disabilities, and significant others. *Adolescence, 16,* 443–451.

Pickering, M. (1991). Interpersonal communication constructs and principles: Applications in clinical work. In C. Simon (Ed.), *Communication skills and classroom success: Assessment and therapy methodologies for language and learning disabled students* (pp. 268–279). Eau Claire, WI: Thinking Publications.

Prillaman, D. (1981). Acceptance of learning disabled students in the mainstream environment: A failure to replicate. *Journal of Learning Disabilities, 14,* 344–346.

Prizant, B., Audet, L., Burke, G., Hummel, L., Maher, S., and Theadore, G. (1990). Communication disorders and emotional/behavioral disorders in children and adolescents. *Journal of Speech and Hearing Disorders, 55,* 179–192.

Prizant, B., and Wetherby, A. (1990). Toward an integrated view of early language and communication development and socio-emotional development. *Topics in Language Disorders, 10,* 1–16.

Prutting, C. (1982). Pragmatics as social competence. *Journal of Speech and Hearing Disorders, 47,* 123–133.

Prutting, C., and Kirchner, D. (1983). Applied pragmatics. In T. Gallagher and C. Prutting (Eds.), *Pragmatic assessment and intervention in language* (pp. 26–64). San Diego, CA: College-Hill Press.

Readability Plus. (1988). Rockville, MD: Scandanavian PC Systems.

Reasoner, R. (1982). *Building self-esteem.* Santa Cruz, CA: Education and Testing Services.

Restak, R. (1984). *The brain.* New York: Bantam Books.

Rice, W. (1986). *Great ideas for small youth groups.* Grand Rapids, MI: Zondervan Publishing House.

Riker, A., and Riker, C. (1977). *Me: Understanding myself and others.* Peoria, IL: Chas. A. Bennett.

Robinson, E., and Brosh, M. (1980). Communication skills training for resource teachers. *Journal of Learning Disabilities, 13,* 55–58.

Roth, F.P., and Spekman, N.J. (1986). Narrative discourse: Spontaneously generated stories of learning disabled and normally achieving students. *Journal of Speech and Hearing Disorders, 51,* 8–23.

Sabornie, E., Kauffman, J., Ellis, E., Marshall, K., and Elksnin, L. (1987-1988). Bi-directional and cross-categorical social status of learning disabled, behaviorally disordered, and nonhandicapped adolescents. *The Journal of Special Education, 21,* 39–56.

Schwartz, L., and McKinley, N. (1984). *Daily communication.* Eau Claire, WI: Thinking Publications.

Simon, C. (1985). The language-learning disabled student: Description and therapy implications. In C. Simon (Ed.), *Communication skills and classroom success: Therapy methodologies for language-learning disabled students* (pp. 1–56). San Diego, CA: College-Hill Press.

Simon, S., Howe, L., and Kirschenbaum, H. (1972). *Values clarification.* New York: Hart Publishing.

Smuin, S. (1978). *Turn ons!* Belmont, CA: David S. Lake Publishers.

Snow, C., Midkiff-Borunda, S., Small, A., and Proctor, A. (1984). Therapy as social interaction: Analyzing the contexts for language remediation. *Topics in Language Disorders, 4,* 72–85.

Spekman, N., and Roth, F. (1984). Intervention strategies for learning disabled children with oral communication disorders. *Learning Disability Quarterly, 7,* 7–18.

Stevens, R., and Pihl, R. (1987). Seventh-grade students at-risk for school failure. *Adolescence, 22,* 333–345.

Street, S. (1988). Feedback and self-concept in high school students. *Adolescence, 23,* 449–456.

Sutton-Smith, B. (1986). The development of fictional narrative performances. *Topics in Language Disorders, 7,* 1–10.

Sweeney, M., and Zionts, P. (1989). The "second skin": Perceptions of disturbed and nondisturbed early adolescents on clothing, self-concept, and body image. *Adolescence, 24,* 411–420.

Tannen, D. (1990). *You just don't understand: Men and women in conversation.* New York: William Morrow.

Toro, P., Weissberg, R., Guare, J., and Liebenstein, N. (1990). A comparison of children with and without learning disabilities on social problem-solving skill, school behavior, and family background. *Journal of Learning Disabilities, 23,* 115–118.

Van Dongen, R., and Westby, C. (1986). Building the narrative mode of thought through children's literature. *Topics in Language Disorders, 7,* 70–83.

Wallach, G., and Miller, L. (1988). *Language intervention and academic success.* Boston, MA: College Hill.

Waksman, S. (1984). A controlled evaluation of assertion training with adolescents. *Adolescence, 19,* 277–282.

Wanat, P. (1983). Social skills: An awareness program with learning disabled adolescents. *Journal of Learning Disabilities, 16,* 35–38.

Wells, G. (1981). *Learning through interaction.* New York: Cambridge University Press.